Richard Chenevix Trench

Sermons preached in Westminster Abbey

Richard Chenevix Trench

Sermons preached in Westminster Abbey

ISBN/EAN: 9783337116651

Printed in Europe, USA, Canada, Australia, Japan

Cover: Foto ©ninafisch / pixelio.de

More available books at **www.hansebooks.com**

SERMONS

PREACHED IN

WESTMINSTER ABBEY

BY

RICHARD CHENEVIX TRENCH, D.D.

DEAN OF WESTMINSTER

NEW YORK
W. J. WIDDLETON
1866

CONTENTS.

CONTENTS.

SERMON XII.

COUNTING THE COST.

Luke xiv. 28–33.

Which of you, intending to build a tower, sitteth not down first and counteth the cost, whether he have sufficient to finish it? Lest haply, after he hath laid the foundation, and is not able to finish it, all that behold it begin to mock him, saying, This man began to build, and was not able to finish. Or what king, going to make war against another king, sitteth not down first

SERMON XXV.

ST. PAUL THROUGH THE LAW DEAD TO THE LAW.

GAL. ii. 19.

SERMON XXVI.

THE DUTY OF ABHORRING EVIL.

ROM. xii. 9.

SERMON XXVII.

CHRIST WEEPING OVER JERUSALEM.

LUKE xix. 41, 42.

SERMON XXVIII.

THRONGING CHRIST, AND TOUCHING CHRIST.

MARK v. 30, 31.

SERMON XXIX.

CHRIST'S PRAYERS, AND THEIR LESSON FOR US.

LUKE v. 16.

SERMON XXX.

THE LONG-SUFFERING OF CHRIST.

PSALM xviii. 35.

SERMON XXXI.

DAVID'S SIN, REPENTANCE, PARDON, AND PUNISHMENT.

2 SAMUEL xii. 13, 14.

SERMON XXXII.

WHAT WE CAN, AND WHAT WE CANNOT, CARRY AWAY · WHEN WE DIE.

PSALM xlix. 17 (Prayer-Book version).

SERMON XXXIII.

WALKING WITH CHRIST IN WHITE.

REV. iii. 4, 5.

SERMONS.

SERMON I.

THE WORKS OF DARKNESS AND THE ARMOR OF LIGHT.

The night is far spent, the day is at hand: let us therefore cast off the works of darkness, and let us put on the armor of light. Let us walk honestly, as in the day. —Rom. xiii. 12, 13.

Advent Sunday.

ALL the services of this Advent season, upon which we are entering to-day, are directed to one single object. They all refer in one way or another to that great event which gives to this season its name,—to the coming of our Lord Jesus Christ in his majesty to judge the quick and the dead. Thus the Gospel of this day was of Christ's triumphal entry into Jerusalem as her king; which has always been considered to have a symbolic prophetic significance, and to prefigure his triumphal entry into the kingdom of his glory. The Gospel of next Sunday will have to do with the signs and warnings which God has graciously given in his Holy Word, to the end that this great and terrible day, however it may overtake the world, may not overtake his people unawares. In the Gospel of the third Sunday in Advent we shall be reminded how God has ordained a living ministry, the ministers and stewards of his mysteries, whose office it is to prepare and make ready the Lord's way, by directing the hearts of his people into an earnest and patient waiting for Him.

So, too, you will find it with all the other services of this holy time; with the Epistles, for example. Thus take the words of my text, and those which go just before them—a portion, as you are aware, of to-day's Epistle. What a trumpet-tone does the Apostle here sound in our ears,—"it is high time to awake out of sleep,"—startling us from the sleep of sin, telling us of a morning that is breaking, of a day that is at hand, of an armor with which we must be clothed, if we would be found upon that day in the ranks of God's army, and acknowledged as true soldiers and servants of Him under whose banner we profess to serve. And assuredly the trumpet of the Apostle gives here no uncertain sound.' It was by these very words that, fifteen hundred years ago, the noblest and chiefest uninspired teacher whom the Western Church has ever known,—I mean St. Agustine—it was in the act of reading these very words that he was at length effectually roused from the death of sin to the life of righteousness. It was by the Spirit of God working through these words that he was strengthened at last to burst those bands of sinful habit which had held him so long, and enabled to enter into the glorious liberty of the children of God. And, brethren, God's Word, if only we will suffer it to work in us, may be as potent now as ever it was of old, showing itself his power unto salvation by the same infallible proofs. Let us believe this as we address ourselves clause by clause to the words which we have before us.

And first: "The night is far spent; the day is at hand." What is here meant by "the night"? It can only be the time of the world's darkness and ignorance, when men walked in darkness and knew not whither they were going; when they did deeds of darkness, unreproved by one another; and at length, being past feeling, unreproved even of their own consciences. But with Christ's first coming this thickest darkness was no more; the day-spring broke. It was not, it is not yet, the full day. That will not be till his second glorious appearing. But the whole time between his first coming and his second may be looked at as the dawn, the daybreak; light still struggling with darkness, the darkness only slowly receding, but yet ever receding; retreating step by step, and pierced through and through as it retreats by the glittering shafts of the true King of day. "The night is far spent;"— even in his own time the Apostle could say this. The long weary night when heathen idolatry and Jewish superstition well-nigh divided the world, was coming to a close. Of the four worldly kingdoms, so fitly typified by the four ravening beasts which Daniel saw coming up out of the sea, three had already passed away; and the fourth, the fiercest of all, "strong exceedingly" as to the eye of sense it still appeared, had received its deadly wound; had received it at that moment when the Babe of Bethlehem was laid in his manger, though as yet it little knew that it was indeed wounded to the death.

But if the night was already far spent when the Apostle wrote, how much nearer must it be now to its close. True, it is still thick darkness in many a heathen land. There is still a conflict of the darkness with the light, even where the true light shineth. Many a time it has seemed even there as though the darkness were about again to cover all—to cover all in our own hearts, to cover all in the church around us. But *we know* that for the church at least this can never be; that the full and perfect day must be drawing nearer— the day when the darkness shall be forever past, and the shadows shall have forever fled away. " The day is at hand "—the day of the Lord Jesus Christ; in other words, the day of *perfect* righteousness, of *perfect* holiness, of *perfect* truth, of *perfect* love (for He *is* all these—He *is* righteousness, He *is* holiness, He *is* truth, He *is* love); the day when He, the King, sitting on His throne, shall scatter all evil with His eyes—shall fulfil the prophetic words of the 101st Psalm : " Mine eyes shall be upon the faithful of the land, that they may dwell with me. He that walketh in a perfect way, he shall serve me. He that worketh deceit shall not dwell within mine house ; he that telleth lies shall not tarry in my sight. I will early destroy all the wicked of the land, that I may cut off all wicked doers from the city of the Lord."

But what does the Apostle urge from this nearness

of the day? "Let us therefore put off the works of darkness, and put on the armor of light;" or, as he has it in another place, still moving in the same circle of images, "Let us, who are of the day, be sober, putting on the breastplate of faith and love, and for an helmet the hope of salvation" (1 Thess. v. 8). I quote the passage, not merely as an instructive parallel to this before us, but because of those precious words, "Let us, *who are of the day*, be sober." You observe he declares in that passage, as in this, that the day has not yet broken; the utmost we can say of the present time being, that it is the twilight dawn; and yet he declares in the same breath that the faithful are "of the day," that they belong, in other words, to the glorious time which is coming; that however they may be *in* this present time, they are not *of* it; they do not belong to it; and upon this he grounds his argument that they should not fashion themselves according to it, that they should not do its works, nor conform themselves to its ways, nor drink in its spirit. They do not belong to it—here is reason sufficient. They have something prophetic about their whole character; they belong to a coming time, and not to the present. They are heirs of a world which is to come, and they must have their conversation already in it.

Here, my dear brethren, is the answer with which you must answer those evil but ever-recurring suggestions of your own hearts—"Why should not I allow myself in those things, wherein I see the greater number around me allowing themselves? Why should I live strictly, when others are living so loosely? Mortify my corrupt affections, when others are plainly allowing free scope to theirs? Deny my appetites, when others are indulging theirs?"—Simply for this reason, because you are not, as they ought not to be, a child of this present world. You are "*of* the day," and must do the works of the day: you are *of* the light, and must put on the armor of light. This is your vocation—to anticipate a coming time; to live as belonging to it, though it has not yet appeared; and your temptation lies in the fact that it has not appeared, that it seems to tarry so long: your temptation is to adapt and conform yourself to the darkness; to let it assimilate you to itself; to become yourself selfish, because selfishness is the law of life for so many round you; to become yourself dark, because there is such darkness round you; forgetting that you are a child of the light, of the light which shall be, and not of the darkness which now is.

As such St. Paul addresses you: "Let us cast off," he says, "the works of darkness, and let us put on the armor of light; let us walk honestly, as in the day." Even though the day be not yet, let us walk honestly, as in it; not making the darkness an excuse for such a walk as would misbecome us, as would prove unseemly, if the day had already broken; for us *it has broken*. His exhortation has two sides, a negative side and a positive; there is something to put off, "the works of darkness," and something to put on, "the armor of light;" these being in fact not so much two duties, as one duty contemplated now from one point of view, and now from another. For indeed the darkness in us only loses ground in exact proportion as the light gains ground; we put *off* the old man only in that measure that we put *on* the new; we die to sin only in the degree that we live to righteousness. Satan must be *cast out* of a heart by a mightier coming to dwell and to make his habitation there; he never *goes out*. There is no such thing as his going out of himself; or if he *does* go out, not being cast out by the finger of God, it is only to return, to find his old habitation empty, swept, and garnished, ready for him, and it may be seven worse spirits than himself, to take a new possession there. Which things being so, if we would fain cast off those works of darkness, there is only one way of doing it, through a putting on of the armor of light.

What those "works of darkness" are is manifest; some of the grosser forms of them St. Paul has enumerated in the verse which follows; and they go by many ugly names in Scripture. They are "the works of the flesh," "dead works," "the hidden things of dishonesty," "the unfruitful works of shame." Whatever is unable to endure the light, whatever shrinks from it rebuked, whatever cannot bear to think of itself as brought out into the open day—that is a work of darkness. Thus the impure thought and the impure deed, every thing in the relation of the sexes which is not according to the law of holiness, that is a work of darkness. Again, the lie is a work of darkness, the flatterer's lie and the slanderer's lie, the buyer's lie and the seller's lie, the lie acted in the life, or looked through the face, or spoken by the lips—they are all works of darkness. And every dishonest dealing between man and man, unfaithfulness in much or in little, unrighteous stewardship of other men's goods, the false balance and the deceitful weights, borrowing without the intention or without the fair prospect of repaying, taking advantage of an oversight or forgetfulness in another, making untruthful returns of the amount of our income, and so laying our proper burden on the shoulders of others—these are all works of darkness. So too the malignant thought against a brother, disparagement of his merits, envy at his successes, secret desires that his blessings might be fewer, pleasure at his calamity, when he does indeed come into misfortune like other folk—all these, with a multitude more that might be named, are works of darkness, which may be hidden now, but which shall be open and manifest in that day which is at hand.

And that you may be the more earnest in casting off these works, think. oh, think what a day is coming ! When the Son of Man shall sit on the throne of his glory, what a flood of light, of light from Him, will surround every one of us ; and not surround us only as from without, but shall penetrate us through and through, piercing and transpiercing, till there be not one dark cranny in our hearts, one unilluminated spot in our lives. In his light our light shall be seen, or our darkness. Whatever there may hitherto have been of hidden in any man, it shall be hidden no more ; that day shall declare it. All things shall be naked and opened unto the eyes of Him with whom we shall then have to do. Ah, brethren, when we consider what are the lives of too many, what our own lives perhaps have been, what our own hearts certainly are, here is an expectation which may well make us tremble. No wonder that we read of some that on that day shall call on the hills to cover them and the rocks to fall on them, choosing these terrible things which at other times they would most have shunned, rather than the wrath of the Lamb, rather than the shame and everlasting contempt that shall then be their portion. No wonder the Psalmist should exclaim, "Blessed is the man whose unrighteousness is forgiven, *whose sin is covered*." Would we inherit this blessedness, would we avoid that shame—there is only one way to do this; to cast off those works of darkness; which, if we cleave to them, if we refuse to let them go, will be to us then a heritage of rebuke and dishonor, a clinging garment of shame and misery and despair.

And if any ask, How shall we cast them off? how cast off these evil habits, sinful practices, unholy thoughts and desires, which, allowed and entertained so long, have become the very robe and garment of our souls, yea, part and parcel of our very selves? there is only one way for any one of us. Through a putting on of the armor of light; in other words, a putting on of the Lord Jesus Christ. Put off the old man, which you can only do by putting on the new. And you can put on this new. Christ was given you, when you were baptized into Him. He was made unto you wisdom and righteousness and sanctification and redemption. Claim Him as all these. He is a *Person*, and therefore can impart not a thing only, but a life—

a *divine* Person, and therefore can impart a divine life. It needs but the act of your faith to obtain all this from Him. This faith indeed is itself the gift of God; but if there is any true longing in you after Christ, any true repentance for having left Him and his righteousness unclaimed so long, He will *give* you that faith whereby you may appropriate all the benefits of his life and death, his resurrection and his glory. Put Him on then, for you may do so; clothe yourself with Him, and He shall be to you armor of light; a light and a defence, a sun and a shield. And then, many darts of the Wicked may fly around you and about you, but they shall not hurt you; they shall fall off or glance aside from those radiant arms: and when Christ, who is our life, shall appear, you shall appear with Him in glory. It must be so. If He has made you here to love holiness, goodness, mercy, truth, his kingdom, the kingdom which He shall set up, shall be a kingdom of all these. How then should you not have your place in it? and the more earnestly you have loved and followed these, the higher place and the nearer to Him.

Put on then this armor, this whole armor of God; put it on piece by piece, the helmet of hope, the breastplate of faith and love, taking in your hand the sword of the Spirit, which is the Word of God; be complete in Him. The kingdom of darkness can only harm those who by natural affinity belong to it—the unloving, the untruthful, the unmerciful, the unholy. These are its victims; against these the powers of darkness prevail, and on these the chains of darkness are laid. But walk in love, walk in holiness, walk in sincerity and truth, walk (which is the same thing) in the light of the Lord, and none of these things shall by any means hurt you. The same which is your glory shall be also your defence; that which is your sun shall be also your shield. And when He comes at length, who is the light as He is the life of men, when there is no longer a foe to be resisted, a darkness to be scattered, a weapon to be turned aside, when therefore armor is needed no more, that *armor* of light will become a *vesture* of light, the garment of peace instead of the panoply of war, a shining garment of immortality, a wedding garment, admitting you without rebuke to the marriage supper of the Lamb.

SERMON II.

TERCENTENARY CELEBRATION OF QUEEN ELIZABETH'S ACCESSION.

He hath filled Zion with judgment and righteousness ; and wisdom and knowledge shall be the stability of thy times.—ISAIAH xxxiii. 5, 6.

THERE are many aspects under which we might contemplate that great event in the annals of this church and nation, namely, the accession of Queen Elizabeth to the throne of this realm, and nearly all of them aspects of gratulation. There is hardly one of these which would not yield matter of devout thanksgiving to Him who orders the destinies of nations no less certainly than those of individuals ; who gives to them kings, and who takes them away, now in His anger, and now in His very faithfulness and love.

Thus we might fitly praise Him that by this auspicious event, and for the elects' sake, those days were shortened,—those days such as England, since she was a nation, had never seen before, such as, we humbly trust, she will never see again ;—I allude, of course, to the last two years of the reign of Queen Mary, the period of the Marian persecution. For, glorious as those days had proved to the English church, making her what else she might have failed in being, a church of martyrs, giving to her her Saviour's own baptism of blood; kindling, as they did, a light in this land which, by God's mercy, shall never again be put out; proving, as triumphantly they did, that those in high place and those in low could alike play the man, that tender women and little children out of weakness could be made strong, and could glorify God in the fires;—still, for all this, we must needs thank God that He now quenched the violence of these fires, bade the fury of that storm to cease, commanded His slain witnesses to stand upon their feet, and, as it were, to ascend into heaven, even in the sight of their enemies; and, to quote, with a little alteration, the words of the translators of our Bible, "at the rising of that bright occidental Star, Queen Elizabeth, of happy memory, scattered those thick and palpable clouds of darkness which had so long overshadowed the land."

This, I say, would be a most just matter of praise and thanksgiving upon this anniversary. Or, not so much looking at the evil which was this day made to cease as at the good which with this day began, we might fitly give God thanks for the inauguration upon it of a reign, one of the most illustrious in our annals, during which she whom He had already so mercifully preserved through the many perils of her youth, wielded with a wise and strong hand the sceptre of this realm, did not suffer any faults and foibles of her private character to intrude into the sphere of her royal duties, or seriously to affect her fulfilment of

them. We might justly praise God for the final set-
tlement and consolidation in her reign of the English
church on such stable foundations that, with the brief
interruption of the Great Rebellion, it has continued
to the present day, shaping and moulding for good
the whole character of this English people. Nor less
might we praise Him for England assuming her rightful place in the very forefront of the great religious
movement of the sixteenth century—assisting, strengthening, and yet at the same time controlling it, where
there was danger that this movement was travelling
too fast and in a wrong direction, where it was rather
seeking to get as far as possible from Rome than as
near as possible to the truth ; or counting that this
and that were absolutely identical with one another.

Nor was it only that these glorious things came to
pass in her reign ; but we must needs recognize in
Queen Elizabeth a main instrument in the hands of
God, by which they were brought about. I know it
is the fashion with some to assert that the personal
character of an English sovereign exerts very little
influence on the course of events, on the tone, temper,
and spirit of the English people. All experience of
the past refutes this assertion. Even at this day, when
other coördinate powers of the state have so much
more influence and importance than once they had,
this is not the case. We are not here to speak flattering words, or to accept the person of any ; but so far
from words of adulation, it is only barest truth, when
we affirm that the personal character of our present
gracious sovereign is felt through almost every house-

hold of the land. Who will dare measure the value of the witness which she has given, that in the bosom of the family, in the charmed circle of home, in the fulfilment of the duties arising there, are found our best and truest and purest blessings ; blessings therefore within the reach of peasant and prince alike ? or who limit the extent to which the whole family life of our land has been strengthened, elevated, and purified by such a pattern set continually before it ? And not otherwise of old in the hour of extreme danger, in the great agony of England's unequal struggle with the might and power of Spain, not otherwise did the heroic spirit of Elizabeth—the undaunted bearing without, true index of the undaunted soul within, thrill like an electric shock through the whole national mind and heart of England, and make itself felt in every pulse of the national life ; and to her, under God, we are in large part indebted for the triumphant issue with which that terrible conflict was crowned.

We might then very fitly, or at least with no inappropriateness, dwell on any or all of these benefits which came to this church and nation upon this day three hundred years ago through the accession of Queen Elizabeth to the English throne. But speaking within these walls, and to this congregation above all, to the assembled members of this foundation, remembering too that we are come together to commemorate not her reign in the general, nor the benefits in the general which that reign brought with it, but to commemorate according to ancient custom, and with a celebration somewhat more emphatic than that annual

one which used to find place in these walls, Queen
Elizabeth as the foundress of this Collegiate Church
of St. Peter's, I cannot but feel that there is a subject
nearer home, and on which it more behoves me to
dwell ; and that is, the close connection, as exemplified in the foundation of this College, between the
cause of the Reformation and that of sound learning.
I have said, as *exemplified* in the foundation of this
College, because this was in fact but one out of num-
berless examples of the same thing.

The grammar-schools of England, which, despite
the abuses which have crept into so many, and caused
them to fall short of the intentions of their founders,
these which have rendered, and will render, such in-
calculable blessings to our land, date back, if I do not
err, almost exclusively to the Reformation, and to the
times which immediately followed ; very many of
them therefore, and certainly the most important, to
the reigns of Edward the Sixth and Elizabeth. When
we contemplate how large a boon they have conferred
on our land, it is indeed sad to think how much more
might have been in this way effected by royal hands,
if greedy and time-serving courtiers had not too often
. intercepted and turned to profane uses that which,
having been once consecrated and dedicated to the
service of God, should have remained, under whatever
altered forms, dedicated and consecrated to this service for ever. Still let us be thankful for what has
been in this way wrought—for the new and healthier
channels in which the liberality of so many now ran,
as compared with those in which during prior ages it

had been wont to run—for the fortresses of light and knowledge, with provision that they should be duly garrisoned for all succeeding ages against the incursions of ignorance and barbarism and error, which were at so many points erected through the land. It was indeed, as we must needs acknowledge, a glorious testimony of the confidence which the Reformation had in itself, and in the eternal foundations of truth on which it rested, that it everywhere sought to ally itself with learning and knowledge as the best human allies which it could have; that it thus everywhere came to the light, that its works might be made manifest that they were wrought in God.

It had been so from the beginning. The Revival of Learning could never of itself have produced a Reformation in the church. That needed hearts and lips touched with fire from heaven—men of whom the Word of God had mightily taken hold, who for that Word's sake were ready to go forward to dungeons and to deaths. The Revival of Learning by itself could have produced but an Erasmus at the best; and, large as is our debt to him, if only Erasmus and such as he had fought against the errors and corruptions of the church, those errors and corruptions might have continued to this day. And yet for all this we should willingly acknowledge that this Revival, though not the motive power, was still a necessary condition, of the Reformation in the church; which could scarcely, indeed could not at all, have been carried successfully through without it. For wherein lay the true strength of the Reformation? First, in the appeal to the Scriptures, to the word and to the testimony; and then in that to *primitive*, as contrasted with a more recent, antiquity; to the stream near its source, and not to the swollen and turbid currents lower down. But without a close and accurate acquaintance with the languages in which the Scriptures were written, how could this appeal to them, to their historical and grammatical sense, lead to any satisfying results? Hence the absolute necessity of schools in which these languages should be taught—the common cause, so to speak, which the Reformation made with human learning, above all with the knowledge of the Greek and Hebrew tongues—the support which they mutually yielded to one another, so that Luther could say with hardly an exaggeration, The best grammarian will be the best theologian. Then too again, as regarded the appeal to primitive antiquity, and the showing that this antiquity was on our side and not on that of Rome, in what way could this be effectually done, how could forged decretals and the like, on which Rome had relied so much, by aid of which had pushed her pretensions so far, be displayed as the forgeries which they were, how could the false be distinguished from the true, without that finer tact and subtler skill which only a long and accurate training in ancient learning could supply?

Then, too, while we of the English church claimed for Scripture that it should receive the law of its interpretation only from itself, with none above it save that Lord from whom it came, we were very far from looking at the Bible as though, like the famous image of Diana,* or the sacred shields of the old Roman religion, it had dropped direct from heaven; or was to be dealt with as if our own were the first human hands into which it had come. We knew, on the contrary, that for long ages it had been in the keeping of men; that many of the wisest and the best had spent themselves and their lives in the searching out of its meaning; that it would be a huge pride and presumption on our part, such as would be most likely to entangle us in error, to slight, and slighting to forego, those helps for its understanding with which they had so richly supplied us. Here was another reason why the Reformed Church required to be familiar with the languages which had as it were the key of knowledge to the treasures of instruction which the writings of these men contained.

Therefore was it, and for reasons such as these, that the authors under God of our Reformation,—the Cranmers, and the Ridleys, and the Whitgifts, with the Kings that were its nursing fathers, and the Queens that were its nursing mothers,—felt by a true instinct, or rather saw with a clear insight, the all-importance of the maintenance of schools and universities of sound learning; and that, if pure religion was to flourish in the land, these must flourish too;—whatever else might love the darkness, it could prosper only in the light, for God from whom it came was light; therefore they saw the need of uniting by the closest possible bands these schools of human learning

---

* Acts xix. 35.

with the schools of divine, since the two must prosper together and decay together.

Let us then, my Christian brethren, all who are here present, as duteous children of the English church, thank and praise God that He put it into the heart of his servant Queen Elizabeth to found this Collegiate Church of St. Peter, for the preaching and teaching of the pure reformed faith of Christ in the land, for the maintenance of that sound learning, which a church like ours, militant here upon earth against so many forms of error, can never afford to be without. And may we who are bound by still closer ties to this grand foundation, to this great historic church of our land, who are here present, not as worshippers only, but have come together to this solemnity as sharers of the high dignity, but also as sharers of the deep responsibilities, which accrue to every member of our body, keep evermore in mind to what a serious extent the credit, the honor, the usefulness of Westminster is in our keeping, yea, is in the keeping of each one of us in particular— and how far we may each one of us hinder a blessing upon it or help one forward ; make it honorable, or make it contemptible in the eyes of men. One of Westminster's worthiest sons, who would have spoken nothing but what he felt to be the truth about it, I mean Bishop Andrews, describing it two centuries and a half ago, could apply to it such titles as these—" Musarum domicilium, virtutis officinam, nobile doctrinæ et pietatis ἀσκητήριον." Will it not need the most earnest zeal, and labor, and diligence, and prayer of every one of us, if it is to be upheld and maintained at the height and level of this praise? God grant that it may not through any fault of ours fall beneath it.

What indeed may be in store for Westminster, for England, for Christendom, for the world, it is not permitted us to know. But it is permitted us to pray, and if in the words of a heathen, yet with a Christian sense, and looking up to Him who alone can make stable, " Stet fortuna domus ;" and when another three hundred years are past, may England be still in the foremost rank among the nations, still holding forth the word of life, the torch of truth, which no competitor outstripping her in the race shall have taken from her ; may the children's children of Queen Victoria still sit on their ancestral throne ; and in this beautiful house a pure offering of prayer and praise be made continually to God.

SERMON III.

CONVICTION AND CONVERSION.

And after certain days, when Felix came with his wife Drusilla, which
was a Jewess, he sent for Paul, and heard him concerning the faith
in Christ. And as he reasoned of righteousness, temperance, and
judgment to come, Felix trembled, and answered, Go thy way for
this time; when I have a convenient season, I will call for thee.
—Acts xxiv. 24, 25.

"YE shall be brought before governors and kings
for my sake, for a testimony against them and
the Gentiles "—such was the announcement of Christ
which He made to the Twelve, as He looked on into
the future fortunes of his church, as with prophetic
eye He beheld it painfully yet gloriously winning its
way, evermore obtaining a wider hearing, awakening
a deeper attention, till at length its sound should go
out into all lands, and his word which it bore into the
ends of the world.

There was one who was not present to hear these
words when they were first uttered ; but in none were
they more signally fulfilled than in that great thir-
teenth apostle, who after the resurrection was aggre-
gated to the other twelve, and labored more abundantly than them all. Sergius Paulus, and Felix, and
Festus, Agrippa and Berenice, yea, in all likelihood

the emperor Nero himself,—St. Paul stood before all these, and in their presence declared that there was a mightier Potentate than them all, a King of kings and Lord of lords, before whose judgment-seat they who now rode on the high places of the earth, they no less than the least and meanest of mankind, must one day appear. Strange and marvellous the leadings of God's providence, which thus brought together, which thus set face to face, the foremost princes of this world, the sceptred monarchs of the earth, and him whom, without wrong and disparagement of others, we may call the first and chiefest among the princes of the new kingdom, the ambassadors of the heavenly King. And few of these meetings were stranger than that whereof in my text we have record. Once indeed it is probable that St. Paul stood before a worse man than this Felix ; but setting aside and excepting that his interview with Nero, the antichrist of the Roman world, it is little likely that at any moment he stood face to face with a man meaner, baser, more unscrupulous, more lustful, more rapacious, than this Felix, in whose power it lay, so far as it lay in any man's power, to open his prison doors, or to shut them ; to deliver him to the will of his enemies, or to throw over him the shield and shelter of the Roman law.

It so happens that we know not a little about this Felix, and all that we know bears me out that I do not paint him in colors darker than he deserved. The great Roman historian of the time tells us that, relying on the protection of a powerful kinsman at the imperial court, he counted that he might commit in his province every atrocity with impunity; and elsewhere, not missing the fact that he was sprung from a servile stock, the same pitiless narrator of the crimes of his age, describes to us this Felix as "exercising in each form of cruelty and lust the jurisdiction of a monarch in the spirit of a slave." And now he sits, this evil man, upon the seat of judgment. Beside him sits Drusilla, "his wife," the sacred historian calls her; for he does not think it needful to interrupt the history by laying bare the shame and scandal of their connexion; nor to bring out that, however wife in name, yet wife in deed she was not; for Felix had enticed her, the first of three queens whom he successively married, from her own husband, one of those petty princes whom the Romans endured within their empire; and in his case and hers the *names* of husband and wife did but palliate and conceal the *realities* of adulterer and adulteress.

I have thought it desirable to enter thus into detail (I might have entered into much larger detail) of what we know from other sources concerning this Felix; for it throws a flood of light on the history before us. We now may see why it was that when Felix "sent for Paul, and heard him concerning the faith of Christ," Paul reasoned before him "of righteousness, temperance," or continence, as perhaps we might better render it, "and judgment to come." It was the glory of the Apostle, his boast, if I may so say, that he became all things to all men; we are here helped to understand what he meant by this boast. There are flatterers,

deceitful handlers of the Word of God, who become
all things to all men, in the hope that they may please
all. There are faithful dealers, who become all things
to all men that if possible they may win some. We
have here one of these faithful dealers. Had he seen
before him one of the weary and heavy-laden, one of
the weary with the burden of their sins, the heavy-laden
with the sense of their guilt, a Philippian jailer,
crying out of the depth of a contrite and penitent
heart, "What must I do to be saved?" the Apostle
would have changed his voice, would have brought
other things out of his treasure-house. "Believe on
the Lord Jesus Christ, and thou shalt be saved"—
"Behold the Lamb of God, which taketh away the sin
of the world"—such would have been his more welcome
message to such a soul; so had he reasoned of the faith
in Christ to him. But he saw none such here; on the
contrary, a proud, stout-hearted sinner, sitting in
the seat of judgment, but executing unrighteous judgment there, his paramour and partner of his guilt sitting shamelessly beside him; and to this man "he reasoned of righteousness, temperance, and judgment to
come." To the spoiler of his province, to the man
whose hands were full of bribes and full of blood, he
spake of righteousness, of the righteousness of God,
which he, Felix, was appointed to execute upon earth
—to the adulterer, the unchaste, the unclean, he spake
of temperance, of that rule and rein which every man
should set over his appetites and desires—to the sinner heaping up wrath against the day of wrath, he
spake of a judgment to come, of a day when God

should judge the world by the Man whom He had ordained.

This was indeed a right dividing of the word of truth ; this was a using of the law lawfully, even as it was made "for the lawless and disobedient, for unholy and profane," for such as this Felix was. For the law, I mean the law as distinct from, and, so to speak, in antithesis to, the Gospel, this law, serving for many ends, serves in the dispensation of grace above all for this end, that it is the hammer of God, with which He will break in pieces, if He may, the hard heart of man ; that, this done and a true contrition brought about, the *grace* of God may reunite the shattered fragments again, and make a whole heart out of a broken heart, a heart which God's grace has made whole out of a heart which God's law has broken. It is only when the law of God has pronounced the sentence of death upon the condemned sinner, and he owns this sentence to be just, that the grace of God in Christ can pronounce the sentence of life on the forgiven sinner, and he can enter into the joy and liberty of the children of God.

But, alas! in Felix's case this law of God did but perform half its work, and was then by him frustrated and defeated before it could perform the other and more blessed part that remained : " as Paul reasoned of righteousness, temperance, and judgment to come, Felix trembled." It did but perform half its work, and yet that half how wonderful! As Paul reasoned, Felix trembled. They still occupied to the eye of sense the same places as before, Paul at the bar, Felix on the judgment-seat, and yet in deed the places of the two are shifted, the tables turned, the conditions reversed. The judge is judged, the prisoner pronounces the doom. Oh wonderful power of conviction that there is in the truth! how does it commend itself, whether he will or no, to the conscience of every man! Paul knew that there was in every man, even in that guilty, miserable man who sat quailing before him, something that would respond to the manifestations of the truth from his lips : he knew that the foundations of man's being were laid in the truth, whatever of lies and falsehood may have overgrown those foundations since ; that wicked men, in his own language elsewhere, might hold the truth in unrighteousness, but that they held it still. He knew that he had a message for Felix, as he had a message for every man—even God's message ; and presently there was that in the bearing of the man whom he addressed which abundantly justified this confidence of his. "Felix trembled." He may have shared, he probably did share, in the wide-spread scepticism or unbelief of the educated heathen of the age. He had overlived all faith in the things which his own religion taught him of the rewards laid up for the good, the punishments reserved for the wicked. Tartarus and Elysium, Minos and Rhadamanthus with their seats of judgment, the wheel of Ixion, the stone of Sisyphus, the whips of the Furies, all these no doubt were poets' fictions, old wives' tales, dotards' dreams for him. Dismissing these, he may have long since dismissed with them the truth which was behind them all, that kernel of truth whereof

these were but the husk and outer covering. But now
that truth, so old and yet so new, revived in him again
—just as by some chemical applications the writing on
parchment, long since apparently effaced by age, may
start into life again—while Paul declared to him that
men were made for righteousness and not for unrighteousness, for temperance and not for lusts, and
how they should all appear one day before a righteous
Judge of the world, to give account to Him of the
deeds done in the body. Felix, I say, could not deny
this. Besides the voice of the Apostle, there was
another voice in his own heart, deep calling unto deep,
which told him that this was true, which compelled
him to set his own seal to the Apostle's words ; and
" Felix trembled."

We read of others who have trembled. We read
of one that sprang in and came trembling and fell before the feet of Paul ;* but he a true candidate for the
kingdom of heaven, whose earnest cry, whose " What
must I do to be saved ?" was the augury of far other
and far better things than the dilatory plea in which
the trembling of this man ended : " Go thy way for
this time ; when I have a convenient season, I will call
for thee." And why " Go thy way for this time"?
why did that fear never ripen into love ? How was it
that a possible conversion was thus stifled and strangled
in the birth ? Alas ! the reason is plain ; he has himself declared it. All which St. Paul declared to him
might be, nay his conscience told him it was, true ; but

* Acts xvi. 29.

that season was not a convenient one. It was not convenient then to cleanse his hands from bribes and his heart from lusts; to put away the adulteress who sat by his side. There was no love of Christ constraining, and making the hard easy, and the painful pleasant, and the rough smooth, and the mountain a plain. And so he trembled—and did nothing more. Unhappy Felix! strange irony of fate which caused him to bear this name! miserable contradiction between the man and his name! The name Happy, the man most unhappy! For who so unhappy as he who just reaches that point of piety which the devils reach, for they too "believe and tremble," and who there stops? who so unhappy as he, the slave of lusts which he knows will be his ruin, but which he cannot, or at least will not, leave? with an ear so far opened that he can hear the thunders of the day of doom already muttering in the distance, while yet his heart is closed to the still small voices of God, which would tell him, would he listen to them, that He who shall be his Judge on that day would fain be his Saviour and his Deliverer now?

Meanwhile he pacifies his conscience with the vague designation of some future day when he will again hear this preacher of righteousness. "When I have a convenient season I will call for thee." Convenient, we are tempted to ask, for what? for his sins? for his lusts? If counsel is asked of them, when will the convenient time for them have arrived? when will they consent to be dispossessed? Oh, no, brethren; that was the "convenient season;" that was his day of visitation, if only he had known it. We cannot affirm of Felix that at any moment he was near to the kingdom of heaven ; and yet we must say that at this moment the kingdom of heaven had come nearer to him than it ever had come before, than it ever should come again. Fear had made a breach, and love might have entered in.

And thou, whosoever thou art, whom at any time God's Word has found out in depths of thy heart where it had not penetrated before, who tremblest for a moment at God's judgments ! at that day when thou shalt stand before his throne, all the secrets of thy life disclosed, all thy hidden things uncovered, beware lest all this thy trembling be as barren and unfruitful and unblest for thee as the like was for Felix. Be true to thine own soul. Cherish that new-born infant desire after God which is behind this trembling ; carry it to Christ, that He may take it in his arms and bless it, and send it and thee strengthened away. Say to no good thought, no holy desire, " Go thy way." It is God's messenger. Thou wouldst never have had it at all if He had not sent it. It is God's messenger to thee for good. As such entertain it. Flatter not thyself that, however thou mayest dismiss it now, at a more convenient time thou wilt call for it again. Thou wilt *not* call for it; or if thou callest it will *not* come ; or if it come, it will not come in power and blessing as it came at the first. See this all exemplified in the case of Felix. He did indeed send for Paul again, but we do not read that he trembled again. He communed with him often. But why? Was it to

deepen these impressions? was it that he might obtain
more perfect knowledge of the way of Christ? was it
that he might better learn how to flee from that wrath
of God at which he shuddered? The sacred historian
shall tell us why he sent for Paul and communed with
him often. "He hoped that money should have been
given him of Paul, that he might loose him."

All that was meanest, all that was basest, all that
was most unrighteous in the man had revived again,
and in all its old strength and malignity. There is no
worse sign of a man than when he forms a miserably
low estimate of the moral condition of every other
man, when, being himself base, he counts every other
man base too. The proverb says well that it is "ill-
doers who are ill-deemers." And Felix thought wick-
edly that Paul, this preacher of righteousness, was
even such an one as himself. He knew that the Apostle at this time was the bearer of alms to his nation,—
had at his disposition no inconsiderable sums of money,
the gift of the richer churches of Greece and Macedo-
nia to the poor saints at Jerusalem; and he dared to
hope that the man of God, after all his fine words
about righteousness and the like, would purchase his
liberty by a bribe, and that with money of which he
was only the dispenser, and which had been entrusted
to him for quite other ends.

I say, this circumstance, this exceeding baseness of
Felix, thus willing to prostitute his office, and to do
for money what he would not do for righteousness'
sake, this belief on his part of a like baseness in St.
Paul, is infinitely significant,—well deserves that we

should lay it, every one of us, to heart; for it teaches us the downward progress of men who are not true to their convictions. It was not much, that trembling of Felix, and yet it might have led to much. He was but in an outer court, the outermost court of all, of the heavenly temple; and yet, if he had pressed on he would have found himself in the innermost sanctuary at last, passing out of the darkness of this world into the clear light of God—from the pollutions of a sensual life into the joyful sanctities of a risen and ascended life in Christ. But he had not courage to advance, so he lost even the little he had gained. He went back again; the defilements of the world—he was entangled in them more deeply than ever; a thicker darkness closed round him than before, and no ray of light that we know of pierced it again; and Felix stands before us a warning that a man may be convinced of his sin, and yet not converted to God; that fear may have torment, but only love a blessing; a lesson, too, that there is but one convenient time for conversion, and that is the present; that each neglected opportunity, each stifled conviction, leaves the sinner in a worse, a more hopeless condition than it found him.

Beware, then, I would beseech you, when the sharp arrows of conviction pierce you, when they pierce, at least for a moment, through your armor of proof, your worldliness, your indifference, your pride,—beware of plucking out these arrows, and then rejoicing that you are heart-whole again. Better to be shot through and through with those shafts, drawn as they are from the armory of heaven ; better that they should drink up your spirit, better that you should go mourning all the day, than that you should be heart-whole, perfect and entire, as the sinner is from whom those arrows have glanced aside, or who has plucked them from his breast again.

And once more, beware by the example of Felix—he stands a beacon to warn you,—beware of the repentance of to-morrow. Break off your sins by righteousness at once. An old Father has said that every lost sinner who finds himself in the pit at the last, has had his own *scala inferni*, his own especial ladder of hell, by which more than by any other he went down into that gulf of woe. Whatever this ladder of hell may be for thee—I cannot tell what it is, but thou knowest—go not down it another step ; leave off, renounce at once that unlawful gain, that unholy connexion, that secret impurity, that purpose of revenge, that neglect of prayer, that absorbing pursuit of wealth or of pleasure, or whatever else it may be, which more than every thing besides threatens to be thy ruin.

This may seem to thee hard, as no doubt it did to Felix. But how many things, which look most hard at a distance, are easy when they are tried. Fear indeed will not enable you to do them, but love will ; that love which may be learned in the near contemplation of the Crucified. Dare not to draw back, when He would draw you out of yourself and nearer to Him. It was for this that He was lifted up upon his cross, for this exalted, that He might draw all men unto Him. Let Him draw you with cords of love (these are the only cords which are never broken), with cords which are at once the cords of a man, and the cords of the everlasting Son of the Father. Reject no impulse, no motion toward God ; rejecting such, you may be rejecting angels unawares—angels who would have blest you, but who, being excluded, turn away with sad countenances, and the sadder as perhaps knowing that they are turning from you, as they turned from Felix, never to return any more.

SERMON IV.

THE INCREDULITY OF THOMAS.

Jesus saith unto him, Because thou hast seen me, thou hast believed: blessed are they that have not seen, and yet have believed.— St. John xx. 29.

HOW many festival days, in which we commemorate the saints of God, cluster round *his* day who is the King of Saints ; and it is only fit that they should, that Christmas-day should have these handmaids, should be thus gloriously attended ; since *He* was on that day *born*, who alone enables any other to be *new* born, from whom alone these saints whom we commemorate derived the beauty which adorned them, the strength wherewith they overcame the world. One of these days, which, as satellites of lesser brightness, wait upon the central brightness of Christmas-day, we have reached this morning—the festival of St. Thomas ; and this fitly precedes the festival of the Incarnation of the Son of God ; for it is the festival of the convinced doubter—of him who searched and sought, for a while too curiously, into the mysteries presented to him ; but whose doubts and difficulties the Lord, even while He rebuked them, graciously met, and for ever overcame. The church, celebrating this one of her saints at the present moment, when she stands at the threshold of the sublimest mystery of all, namely, the incarnation of the Son of God, would teach us that she shrinks from no examination of her claims—that she courts the most searching scrutiny in respect of those great facts on which her faith reposes, and for which she demands the faith of her children—that, only let a doubter be an honest one, one who is desiring to believe, and not one who is seeking excuses for unbelief, and she will stoop even to his somewhat unreasonable requirements, if by so doing she may bring him to see the glory of the Only-begotten of the Father, which hitherto has been hid from his eyes.

We read then of St. Thomas, that, one of the twelve as he was, he was not with the other ten at the first appearance to them of their risen Lord. In that emphatic "one of the twelve" with which the Evangelist notes his absence, we may recognize, I am persuaded, a silent rebuke. "One of the twelve," one chosen to be a witness of Christ and his resurrection, he had yet separated himself from them, and from their hopes, and, as it proved, for a while from their blessing. There are those who account this absence of his to have been accidental, that he was kept from the company of his fellow-apostles by some cause which had no moral significance in it. But we must not so regard it; we should thus lose the right point of view from which to judge of the whole narrative on which we are entering. Putting the three passages together in which St. Thomas is mentioned,—one in the 11th chapter of this Gospel, another in the 14th, and this present,—the great outlines of his character stand clearly and distinctly before us. On the first of these occasions, when he finds his Lord determined to return to Judæa and to brave the utmost malice of the Jews, Thomas says to his fellow-disciples with something of a sad resolution, "Let us also go, that we may die with Him." On the second occasion, when Christ, who would fain cheer their sinking hearts, reminds them, "Whither I go ye know, and the way ye know," Thomas doubtfully and despondingly rejoins, "Lord, we know not whither thou goest, and how can we know the way?" And on this present occasion, when the other disciples in the joy of their souls declare to him, "We have seen the Lord," he has no share in their joy, but only replies, "Except I shall see in his hands the print of the nails, and put my finger into the print of the nails, and thrust my hand into his side, I will not believe."

By the aid of these three scriptures, and by the light which they cast upon one another, we may recognize, I think, in Thomas a most true affection and hearty devotion to his Lord,—if his Lord goes into danger, he will go and *die* with Him,—yet at the same time a certain slowness of faith; for why not go and *live* with that Lord? why anticipate danger and death in his company? We see in him a readiness to look at things on their sadder and darker side, a temperament naturally melancholic and desponding—a certain amount of self-will and determined adherence to an opinion of his own once taken up. He and Nathanael formed, as one has said, the two opposite extremes in the line of the Apostles, if indeed Nathanael was such; the one of a childlike faith, the other tempted to give over-much scope to the critical faculties of the mind.

And may we not thus only too easily account for his absence on that Easter morn? The other disciples have come together with a trembling expectation, which they hardly perhaps dare own to themselves, that the Crucified shall yet be the Risen; they remember words which fell strangely once upon their ears, but which haunt them now, in which He spoke of a rising after three days. What if He should prove the Prince of Life after all? and that bitter cross, those mists of darkness which hung on his brow, that wrapping in the clean linen of his lifeless body, that sealing and making sure of his sepulchre, not pledges of death, but passages to life? The thought of this, or rather a dim unacknowledged hope of this, has drawn them together; the bond that bound them with one another they will not admit that it is snapped. Thus is it with them; but not so with Thomas. He will not hear of any hope; he will tread his own dark way alone; his Lord, the Lord whom he loved so well, is dead; he can attend Him with faithful, loving thoughts to his grave; but all is over there: who ever heard of one rising from the dead, and bursting the barriers of the grave? When therefore the others surround him with their joyful annunciation, "*We* have seen the Lord," even this is not enough to change his sorrow into joy, to cause him to put off his sackcloth, and gird himself with gladness. He cleaves with a certain fixed pertinacity to his own conclusion. The

Lord is dead; and they who speak of having seen Him living, *must* be deceived. Thomas does not so sin against his fellow-disciples as to imagine that they are deceiving him, but only that they have been themselves deceived. They have believed too lightly, and on evidence which a wise man would count insufficient. They have *seen*, as they say; but have they *touched?* have they *handled?* It might have been a ghost, a phantom, an unreal mockery, an imposture; why did they not, when they had the opportunity, put this to the proof? And if they did, if in obedience to Christ's command they actually touched and handled,* and only so believed, why do they demand belief from him on slighter evidence than satisfied themselves? For his part he will not believe till he has himself touched and handled—till he has the evidence of his own senses—till by actual sight and touch he is able to connect this appearance, this apparition, as he would imply, with his own Lord who three days since hung pierced and wounded on the cross, and was laid in his grave. Unless he may do this, he *will not* believe.

For eight days, in just punishment of this his unbelief, he walks in gloom, while the other apostles, and the faithful women, and many a humble disciple, are walking in the light; he like some low and gloomy vale, untouched, ungladdened by the rays of the risen sun, while all the neighboring heights long since were smitten and lighted up with his glory. At the end of

---

* Luke xxiv. 39

these eight days, on the ensuing Lord's day, for the Lord again claimed the first day of the week for his own, they are once more gathered together, and this time Thomas is with them; the others, it may be, waiting for their Lord's reappearance, and he still closing his heart against their joy. Once more that Lord is among them—He stands in their midst—He greets them with his former salutation, with his " Peace be unto you"—and then, turning to Thomas, shows plainly for what He is chiefly come, namely, to convince and put to shame, to a shame most wholesome to him, this doubter; whose doubt should thus be overruled not merely to his own stronger establishment in the faith, but to that of all who come after; so that we may say in the language of Augustine, which the church has embodied in her Collect of this day, the doubtfulness of Thomas, the confirmation of the church (*Dubitatio Thomæ, confirmatio Ecclesiæ*). And first, He gives back to Thomas his own speech, almost word for word, witnessing in this way for his own divine omniscience and omnipresence, showing plainly that those unbelieving and somewhat over-bold and irreverent words, for they lie under this fault as well, had not been unheard by Him. Thou hast declared that nothing short of this evidence will suffice; well then, thou shalt have it: " Reach hither thy finger, and behold my hands; and reach hither thy hand, and thrust it into my side; and be not faithless, but believing."

Observe, I would entreat you, these last words— this *command* to believe; which therefore to do, or not to do, must lie in the power of the will. How many complain that they *cannot*, when indeed they *will not*, believe ; for the root of unbelief for us all is not in the error of our understandings, but in the wrong condition of our hearts and affections. The command, however, was not addressed in vain to St. Thomas. But did he, we may ask with no vain curiosity, did he put his finger into the print of the nails, thrust his hand into the pierced side of his Lord? Some count that he must have done so—that this too was a divine *command ;* and that he who is presently after praised, must needs have obeyed that command. But was it a command? was it not rather a permission, which the Lord was far better pleased that he did not embrace? If nothing else will convince thee, then convince thyself in the way thou hast demanded. Better this, than that thou shouldst remain in thy doubts. It was a permission, but such a permission as God gave to Balaam, when He bade him to go with Balak's messengers,*—a permission which, even while He gave it, He gave in displeasure, and he who received it would have done far better to have left it unused. You will note that St. John records nothing which would imply that Thomas touched ; neither does the Lord say in my text, " Thomas, because thou hast *touched* me," but rather, " because thou hast *seen* me, thou hast believed." To me it seems certain that Thomas did *not* touch. Indeed, a great part of the glory of the scene would depart, if instead of the electric shock of an intuitive and instantaneous convic-

* Num. xxii. 20.

tion, we assume the slow process of the discursive faculty, which being satisfactorily completed, he finally dismissed his doubts, and for a moral substitute a merely sensuous proof. Oh, no; there is nothing in the narration which implies this; but rather that all his doubts and hesitations were scattered in an instant, like morning mists before the sun in his strength; and deeply ashamed and humbled that he should ever have entertained them, he broke out at once into that adoring exclamation, " My Lord and my God."

But to whom are these words addressed? to Christ Himself? or are they, as some would persuade us, a burst of gratitude and adoration addressed to the Father, who had so plainly raised this his Son Jesus from the dead? Some, I say, have sought to persuade us this last. But who that deals honestly with the words can doubt that they are addressed to the risen Saviour Himself? or can regard the other application as aught but a shift and an evasion of theirs who cannot endure an interpretation of the passage which would make Christ so plainly to be called God? For, in the first place, nothing was more alien to the religious habits of the Jews than that sort of profane, or at least irreverent, employment of the name of God on any occasion of sudden surprise, which is too much in use among ourselves, and which would be thus ascribed to St. Thomas. Then, too, we are expressly told that he answered and said *to Christ*, " My Lord and my God." Which being so, we may urge lastly, that had this name *not* belonged to Christ, had it not been his by right, He would have repelled it with horror ; with a horror like that wherewith Paul and Barnabas regarded the divine honors which the Lycaonians where preparing to offer to them.* As it was, He accepted these names of Lord and God, and, in accepting, declared that they were rightfully his own ; that Thomas had only uttered the truth concerning his person, when he gave Him the honor of these incommunicable names. And thus the convinced doubter becomes, as is sometimes the case, the deepest believer ; the very powers and peculiarities of his mind which make him hold off so long, which make him so hard to win, making him, when he is won, to be won more mightily for the truth, to have a firmer grasp of it than any. No other apostle had hitherto distinctly called Jesus God ; this might have been implicitly involved in the confession of Peter,† in much which they felt concerning Him, but it had not found utterance from the lips of any until now.

A gentle rebuke for the doubt which he had cherished so long, with a new beatitude added to the eight of the Sermon on the Mount, closes this wondrous scene—"Because thou hast seen me, thou hast believed : blessed are they that have not seen, and yet have believed "—a blessing, dearly beloved, for us, if we choose to make it our own ; if only faith, which is indeed " the evidence of things not seen," shall supply the place of sight, so that we shall be able to say with Peter, " Whom having not seen, we love."

Let us seek to sum up very briefly what has been

* Acts xiv. 13, 14.   † Matt. xvi. 16.

spoken, and to draw from it one or two lessons which it naturally suggests. The little history which has occupied us to-day is commonly called, Thomas's unbelief. The word is a hard one—yet not too hard. We must not seek to clear him of a grave fault whom the Scripture does not clear. But at the same time there was much to mitigate the gravity of it—to explain the condescending love of his Lord to him ; to difference his case from that of many a doubter and a sceptic who is never like him brought from darkness into light, from error to truth, but is rather each day entangled more deeply therein. Thomas doubted in his Lord's resurrection—but there was no secret desire in his heart, out of which this doubt had grown, that such a resurrection, setting its seal to the mission and divine authority of Christ, might never have taken place. On the contrary, he doubted as one who felt the news too good to be true. Every desire and longing of his heart yearned and stretched toward that thing which yet his understanding for a while was unable to take in. How different is such a doubter as this, who would give worlds to get rid of his doubt,—for it stands between him and his blessedness, between him and his God—from the doubter who hugs his doubt, who would not be rid of it, if he might, to whom every difficulty which besets Revelation is welcome, because it stands between him and that submission which he is determined not to yield to the Gospel of Christ ; because it serves him as an excuse, almost as a justification, for the disobedience of heart, it may be also the disobedience of life, which he will not renounce. Shall Christ work a miracle for such as these? Shall He touch their eyes, that the scales may fall away from them? Shall He offer to them his hands and his side? He will not do so. It were useless if He did it; would only add to their guilt. Were they delivered from one doubt, they would presently entrench themselves in another. In no speculative difficulties, which move in the region of the understanding, but in the disaffection, the alienation of heart and will from God, is the real seat of their unbelief; and only when this alienation is removed, will the unbelief be removed.

Therefore, O my brethren, should there be any among us visited with doubts, beset with difficulties in regard of any part of that which God has revealed of Himself (and in so vast an assembly we can scarcely hope that some such an one there should not be), it greatly behoves such diligently to examine in what temper they entertain and deal with these perplexities of their spirits. Are these doubts welcome to you? these apparent contradictions of Scripture to some of the later discoveries of science, or apparent contradictions of one part of it to another, or difficulties of reconciling its statements with your notions of the righteousness of God, greedily snatched at by you, that so you may escape the unwelcome necessity of yielding obedience to its precepts and commands? Be sure that for you, continuing in this temper, there is no blessing in store such as that which overtook him whose memory the church celebrates to-day.

But are you yearning to believe, to see removed out

of your way every obstacle which stands between you
and the full affiance of faith ; do you long to yield
yourself to Him, of whom you feel that He alone could
satisfy all the deepest needs of your soul, that if there
are words of eternal life any where, He *has* those
words ; if there is truth any where, He *is* that truth ;
are your doubts your misery, because they stand between you and this your highest blessedness? then we
dare to hope that this, the blessedness of Thomas, may
one day be yours.   We do not indeed dare to say that
there is not a sinful element in every difficulty which
keeps us from God.   There was such, an overweening
estimate of self, of the powers of his own mind, with
other faults, in that blessed Apostle of whom we have
been speaking to-day.   But still our God is one who
does not deal with us after our sins ; and to you thus
minded, to you, if only you thus reach out after this
Saviour, He will yet show Himself alive by many infallible proofs.   He will stand before you—He will show
you his hands and his side, his hands wounded, his
side pierced for you.   There will be something of a
sad rebuke in this showing—a rebuke that you should
have stood out so long, that when your brethren were
satisfied, you should not have been satisfied—should
have refused to accept their testimony, the testimony
of the wise and good, the church of all the ages, that
this was the Christ, the Saviour of the world—who
was dead, and is alive, and now liveth for evermore ;
but a rebuke of which the sadness, with all the shame
for those doubts entertained too long, shall be swallowed up in joy, in the joy that you have found Him at

length, Him who was all along the desire of your soul, and to whom you are now able at length to say from the depths of a convinced and worshipping heart— "My Lord and my God."

SERMON V.

THE COATS OF SKINS.

Unto Adam also and to his wife did the Lord God make coats of skins,
and clothed them.—Gen. iii. 21.

AN ancient interpreter of Scripture, one of the early
Fathers, extolling the worth and dignity of the
book of Revelation, and inviting to a close and patient study of it, has not scrupled to declare that there
are in it as many mysteries as there are words. True
as these words are, taken with that natural limitation
which of course they demand, as applied to that wonderful book, they may be affirmed to be truer still in
regard of the first three chapters of Genesis, above all
in regard of this third chapter from which my text is
derived ; for this assuredly is the most important
chapter in the whole Bible. It is the only chapter
which, if we could conceive it as being withdrawn,
would leave all the rest of Scripture unintelligible.
Take this away, this record of the fall, and of the
penal consequences of the fall, and of the provision
which God so graciously made to repair these consequences, to build up the breach which Adam had made,
take this away, and you take away the key of knowledge to all the rest of the Bible. Nor is it the Bible

alone which would thus become unintelligible; but the whole condition of the world around us, of man and of nature, of our own selves above all, would present itself to us as an inexplicable riddle. What a riddle, indeed, does it evermore continue to all those who refuse to accept the solution of it here offered! There are indeed in this chapter almost as many mysteries as there are words.

But among all these mysteries I must limit myself to one,—to that contained in the words of my text: "Unto Adam also and to his wife did the Lord God make coats of skins, and clothed them." I say, and I am uttering in this no mere fancy of my own, that much is hidden in these words; with a sense upon the surface, there is also a sense below the surface; and yet how easily we might miss the latter. How easily we might pass by, as doubtless thousands have passed by, the profound significance of this notice, made with so little pomp of words, and read in it nothing more than an act of ordinary kindness whereby God ministered to the bodily needs of his fallen children, for whom with sin had come shame; and who, exiles from Eden, should henceforth be exposed to the sharp and wintry blasts, and all those distemperatures of the air which were among the secondary consequences of the fall. As such a record of the kindness of God at such a moment, the words would indeed be precious; but how infinitely more precious when we read in them, and draw out of them, what better they contain even than this; when they reveal to us the deeper mystery which lies behind.

Let us look back for an instant at the history preceding. Our first parents, so long as they stood in their original uprightness, were clothed with their own innocency as with a garment, and needed no other. But shame followed close on sin, and under the influence of this shame they proceeded to make *for themselves* such coverings as they could, yet such as they were conscious themselves to be slight and insufficient; and in proof that they felt them so, when they heard the voice of the Lord God calling them in the garden they were afraid, because, in Adam's own words, they were naked, and they went and hid themselves from Him. But now being drawn from their hiding-place, and having received from the mouth of their Judge at once the sentence of death and the sentence of life, the Lord God proceeds Himself to do for them what they had vainly attempted to do for themselves,—to make clothing for them, such as shall be indeed effectual, such as shall enable them to endure his else intolerable eye. This, however, He can only do at the cost of a life. Some harmless beast, which would never have died if they had not sinned, must perish, and perish by God's immediate decree and act, that they may be clothed; that its covering may henceforth be their covering, in which they may not be ashamed to appear before God.

Is not, I ask you, the whole mystery of our justification wrapped up in these most precious details? have we not here a clear prophecy of the Lamb slain, to the end that the righteousness which was his might become ours? Trace it through all its steps. For, first, we have here the fact, as in a parable, that man is utterly impotent to bring to pass any satisfying righteousness of his own. He can see his shame, but he cannot effectually cover or conceal it. Adam and Eve, they could see and feel that they were guilty, miserable, naked—unfit for one another's company, (for it is only the pardoned that have fellowship one with another,) still more utterly unfit for the presence of God ; but when they endeavored to help themselves, what profited· all the cloaks and coverings of their shame which they devised for their own selves? No sooner did they hear the voice of the Lord God in the garden than they confessed in that act of hiding themselves their sense of the worthlessness of these.

And wherein, O my brethren, is any garment of our own righteousness which we devise for ourselves better than those aprons of fig-leaves of theirs? What is it but a garment narrower than we can wrap ourselves withal? It may seem to serve its purposes for a while, to constitute a sufficient protection for us ; we may rest upon it, upon our decency of behavior, the absence of any gross vices from our lives, our diligence in the performance of the duties of our calling, our kindness to others, our forwardness in good works. Fig-leaves all! and we shall prove them such. Let God once call to us, let us once hear his voice singling out us in particular, let Him speak to us out of the whirlwind, show us a glimpse of his glory, and in his glory of our own shame, let it once come to this that we stand face to face with Him the Holy One, and we shall find how little all these devices of our own can ao for us, we shall stand shivering, naked, and ashamed before Him. Like Job we may have washed ourselves with snow water, and made our hands never so clean ; but He can plunge us in the ditch, so that our own clothes shall abhor us.* And if we are only drawn out of our refuges of lies, if we only make this discovery of our nakedness and defilement, when it is too late to seek and to obtain any better covering, we may then cry to the rocks to cover us, and to the hills to hide us ; but neither they, nor any other shelter, neither height nor depth, shall conceal us from those eyes of fire which shall at once look us through and consume us.

But while we thus learn that man cannot clothe himself, we learn also that God undertakes to clothe him. They were his hands which made the skins of beasts into garments for Adam and for Eve. What a blessed mystery is here! How much is contained for us in this gracious, this condescending act of God toward them whom just before He had judged! The hands which bind man to God have not been broken by man's sin—or rather, though broken once, they have been reunited again. He can yet devise a way by which his banished shall return home. As elsewhere He has said *in word*, "I am the Lord that *healeth* thee," so here He says *in act*, "I am the Lord that *clotheth* thee." He does not abhor man in his fallen estate, however that state may be one in itself sufficient to provoke abhorring. He beholds man, to use

* Job ix. 30, 31.

the image of Ezekiel, as a new-born infant cast out at the moment of its nativity to the loathing of its person, polluted in its own blood ; and He spreads his skirt over it, and says unto it, Live. This is the second lesson of our history—that when man has, so to speak, unclothed himself, stripped himself bare of that righteousness with which he was arrayed at the first, God Himself undertakes to find garments for him, to the end that the shame of his nakedness may not appear.

But, thirdly, we note in this Scripture that the clothing which God found for Adam could only have been obtained at the cost of a life, and *that* the life of one unguilty, of one who had no share nor part in the sin which made the providing of it needful. So it must necessarily have been. A beast, one or more, must have been slain before these coats of skins could have been prepared ; and it must have been slain by the act of God. I do not scruple to say that we have here the first institution of sacrifice ; and what is more noticeable still, God Himself the institutor ; not merely enjoining, commanding, but Himself ordaining, showing the way ; and the central idea of sacrifice, as it afterwards unfolded itself in manifold rites, is wrapped up in this first sacrifice of Paradise. In proof that here we have nothing less than the first of that long series of sacrifices which were to follow, a type and shadow, a prelude and prophecy, of that crowning sacrifice on Calvary, in which all others were to find their consummation and their end, I ask you to note how close the similarity between that and

this,—in what wonderful ways this points to and pre-
signifies that. Already in Paradise there is not merely
a prophecy of Christ in words, "The seed of the
woman shall bruise the serpent's head," but a prophecy
in act. A creature which has known no sin comes
here notwithstanding, and by the will and act of God,
under the law of death, under all the penal consequences of sin, dies, that so from man the sinner those
same penal consequences of his sin may be turned
away,—that man, who had stripped himself of the
robe of his own innocency, may yet be clothed, though
not now in anything of his own, but in a garment
which is furnished him by another. What can all this
point to but to Him, the Lamb of God, in whom was
no sin, and who yet endured the penalty of our sin,
died that we might live, and who thus died by the de-
terminate counsel and foreknowledge of God,—God
Himself putting Him to grief, bidding his sword to
awake against the Man that was his fellow, and all
for our sakes, that He might thus lay on our divine
Substitute the iniquities of us all, that He might thus
find a ransom for us, and One by whose stripes we
should be healed, and by whose righteousness we
should be clothed. O my brethren, we hear in the
New Testament of the Lord our righteousness, of
Christ our righteousness; He is *plainly* declared to
us there: but He is not obscurely intimated in these
words of Genesis, in this sacrament, for so we may
call it, which was accomplished in Paradise, when to
" Adam and to his wife did the Lord God make coats
of skins, and clothed them."

And are not the lessons which we may draw from all this plain and palpable enough? As for instance, this first,—that there is no robe of our own righteousness which can cover us, which can conceal our shame. Those were poor miserable palliations of their dishonor which the guilty progenitors of our race invented and contrived for themselves; and ours, be sure, will be as poor, or poorer still. What! will you stand before God, before Him of the eyes of fire, before Him who charges his angels with folly, before Him in whose sight the heavens themselves are not pure, with nothing better to cover you than the rags of your own well-doings,—boasting, it may be, like that wretched Pharisee, that you are not as other men, adulterers, extortioners, and the like,—glorying in your virtues, your uprightness, your honesty, your almsdeeds, your diligence in good works, your constant attendance at God's house, your frequent participation in holy sacraments?—all of them good, all more or less indispensable for any who would see life, but yet constituting no part of the righteousness of a man in which he is to stand accepted and justified before God; and he is miserably mistaken if he so regard them.

But, secondly, that righteousness which we have not in ourselves we must be content, yea glad, yea thankful, to receive it at the hands of God. Pride may revolt at this; the old Adam may kick at this; but till a man is content to put his mouth in the dust, to give all glory to God, and to take all shame to himself, to renounce all trust in anything which he has wrought or ever will have wrought for himself, to place all trust in what God has wrought for him, he is not near to the kingdom of God. How gladly must our first parents have cast aside the poor, ineffectual makeshifts which they had sewn together for themselves, when God had supplied them with clothing sufficient for their utmost needs? With like gladness let us cast everything away which would hinder us from making our own that durable clothing, those garments at once of use and of beauty, which God has in Christ provided for us.

But, lastly, not Christ by his life, but by his life *and death*, and mainly by his death, supplies these garments for our spirits' need. It is not to the Lamb of God, but to the Lamb *slain*, that we must look. Those coats of skins of which we have been speaking to-day were so far dearly bought, that they were bought at the price of a life, and the very existence of them involved and implied a death. And so it was ever after in every sacrifice which followed. The sacrifice must die, if he on whose behalf it was offered was to have any profit by it. Without shedding of blood was no remission. It was so with Him who crowned and completed all the sacrifices which went before, to whom they had all pointed. It is his death which is our life. It is because He was stripped that we are clothed ; because He hung naked upon his cross, therefore is it that the shame of our nakedness shall not appear ;—that is, if indeed it shall not ; for it is for us to determine whether it shall appear or no. If we would not have it appear, then let us buy of Him white raiment ; let us seek to stand before God accepted in Him ; his righteousness imputed to us, and all our sins covered by that ample robe. Yet even this is not all ; as we must ever seek to preserve the due balance between one truth of God and another, I will therefore conclude with this warning word, namely, that to put on Christ is something more even than this. It is so to appropriate the righteousness of Christ that it becomes our righteousness, life of our life, woven into the web and tissue of our own moral and spiritual being ; if in one sense a garment separable from us, yet in another as our own flesh and blood, having become part and parcel of our very selves ; a Christ *for* us, who is a Christ *in* us as well. Let us as little dare to separate these two truths as to confound them.

3*

SERMON VI.

THE SLAVERY OF SIN.

Whosoever committeth sin is the servant of sin.—JOHN viii. 34.

WE are unhappily so used to take words, even words of God, in a vague, general way, without attaching any very distinct force or meaning to them, that an announcement like that we have just heard may sometimes almost sound like a truism in our ears. "He that committeth sin is the servant of sin." We hear these words, and they do not reveal to us the consequences of sin under a new and terrible aspect. This they will only do, when we give to the word "servant," or "slave" as it might be rendered, the emphasis which the divine Speaker meant it should have. "He that committeth sin is the *slave* of sin." That Lord who in so many gracious ways has sought to scare and separate us from evil, does so here by setting forth to us that it is a slavery; that however men may think and fancy at the beginning that their sins shall be servants to them, it is never long before they inevitably become the servants to their sins.

He would teach us this, and all experience confirms it, that any wilful sin, admitted into the heart, having once gained a footing there, cannot remain at a stand-

(58)

still, but must ever bring more and more the whole man under its dominion, laying ever new and ever stronger fetters upon him ; so that the chains of evil habits which may have been but as spiders' threads at the first, so easily might they by a vigorous effort of the will have been snapped asunder, become links of iron at the last. He would bid us know that sin, this tyrannous mistress of our lives, puts him who has accepted her yoke ever to viler drudgeries than before ; so that many things which he would have shrunk back from at first, while his conscience was yet unseared, being past feeling he does greedily at the last, and without hesitation or remorse : small sins in him growing into great, the petty purloiner from the common stock into the traitor who sold his Lord ; sins of desire turning into sins of act ; the cockatrice's egg hatching into the fiery flying serpent ; the man falling from one wickedness to another ; and because he did not like to retain God in his knowledge, being given over to vile affections and to those penal blindnesses with which, by an inexorable law, God visits and avenges the free indulgence in unlawful desires.

But here let me pause an instant, and ask you to consider with me *why* it is that sin has this fearful power of enslaving those who had no intention of yielding themselves absolutely and without reserve to its dominion—of growing, increasing, more and more leavening the whole life, penetrating it through and through, till, it may be, the whole is leavened ;—how it comes to pass that no man can say, Thus far I will advance in sin and no further ; or, In this I will allow myself, but then I will stop short ;—why it is that all such calculations are sure to be defeated, and that none can measure out to himself the exact amount of evil which he will commit. The reason is, that no sin, however separable or separate from other sins it may seem, can be regarded as an isolated thing ; every sin stands in connection with a whole spiritual kingdom of darkness, from which it came forth, and with which it maintains correspondencies and relations still, even after it has found lodgement in the sinner's heart. The existence of this dark kingdom, this kingdom of envy and hate and lust and pride, which is around us, and would fain be within us—the existence of Satan and his angels, of these tempters ever watchful to find an open door in the heart, and where that door has been opened but for one sin, by force or fraud to make an entrance for many—this fact that there is a kingdom of darkness around us, as well as a kingdom of light, that we have affinities with the one no less than with the other, and that sins no less than graces are linked together by a mysterious law one with another, it is this which explains to us the deep significance of the Psalmist's prayer, " Keep thy servant from presumptuous sins, lest they get the dominion over me." It is this which forbids us to believe that any sin, wilfully admitted into a heart, will remain quiescent there ; which makes us sure that it must stir and move, must cast forth its roots and fibres on every side, must gradually vitiate and corrupt portions hitherto sounder and sincerer of the life no less than that part which it originally claimed for its own. Nay, not merely *some* portions, but *all*—perhaps itself gradually taking possession of all. For oftentimes a ruling sin will have power little by little to color the whole life with its own tints ; to assimilate everything there to itself —as in ever wider circles to absorb all into its own vortex, being as it were a gulf, a maelstrom, into which all which was better and nobler in the man is irresistibly attracted and drawn, and is there swallowed up, and for ever disappears.

There are many sins which have this absorbing character, whose property it is ever to encroach more and more on the regions of the moral and spiritual life not as yet possessed by them, never content till they have reared their trophies on the wreck and ruin of every nobler faculty and power. All sins perhaps have more or less this character ; yet we may signalize two or three, concerning which it is eminently true. Vanity is such a sin. This may seem to us often little worse than a harmless foible ; yet physicians will tell you that there is almost no sin which gives more inmates to the madhouse than does this ; and how many through it shall have missed the crown of life only the last day shall declare. The love of money is another such a sin, growing by what it feeds on ; and ever claiming to exercise a wider, a fiercer, a more relentless tyranny and dominion in the soul where it rules as lord ; ever resenting more and more any freedom of action, any generosity in dealing, any openhandedness in giving, any bowels of compassion shown on the part of him, who meant indeed to allow this sin, but did not intend at the first that it should bear sway in his heart and life as sole and absolute and tyrannous lord.

The lust of the flesh indulged and allowed proves oftentimes another such a sin ; it has a fearful tendency to become such. And then what a hideous tyranny will this be! In the nature of things, sin in act will be only from time to time ; but, perhaps more defiling still, as more cold-blooded, sin in thought and imagination may be, and often will be, almost continual. What a workshop of unholy, impure fancies will the heart of the man be who has given himself over to this spirit of uncleanness! On the anvil of that heart what foul and ugly imagination will be forging and fashioning for evermore ; and the unholy fires which have been kindled there, how will they in their fierce devouring hunger be seeking every where and in every thing for the pabulum which should nourish and the fuel which should feed them! There is nothing for such a man which will not be made to minister to impurity ; " having eyes full of adultery, which cannot cease from sin." By a dreadful alchemy of hell he will extract what is foul from the fairest ; what will yield healthful nourishment to others will only yield poison to him. Noble books of antiquity, or famous poems of the modern world, if there should be, alas! one tainted spot in them, passing over whatever of pure and elevating and ennobling they may offer, he will fasten upon this, as one who can feed upon rottenness and corruption, and can feed only upon these. O fearful condition of him, for whom all which contributes most to the beauty of earth, or which will go far to make up the glory of heaven, the purity of womanhood, the innocency of children, the continence of manhood, is as something which he would fain see to disappear ; for it stands in his way, its mere presence rebukes him, who now knows of no other joys than those which are to be found in the sty of Epicurus, and the wallowing in the mire. O fearful condition of him for whom no simple pleasures, no pure delights exist any more ; whom nothing can please which has not the serpent's slime upon it ; to whom literally " nothing is pure," for his very " mind and conscience is defiled."

Oh, if some young man, timidly beginning a course of departure from God, with as yet many restraints of conscience, of a godly education upon him, still dwelling within the charmed circle of a mother's prayers, not yet having quite escaped the influence and remembrances of a holy home, could realize himself to himself, as hereafter he shall be, how low he will fall, what swine's husks he will come to, could he picture to himself his future boldness in vice, his shamelessness in sinning, the day, not so far off, when he, now timidly sipping at the cup of a forbidden joy, shall drink up iniquity like water, and work all uncleanness with greediness, foaming out his own shame—could he thus picture his future self to himself, he would perhaps start back in horror and amazement : it may be that he would not venture on that step which shall be as the first term of so fatal a series. Or again, if in the confidence and jollity with which presently, somewhat bolder grown, the prodigal launches forth on ways of his own choosing, saying to himself that to-morrow shall be as to-day, and much more abundant, that he shall have peace though he add drunkenness to thirst, and walk in the imaginations of his own heart—he could see the waste desolations of his life at some future and it may be not distant day, the blight of his hopes, the withering of his affections, the garlands of a fresh-springing joy for ever struck from his brow, the life run to the lees, empty of joy, because empty of God who is the source of joy,—if he could see the days which shall so soon overtake him, when he shall exclaim, " What good shall my life do me?" when friends shall have forsaken him, opportunities have passed from him, when the talent he would not use shall have been transferred to another, and the crown which he might have worn another shall have taken, when the dreary present shall be shut in by a threatening future and an accusing past, when his feet shall be already stumbling upon the dark mountains,—if he could see all this, this bankruptcy of all things which is so near before him, perhaps he would pause, perhaps even now he will pause, and retrace his steps, while to retrace them is still possible for him.

But too often he does *not* see. His eyes are holden ; or, in the flattering glass which the arch-deceiver holds up before his eyes, he sees quite another sight,—lying prophecies of the future, sin not bitter, the world not false, pleasures never palling, judgment never arriving. There is a glass, the glass of God's Word, which would have shown him these ; but *that* he has put far from him ; for, like Micaiah of Ahab, it prophecies no good concerning him, but evil.

But *we*, my Christian brethren, we who, I trust, have believed, and *that*, without having made miserable proof of it in our own selves, that it is an evil and a bitter thing to forsake the Lord our God, what shall *we* say to these things? Shall it not be this? If there be this rank growth of sin, if it have this power of pervading the whole moral being, and subduing all things to itself, of laying waste and ruining all, what is there which can resist this death but a life? what can resist this growth of sin but a growth of grace? or, in other words, a growth and increase from God and in God? If such as we have described it, is, or at least may be, in every one of us the life of nature, a life which is not life, but death, what remains but that we seek the life of grace, which is life indeed? If it be thus to grow out of the root of Adam, if that bitter root of the old Adam *may* in all of us, and *will* assuredly in many, put forth these bitterest fruits, what is there for us but to seek of God that we of his grace may evermore grow out of the sweet root of the new Adam, which is Christ? Nothing short of this will meet our needs. Sin seeks to possess us wholly. It is, as I have said, a leaven which would fain not cease its working in us, till the whole lump of our nature is leavened by it. To counterwork, to defeat, to expel this, we must seek a principle of good which in like manner will embrace our whole life, will penetrate, transform, transfigure every part of it into its own image and likeness. And where shall this be found except in the regeneration, in that transformation and transfiguration from above which was made possible, and the germs of it planted in us, on the day when we were baptized, and potentially were made partakers of Christ and of all powers of the world to come? It is not a bettering of the old man which will serve, but the putting on of a new man ; not the putting here and there a new patch on the old garment of nature, for this patchwork will not hold, and the rents will only be made worse,—but the web and woof must be made new throughout. Sin is a central principle of disobedience to the will and law of God ; nothing can overcome this, but a central principle of holiness and conformity to that will, which only can in Christ be made ours, which can only be Christ in us.

He, and He only, can make us free. Say not then, as the proud Jews of old, proud and blind at once, "We never were in bondage to any." So far as we have committed, or are committing, any sin, we are in bondage to it ; "he that committeth sin is the servant of sin ;" and that bondage, that servitude will increase upon us more and more. But He, who is the Truth, has said concerning the Truth, that is, concerning Himself, "the *Truth* shall make you free." Let us make trial whether these are not true words, which He who is the Truth has spoken, and whether there is not indeed for us a freedom in the Truth, that is, in Him, which we have vainly looked for elsewhere.

SERMON VII.

THE ANGELS' HYMN.

And suddenly there was with the angel a multitude of the heavenly
host praising God, and saying, Glory to God in the highest, and on
earth peace, good-will toward men.—LUKE ii. 13, 14.

Christmas-Day.

THIS is not the earliest angelic hymn which is recorded or alluded to in Scripture. At the first
creation, when God had laid the corner-stone of the
earth, and it stood forth in all its primal beauty and
perfection, then too " the morning stars sang together,
and all the sons of God shouted for joy."* Whatever doubt there may be in respect of those " sons of
God " mentioned in Genesis,† whose apostasy from
Him did so much to hasten the flood, there can be no
doubt or difficulty in regard of these. The " sons of
God " here can be only the angels of heaven, the heavenly host ; for there as yet existed no other who
could claim, or be competitors with them for this
name. So was it at the first creation ; and it might
almost seem on this night of the nativity as if a new
creation had taken place, for now again we hear of

---

* Job xxxviii. 7.   † vi. 2.

"a multitude of the heavenly host praising God, and saying, Glory to God in the highest, and on earth peace, good-will toward men." Nor, if we thus judged, should we prove very wide of the truth. There is indeed now a new creation, and a new which is more glorious than the old. In the creation of the *world* God showed forth his power, his wisdom, his love; but in the foundation of the *Church* all these his attributes shine far more gloriously forth: and that church was founded, the corner-stone of it, elect, precious, was securely laid, on that day when the Son of God, having taken upon Him our flesh, was born of a pure Virgin, and was laid in the manger at Bethlehem. Most fitly therefore was that day of the New Creation, which should repair and restore the breaches of the old, ushered in with hymns of gladness; most fitly did "the sons of God" once again shout for joy, and welcome with that first Christmas carol which this dull earth ever heard, the birth of a Saviour and Restorer into the world.

They witnessed for themselves that they *were* the hosts of heaven, of that heaven in which love only dwells, where there is no envy, no evil eye, no grudging at another's good, in these songs and praises of theirs. For wherefore did they break the stillness of that Christmas night with these their hymns of thanksgiving? Was it for any restoration or addition of happiness to themselves or to their fellows? Oh, no! but for peace on earth, and good-will toward men. He that was now born took not upon Him the nature of angels, but of men. He came not into the world to save angels, but for the salvation of the children of men. Nor was the state and condition of angels to receive advancement and glory by his coming, but the state and condition of men ; nay, more, to receive it in such a sort as might seem to impeach the dignity, and in part diminish the lustre, of those excellent creatures, seeing that an inferior nature, the nature of man, was now in the person of Him who had become a man to be advanced to a throne of divine majesty, and to become Head and King not only over men, but of the heavenly host itself ; that Child, whose birth these were celebrating this night, to be exalted at the right hand of God, "angels and authorities and powers being made subject unto Him."

This hindered not their joy, nor yet did they repine and grudge that there were mercy and deliverance for the children of men, while there was no deliverance, no restoration for such of their own hosts as had fallen. When these, the angels, left their first estate, fell from their golden seats, there was no attempt to break their fall ; no mystery of redemption for their recovery, for the drawing them up again from the gulf of perdition to those glorious thrones which they had left vacant in heaven. Nay rather, it was now plainly seen who were to occupy the room which they had left empty there. It is this mystery of God's love, not to themselves, but to us, this unsearchable wisdom of God, planning our redemption, not their advancement in glory, which causes them to sing their *Te Deums* in heaven. Woe indeed to us, if we find no argument for praise in that which concerns us so much more nearly than it concerned them ; if they could praise God for the salvation of another race, and we cannot, or with cold dead, hearts will not, praise Him for the salvation of our own.

What is the burden of their song ? It is brief. It is comprised in two, or in three short clauses at the most ; and yet in this narrow compass it contains how much, contains everything. All that Peter and Paul and John and the other Evangelists and apostles laboriously unfolded, the whole Gospel of the grace of God, is shut up in these words ; shut up in them as truly as the oak is shut up in the acorn, and to be unfolded in due time.

And first, " Glory to God in the highest." This is the first jubilant adoring exclamation of the angels, as they beheld the fulfilment of that eternal counsel of God, which, partially known no doubt long since and foreseen in heaven, was now at length actually accomplished upon earth ; as they behold the Lord of glory, Him whom they had worshipped in heaven, become an infant of days, and as such laid in that rugged cradle at Bethlehem. But what is the exact force of these words ? Can God receive increase of glory, more than He has already ? Is it not the very idea of God that He is *infinitely* glorious, and that this He always has been and ever will be ? Assuredly so : in Himself He is as incapable of increase as of diminution of glory. But *we* may *ascribe* more glory to Him, more, that is, of the honor due unto his name, as we know Him more, as the infinite perfection of his being, his power, his wisdom, his love, is gradually revealed to us. So too may angels; and the heavenly host declare in this voice of theirs, that the incarnation of the Son of God was a new revelation, a new outcoming to them of the unsearchable riches of the wisdom, the power, the love, that are in God; that in that church of the redeemed which now had become possible, would be displayed mysteries of grace and goodness which transcended and surpassed all God's past dealings with men or with angels.

We have St. Paul in the Epistle to the Ephesians declaring the same thing; that heaven was taught by what was done upon earth; that angels, as they stooped from the shining battlements on high and looked toward this dim speck of earth, and on one obscure province of it, and at a little village, and to one lowliest household there, learned about the mind of God things which they had not learned, standing upon the steps of the throne, and beholding the unapproachable brightness of Him who sat thereon. Can we doubt this? Does not St. Paul declare that he was himself set to proclaim the mystery which from the beginning of the world had been hid in God, more or less concealed therefore from men and angels alike? And why to proclaim it? he proceeds to give the answer; —" to the intent that now unto the principalities and powers in heavenly places," in other words, to the angelic host, " might be known by the church the manifold wisdom of God."* Here then is the explanation of the angels' song, of this " Glory to God in the

* Ephes. iii. 8–10.

highest"—this melody of heaven, to bear a part in which they invite and challenge the listening children of men upon earth.

And indeed that way of salvation which God has thus devised was worthy of the admiration of angels; so original, so grand, implying such infinite love and condescension, that it must have been in great part inconceivable before it actually took place. Many, alas! have found it inconceivable even after it has taken place. Not merely was it the best way, but we may be bold to say, it was the only way whereby men could be saved. It is sometimes contended that we speak presumptuously, when we speak thus; that we have no right to limit the power of God, or to affirm that anything is impossible for Him, or that He could have devised no other way for bringing his banished home. Now, doubtless all things are possible to God; but yet with one limitation, that they must be things consistent with those supreme moral attributes, that truth, that righteousness, that love, stript of which, God would not be God any more. And keeping all this in view, it is not, I think, too much to affirm, it is not overboldly said, that there was no other way but this of the incarnation of the Son of God, followed as that was by his life of obedience, his death of propitiation, his resurrection in power, his ascension in glory, whereby men could be saved. What should we think of a king, some of whose people were in bitter bondage in a foreign land, if he, knowing that he might have them back by simply sending for them, or at most by paying a ransom of silver and gold, chose

instead of this, and when this was free to him, to send
his own son to serve that bitter bondage in their stead,
to endure all outrages, indignities, wrongs, even death
itself in obtaining their release? Would either wisdom or love shine out gloriously here? Could he
reasonably demand the boundless gratitude of the
ransomed on the ground of the costly sacrifice which
their deliverance entailed, when that deliverance might
have been effected at so much easier and cheaper a
rate? No, dear brethren; when God chose that cost-
liest means of our deliverance, sending his own Son
in likeness of sinful flesh and for sin, we may be quite
sure that at no lower price would our redemption have
been possible, that nothing short of this could have
satisfied that righteousness of his, which He was bound
to maintain; which He could not forego, without
shaking to their strong foundation those eternal pillars on which the moral universe reposes; we may
be quite sure that no weaker, poorer motives than
those in this way presented to man, would have ever
succeeded in making him holy, and thus capable of
blessedness.

But here was a way effectual. God could continue
just, and yet a justifier of sinners, showing in the same
act his hatred of sin and his love of the sinner; and
therefore did the angels sing at the incarnation of the
Son of God, " Glory to God in the highest," while at
the same time they added to this, as not inconsistent
with this, nay rather as following from this, " and on
earth peace, good-will toward men." That same wondrous act which brought such glory to God, namely,

the taking of our flesh by the Son of God, brought also peace on earth, and declared God's good-will towards men. For He who was upon this day born was no other than the very Prince of Peace, the author of all peace, who not merely spoke peace, but who made peace, peace for man with his God, peace for man with himself, peace for man with his brother. Christ in all these three aspects is the author of our peace.

First, He made peace for man with his God. Man was alienated and estranged from God by wicked works; he knew that he hated God, and he feared that God hated him; his whole life was a fighting with God, or a flying from God. They could not walk together; for they were not agreed. And God, though He did not hate man, yet hated his sin, and neither would nor could bless him so long as he continued in his sin. But now the Child was born who should kill the enmity in the heart of man, who should make a propitiation to enable the love of God to flow freely forth on the sinner as it could not flow before. Thus peace in the highest and most blessed sense of all came down from heaven, and made its dwelling-place upon earth, when the Son of God was born.

But He is the Prince of Peace in another sense. In setting men at peace with God, He sets them at peace with themselves. Oh, what turmoil, what strife, what ceaseless agitation are in the hearts of sinful men! what vain hopes, what eating cares, what passionate regrets, what impotent struggles of the better nature within them against the worse which is mastering it more and more. Nor only this helpless struggle of the weaker good against the stronger evil, but one evil fighting within them against another, and sin in arms against sin. And then too oftentimes, what black remorse, what fierce hatred of the sinner against himself, what innermost self-loathing, as in memory he paces back through the hideous gallery of the evils which he has done. "There is no peace, saith my God, for the wicked." But Christ comes, and speaks the word of peace, the word of forgiveness; and there is a great calm upon the stormy sea; and he that a little while ago was crying and cutting himself with stones, is sitting at Jesus' feet, clothed and in his right mind. In this sense also the birth of the Saviour deserved to be proclaimed as the advent of peace upon earth.

But man, at enmity with God and with himself, is also at enmity with his brother. "From whence come wars and fightings among you? Come they not hence, even of your lusts that war in your members?" Selfishness, or an undue love of self, is the root of all the divisions upon earth, from the trivial brawl that disturbs the peace of a village, to the mighty war which makes a desolation over half the world. But He who was as upon this day born came to uproot this selfishness in the heart of man, to plant love there in its room; and, distant as that day may be still, it will yet arrive, when the nations shall not learn war any more. Whenever that day shall come, it will be Christ, and Christ only, who shall have persuaded men to beat their swords into plowshares, and to unlearn all those arts of mutual destruction which now claim so much of their skill, and occupy so large a portion of their thoughts. This Man shall be the peace. It was then with threefold right that the angels hailed his advent as the advent of "peace on earth, good-will toward men."

And now, brethren, one or two very brief words in conclusion. And first, let us praise God for the inestimable gift which was this day given to men. The angels praised Him, whom by comparison it concerned so little; let us praise Him whom it concerns so much. Let us praise Him that heaven and earth have been so knit together; that in Christ Jesus we have the golden clasp which, having once knit them in one, has knit them for evermore; that in this incarnate Son of God the Jacob's ladder, let down from heaven to earth, and spanning the gulf between them, is no longer a dream, but a waking truth and reality; so that if these shining stairs seen by the patriarch were the prophecy, the coming of the Son of God in our nature is the fulfilment of that prophecy; let us praise Him too, that not angels only, but men, may by these stairs ascend into heaven.

And secondly, as we see in Christ and in his Incarnation the bond and bann which knits heaven and earth in one, so too let us see in Him the true maker, upholder, maintainer of all genuine fellowship and brotherhood between man and man. He did not merely proclaim this fellowship; it is actually constituted in Him. He is every man's Brother; and all men, thus akin to Him, are akin also in Him to each other. Christ's brethren are our brethren. All philanthropy, all love of our fellow-men, which does not grow out of this root, which does not nourish itself on this faith, is a poor sickly plant at the best, and will bring no fruit to perfection. But this faith in Christ, that He took the nature of every man, that in Him we have, as many as believe on his name, adoption into the family of God, this and this alone will be effectual to maintain any true fellowship between men.

And you, my Christian brethren, to whom any portion of this world's goods are given, while you show at all times, above all things show at this present, that you believe these things to be true; that you do indeed count the poor, the naked, the hungry, the houseless, your brethren in Christ. Oh, be ashamed to be warm while you have done nothing to hinder them from being cold ; be ashamed to feed without fear, while not so much as a crumb from your table relieves their necessities ; be ashamed of the voices of joy and gladness within your doors, so long as you have done nothing to still the cries of want and woe in that waste wilderness of suffering and sorrow, which, however we may hide our eyes from it, is day and night around us and about us ; and nowhere nearer to us than in that great city, itself also a wilderness, wherein we dwell.

SERMON VIII.

ST. STEPHEN.

And they stoned Stephen, calling upon God, and saying, Lord Jesus,
receive my spirit. And he kneeled down, and cried with a loud
voice, Lord, lay not this sin to their charge. And when he had said
this, he fell asleep.—ACTS vii. 59, 60.

YESTERDAY we celebrated the birth of Christ;
to-day we celebrate the death of his first witness
and confessor, St. Stephen. It was Christ's birth, but
it is Stephen's death; for with the exception of the
Baptist, who was wonderfully born, we do not commemorate the birth of any, save only of the King of
saints. And there is reason in this; seeing that to be
born into an evil world is not the blessed thing for
sinful man; but to be new born into the kingdom of
grace, which is blessed; even as to be fully born into
the perfected kingdom of glory, which is most blessed
all. Of one Man only could his birth be regarded as
a matter of pure and unmingled rejoicing—the Man
whose generation did not require a regeneration to
complete it, and was not therefore followed by one.
But of all other among her saints the church commemorates not the day of their birth, but that of their
death, which was indeed their passage into life, the
seal of their final triumph over sin, and the pledge that
henceforth nothing should by any means hurt them.

And the day of St. Stephen's martyrdom follows close (it could not follow closer) on the day of Christ's nativity. The fact has its lesson. Of course, as we do not pretend to know exactly at what period of the year this glorious martyr suffered, it lay open to choose any day for the celebration of his faith and patience and victorious martyrdom. But this day was not chosen at random. A profound Christian feeling dictated the selection; and the mere juxtaposition of the two is eminently instructive for us. We are thus reminded in whose strength it was that this martyr triumphed, even in the strength of the incarnate Son of God. We are thus taught that it was because Christ had lived for Stephen, that therefore Stephen was enabled to die for Christ. The self-denying life of Christ, crowned with his holy death, was for those who followed at once the pattern and the power—the pattern of what they ought to be, the power by which they were enabled to be what they ought. We have here a commentary, not in word but in life, on the declaration of the Apostle, "I can do all things through Christ which strengtheneth me."

But concerning Stephen, foremost in the glorious army of martyrs, first of those golden grains beaten out by the persecutor's flail to enrich the barn-floor of the Lord,* it is probable from his name, which is a Greek one, that he was not a Jew of Palestine, not, that is, a Hebrew Jew; but one of the Dispersion, who

---

* "Primum granum trituratum, Christi, ditans arcam." *Ancient Hymn.*

had retained the faith, but who had lost, or left off to use, the language of his fathers—a Hellenist, or 'Grecian,' as such are called in our Bible. This, it will be well to remember, means something quite different there from a 'Greek.' A 'Greek' is a Gentile, one of Gentile birth and heathen religion; but a 'Grecian' is a Jew, quite as much a Jew, as truly of the stock of Abraham, as the Hebrew; and with only the difference that, through long dwelling in foreign lands, he, or his fathers before him, had unlearned the Hebrew tongue, and spake the Greek language, and used the Septuagint translation of the Bible; being for all this quite as much an heir of the promises as the other.

Such a Grecian, it can hardly be doubted, we have in St. Stephen. When the Twelve, willing to devote themselves exclusively to the spiritual duties of their great apostleship, required of the congregation that it should designate "seven men full of the Holy Ghost and of wisdom," whom they might appoint over the secular business of the church, Stephen is the first among those named, and with this most honorable addition, " a man full of faith and of the Holy Ghost." Being thus brought forward into a prominent place in the church, he speedily drew upon himself the peculiar enmity of the unbelieving Jews; partly by the great wonders and miracles which he did, thus confirming and spreading the faith of Jesus of Nazareth; but chiefly no doubt by the boldness with which he proclaimed the significance of that new society which Christ had founded; that in it Jew and Gentile stood on equal terms; for the middle wall of partition which had separated them hitherto, and set one nearer and one farther off from God, had been broken down by his death; that all now were near;—a doctrine above all other unwelcome to Jewish ears.

This much we are justified in affirming; for it is this which must evidently lie behind the charge which his accusers bring against him: "We have heard him 'say that this Jesus of Nazareth shall destroy this place, and shall change the customs which Moses delivered." The charge was an untrue one; they are declared "false witnesses" who bring it; but like so many lies, like the very similar accusations made against Stephen's Lord,* it was the perversion and caricature of a truth. It did no doubt lie involved in that mighty truth which Stephen perhaps was the first to proclaim with power, and of which St. Paul was afterwards raised up to be the witness,—namely, in the universal character of that church which Christ had founded,— that sooner or later the temple-worship should cease, the ceremonial law be done away, that no longer in that mountain, nor in Gerizim, but that every where men should worship God in spirit and in truth; that Christianity, whose true centre was every where, inasmuch as Christ was every where, could have no local centre, as the Jewish religion had.

But neither Stephen now, nor Paul at a later day, spake *against* the Temple or *against* the law. These were of God; and, albeit now they had done their

* Matt. xxvi. 61.

4*

work, were to be set aside not rudely nor violently, but gently, and with all reverence and honor, and, as far as possible, with no outrage done to the feelings of any; the church detaching itself from its Jewish integuments with as little violence as the full-formed fruit from the shell or husk which protected it while as yet it was not fully formed. Still the doom of the Temple, the doom of the law, did most plainly lie in the doctrine which Stephen preached (and this much right his accusers had); of the Temple, for not in one temple made with hands more than in another, but in prepared hearts of all faithful worshippers, would the Lord's habitation henceforth be: of the law, for a main purpose of that law had been to separate the Jew from the Gentile, while that of Christ had been, for now the time was come, to unite them.

No wonder then that Stephen should have stirred up the bitterest hatred of all who in the pride and narrowness of their hearts desired that the exclusive privileges of the Jew should be for ever, of the wicked husbandmen who, having killed the Son, hoped that the inheritance might be theirs: no wonder that the lot of martyrdom should first have fallen on him, the newly-elected deacon, rather than on Peter or James or John, foremost pillars of the church. The great truth of the calling of the Gentiles, and that upon entirely equal terms with the Jew, he had seized with a far firmer grasp even than these chiefest apostles (at a later day, you may remember how Peter needed an especial vision to reconcile him to it), he proclaimed it more boldly than all; and thus he concentrated on himself, as Paul, the inheritor of this mighty truth, at a later day concentrated on himself, well-nigh all the hostility and all the enmity of the Jewish opponents of the Gospel.

The relation of these two with one another is one of profoundest interest; for Stephen is evidently the precursor of Paul; and when in that fire-chariot of pain the first martyr was taken up to heaven, it was on Paul that indeed his mantle fell. And yet it little seemed so at the time. In all probability they had actually disputed with one another concerning the faith of Christ. Stephen, we know, had disputed with them at Jerusalem of the synagogue of Cilicia;* and who so likely as Saul of Tarsus to have been the chief disputer among these? and when the matter came to a sterner arbitrament than that of words, it was at a young man's feet whose name was Saul that the witnesses, who were bound to cast the first stone at him who died by their witness, laid down their clothes; he, as it were, not being content to have one hand in Stephen's death but many, helping many to slay, even all whose clothes he kept.

And yet here was indeed the turning-point of St. Paul's life. We dare not indeed say, as some have said, that all his earlier convictions, all his fierce zeal for the Jewish religion, and hatred of the Christian name, were shaken by what he saw of Stephen's patience, courage, meekness, love, by the sight of his face shining like an angel's, so that inwardly he was half a

* Acts vi. 9.

convert even before the Lord met him on the way to Damascus. We dare not say this. There is no sign, no indication of any thing of the kind in Scripture. So far from this, he was holding on in all his heat of pride, in all his fanatic hatred against the name of Jesus, unabated to the last, even to the very instant of his conversion. And yet for all this, we may say that here was the turning-point of all; for it has ever been the faith of the church that to Stephen's prayer we owe Paul's conversion.

And if this was so, (which who would willingly deny?) how does it explain much that else is strange and perplexing in the protomartyr's story. Here we behold a man full of wisdom, of the Holy Ghost, and of power; whose adversaries were not able to resist the wisdom by which he spake; equipped as few were, in some respects it might be, equipped as no other was. for a great work in the kingdom of God; and yet scarcely has his career commenced when it is brought to a close. This burning and shining light is hardly kindled before it is quenched in darkness again. And yet not so; only to the eye of sense does it so appear: from that candle another has been lighted, which shall burn long, and give light to all that are in the house. One has fallen at the first onset and in the foremost ranks of the battle; but another, kindled by his example, has stepped into his room. And how many other lives may perhaps find their explanation here. How often the life of some good man. of some man signally furnished for the serving of God in his church, seems brought prematurely to a close. Shut up while he lived within some narrow sphere, and not occupying even that for long, he may yet have left some inheritor of his grace behind him,—the fruit of his prayers, of his labors, of his holy example,—as great, or it may be much greater, than himself. Can he be then esteemed to have lived in vain? does he not live on in this his spiritual heir?

But these considerations of the great Apostle of the Gentiles, as at once this spiritual heir to Stephen, and successor to his unfinished life-task, must not lead us altogether away from the latter. I must ask you before we conclude, to consider three or four principal Christian graces which shine out in him; and may we, at however remote a distance, be followers of him, as he was of Christ.

Note then, first, his wisdom. He was a man, we know, full of wisdom. Put on his defence, he does not rudely affront the prejudices of his Jewish hearers; for indeed they are "brethren and fathers." Where he has common ground with them, he takes it. We have here an explanation of that which has perplexed many, namely, the long and particular recapitulation which he makes of the early history of the elect people. He may have higher objects too, but with those higher he has this—to show how that history is as dear to him as to them; that he is no enemy of the law, or of Moses, or of the Temple, however he may now believe that in Jesus of Nazareth better things are theirs, or may be theirs, than their fathers ever knew.

But with all his wisdom, admire also his courage. There is no shrinking upon his part from the utterance of unwelcome truths; no flattering of the fatal prejudices of his Jewish audience. Where need is, and when the right time has arrived, he addresses to them the most cutting rebukes. The ingratitude, the revolt, the rebellion of the people in the wilderness was but a type and pattern and prelude of theirs: " Ye stiff-necked and uncircumcised in heart and ears, ye do always resist the Holy Ghost: as your fathers did, so do ye."

But next, admire his love. He speaks so sharply, one may say so fiercely, that it would lie very near to think that there was no love in his heart. And yet what were a martyr without love? " Though I give my body to be burned, and have not charity, it profiteth me nothing." Not so, however. His rage is but the rage of the dove, in which there is no gall, no bitterness. The wounds which he inflicts are the faithful wounds of a friend, if only they had been accepted as such. And this he plainly shows when, amid that shower of cruel stones, he answers evil with good, cursings with blessings, despiteful usage with prayers; in all this following hard on the footsteps of his blessed Lord, and in that more excellent way which He had shown. When Zacharias, son of Barachias, a martyr of the elder covenant, was slain between the Temple and altar, he, in harmony with that covenant of righteousness wherein he served. exclaimed with his dying breath. " The Lord look upon it, and require it." *
But as the blood of Christ speaketh better things than the blood of Abel, cries from the earth for pardon and

* 2 Chron xxiv. 22.

not for vengeance, so better than the prayer of Zacharias is the prayer of Stephen : "Lord, lay not this sin to their charge."

But lastly, my brethren, observe, and at whatever distance imitate, this blessed martyr's faith. How was it, it may be asked, that he endured? He endured as seeing Him that is invisible. Others might not see, but he saw heaven opened, and saw the glory of God, and the Son of Man standing at the right hand of God. Observe, I beseech you, that 'standing.' Often as we read of Christ *sitting* at the right hand of God, this is the only occasion upon which He is spoken of in Scripture as standing there. And why standing? As in act to help, as rising from his throne to succor and to save, to uphold his servant in this the hour of his extremest need. Such was the latest sight which his closing eyes beheld on earth. No wonder that those who looked on him should have seen his face as it had been the face of an angel. And then, after a sharp short agony, his eyes opened once more, and he beheld that same Lord, not now far off but near ; and he was ever with Him. Earth and earth's toil, and the gnashing teeth and the fierce faces of foes, and whatever of mortal pain this flesh can suffer, had for him for ever passed away. His was the crown which his name 'Stephen' had prophesied for him from the beginning, and his the rest of Paradise, and the beatific vision, and the exceeding weight of glory. May God give us grace in our humbler sphere, according to our smaller strength, that we too may be faithful unto death, and may so receive a crown of life!

SERMON IX.

THE CALL OUT OF EGYPT.

Out of Egypt have I called my Son.—MATT. ii. 15.

THESE words are quoted by St. Matthew as having
found their fulfilment when the infant Saviour, at
the bidding of the angel of the Lord, was carried into
Egypt, and having there abode till the tyranny of
Herod's wrath was overpast, did again, at the same
bidding, return with Joseph and his mother out of
Egypt, and dwell once more in the land of his nativity.
At first we are somewhat startled and surprised at the
use to which the Evangelist puts these words of the
prophet. We turn to Hosea ii. 1, and it is evident
that in their primary intention they do *not* refer to the
child Jesus, but to the children of Israel collectively
regarded as God's dear Son ; and the calling out of
Egypt is *their* deliverance by the mighty power of God
from their house of bondage there, and from the yoke
of their Egyptian taskmasters.

Shall we say then that St. Matthew only accommo-
dates these words; that although they have no real
or direct reference to the later event which he is re-
cording, he notwithstanding adapts them to it: and
that this is all? I think we must every one acknowledge that such would not be a reverential dealing with

the Word of God; that, when St. Matthew speaks of the infant Christ's return out of Egypt as the *fulfilment* of a prophecy, we ought not so to interpret his words as to find in them only the adaptation or accommodation of a prophecy, and of one spoken originally in quite another sense, and having properly no allusion to Him at all.

What then? how shall we understand the declaration of the Evangelist, that in this event a scripture was fulfilled, which we know had direct and immediate reference to an event which had happened two thousand years before? In this way. Words of Scripture being words of God, and being therefore deep words, central words, words which take their stand at the heart of things, look many ways, have many aspects, may have one fulfilment, and then another, a commencing fulfilment, and then another, and another, and at last a crowning fulfilment. It is not easy to exhaust them; so to draw out all their meaning, that no more remains behind to be drawn out from them still. No doubt the words of Hosea—the exact words, as I will remind you, are these, "When Israel was a child, then I loved him, and called my son out of Egypt"— did look back to the calling of the children of Israel out of Egypt; but they were so overruled by the Holy Ghost, that while they thus looked back to one signal mercy of God to his church, they looked on to a far greater mercy; but one of exactly the same kind, with an inner as well as an outer resemblance; which therefore could be fitly included under the same words.

For why were the children of Israel called out of

Egypt? For this reason, that they might be bearers of God's word, witnesses of God's truth, to the nations, that they might declare His name to the world, that they might be a light to lighten the Gentiles. I do not stop to inquire how far they were true to this their high calling ; but it was for this that God called them out of Egypt, acknowledged them his people, gave them his law, drove out their enemies before them, and caused them to ride upon the high places of the earth. And why was Christ preserved from Herod's sword and all the perils of his infancy, sheltered for a while in Egypt, and then in due time called out of Egypt, and brought back again to the Holy Land? Why, but for this same reason—that, growing in grace and favor with God and man, He might indeed be that which the natural Israel ought to have been, and was not, the Light of the World, the true and faithful Witness, who should declare the name and worship of the true God to the ends of the earth.

For indeed in Christ were gathered up and fulfilled all the purposes of God, all the intentions with which the Jewish people was constituted from the beginning. We might not unfitly compare that people to the aloe-plant, which is said, and I believe rightly, only to flower once during its lifetime, and that after a long lapse of years ; and having put forth its single flower once for all, that indeed a flower of exquisite beauty and richness, then, as having lived but for this, to droop and wither and die. Christ, the fairer than the children of men, the One among ten thousand, the Virgin-born, was in some sort the one glorious and perfect Flower which the rough and hard aloe-stem of the Jewish church and nation, barren so long, at length bore ; and having borne this, having fulfilled the purpose of its existence in that wondrous birth, it also drooped and died. Thus, as gathering up and concentrating all the life, strength, and beauty of that stalk and stem in Himself, as the consummation of all that went before, Christ *was* Israel ; He is often so called in the Prophets. He, a Jew, at once embodied and represented the Jewish nation before his Heavenly Father in their noblest aspect, in their highest fulfilment of that great mission which was theirs, namely, to declare the name of God to the world ; and every gracious dealing of God with his people had reference and respect to that one crowning act for which the nation existed, namely, that a Child might be born out of the bosom of the people, a Son of Abraham, a Son of David, in whom all the nations of the world should be blest. With good right, therefore, could St. Matthew claim all the promises which were made to Israel, as having been made to Him who by best right *was* Israel, all past deliverance of the people as typical and prophetical of that mightier deliverance with which God would deliver his elect, in whom his soul delighted, from every danger and from every fear, saying to Him, " Thou art my servant, O Israel, by whom I will be glorified."

The words, therefore, spoken by the prophet Hosea are not accommodated to Christ, but were most truly fulfilled in Him. They had thus a double fulfilment, the second more glorious than the first. Nor should we err if we ascribed to them one fulfilment more. That which was on these two occasions literally fulfilled, "Out of Egypt have I called my Son," is ever more finding its spiritual fulfilment in the church of the redeemed. It collectively is God's Son, even as one by one the true members who compose it are his sons; and they too have been called out of Egypt, and are living members of his church, in so far as they have not been disobedient to that heavenly calling; and it is to this, the third fulfilment of this memorable prophecy, that I would ask your attention for the time which remains, and to some of the practical considerations which may thus be naturally suggested to us.

Egypt, as I need hardly remind you, is always represented to us in Scripture as a land of darkness, a land of superstition, of low grovelling idolatry, of slavery and oppression at once for the bodies and the spirits of men. Nowhere had idolatry assumed so degrading a form. In other heathen lands men worshipped the sun and the moon, and the shining host of heaven, or gods made in the likeness of men; but in Egypt they had sunk to the worship of birds and four-footed beasts and creeping things. If thick darkness rested over the whole of heathendom, yet the thickest darkness of all was over Egypt. Then, too, Egypt was the land where the children of Israel had served their hard service, their cruel bondage, under tyrannous taskmasters and unrighteous lords. What wonder then that Egypt in Scripture should be the standing type and symbol of the world, as it lieth in the Evil One, as it is full of darkness and ignorance of God, alienated from the life of God, as it lays its heavy bondage on the hearts and spirits of men, draws them away from the worship of their Father in heaven to the worship of the meanest objects of sense? What wonder, then, that when God calls us with a holy calling, from darkness to light, from slavery to freedom, from the worship of idols, of the idols of sense, of the things beneath us, to the worship of Himself, it should be styled a calling out of Egypt?

Such indeed it is. It is a coming out of Egypt; and it is a coming out in obedience to a heavenly calling. The children of Israel might have groaned under their tasks, they might have cursed the imposers of those tasks; but they would never have thought of freedom, of deliverance, unless God had put that thought into their hearts. It was his voice, his calling, wakening in them higher hopes, nobler desires, which changed them from a servile band of cowering slaves into an army of freemen; which strengthened them to go forth from the land of their bondage—not fearing the wrath of the king, but seeing Him that was invisible, and nothing doubting but that He would lead them through the waves of the Red sea, through all the perils of the wilderness, even to the promised land of their inheritance at the last. And our Egypt, believe me, we should never leave it, if God, even the God of the spirits of all flesh, did not quicken our spirits, did not summon us to a nobler life—to something better than a slavish bondage to our fleshly appetites and grovelling desires. And God calls us *as his sons:* "Out of Egypt have I called my *sons.*" In one sense all men are his sons. "We are his offspring," as is declared in words to which the apostle Paul has set his seal. But this original sonship has been lost; if not effaced, it has been suspended, through sin, and we need a new adoption into the family of God, which we have in Christ Jesus our Lord; for as many as believe on Him, to them gives He power to become the sons of God.

If, my Christian brethren, it is thus with us, if we have been called out of Egypt by the voice of God, to be his children, what are some of the duties which flow out from our high vocation as in this light regarded?

And, first, this surely is one—to leave Egypt altogether behind us, to have no going back to it even in thought, much less drawing back to it in deed. You remember how it fared with the children of Israel, the temptations which assailed *them ;* how they called to mind the fleshpots of Egypt, said it was well with them when they were sitting beside these ; would fain have chosen some new leader who might bring them back to these coarse delights,—even though he brought them back to their house of bondage too ; and because Moses was hidden in the mount of glory with God, " as for this Moses," they said, " we wot not what is become of him." And though they did not actually *go* back, one cause or another preventing, yet when they committed the sins of Egypt in the midst of the church of God,— when they set up the golden calf, when they committed fornication with the daughters of Moab,—they had in spirit returned thither, and were dealt with by God as guilty of this extreme revolt from Him.

Is there not something only too like this in the spiritual history of men? By the grace of God it is only a temptation, and a temptation which is overcome, in many ; while others, alas! succumb to the temptation, and are again entangled in that yoke of bondage, return to that darkness and slavery, from which they had been once delivered. But the temptation is common to all—to cast after a while a longing, lingering look on that which has been forgone and renounced, yea, even to loathe, as light food, the heavenly manna, the bread that cometh down from heaven, and to yearn for some coarser fare, some of the sinful dainties of the world, in its stead; to lose trust in the Heavenly Guide ; and, because He is unseen, because He is withdrawn for a little from our sight, because He is in the Mount of God, beholding the glory of his Father's countenance, to say of Him, "We wot not what is become of Him." Let us watch against this temptation. Our course is onward ; our salvation is before us and not behind, above us and not beneath ; behind and beneath are slavery and darkness, despair and death ; before us and above us is the light of life, with Him who is Himself that Light for our guardian and our guide.

But again, let us remember that if we have been called out of Egypt, it is not that we may enter the promised land at once ; that there is a time and space between, in which our God will prove us, and humble us, and show us what is in our hearts ; and that this, being a proving time, is also a sifting time, a separating of the true members of the church from the false. There were many who came out of Egypt, who never entered into Canaan. Their carcasses fell in the wilderness. And why? For many reasons; and among other reasons for this—they murmured at the greatness of the way, and the difficulties of it. They had not laid their account for this; and thus they became murmurers and complainers; unthankful for past mercies, distrustful of future; at every little check or annoyance fretting against God; or it might be, worse than this, in an evil heart of unbelief counting that the wonders of God's power and of his love were exhausted, and that He had brought them out into that wilderness only that they might perish, or even that He might slay them, there. And these things—the records, that is, of their impatience, ingratitude, unbelief, rebellion— were written, as the apostle expressly tells us, for our admonition. Truly such admonition drawn from such ensamples is not superfluous. How easily, not to speak of yet graver sins, *we* give way to the same evil spirit of fretfulness or impatience! If one little thing is withheld, we forget a thousand great things which are freely given. It is nothing to us that God has called us out of Egypt, has given to us the adoption of sons, that He is leading us to a good land and a large, the glory of all lands, even the land of everlasting life. If any little thing goes wrong on our journey thither,— if the water of the wells at one of our halting-places is but a little brackish, if earthly comforts at all fail, if we cannot have the quails for our lust as well as the bread for our need,—how prone we are to discontent and to displeasure, to act over again the sin of Jonah, who, because his paltry gourd had perished, wished in himself to die, and said, " It is better for me to die than to live ; " yes, and like him to defend this impatience, and to affirm even in the face of God, that we do well and not ill in being thus angry for the withering of our gourd. Fretfulness, irritation of spirit, discontent at God's dealings with us, not, it may be, manifested without, but nourished and entertained within, is a sin against which it behoves us, partakers of a heavenly calling, travellers to a heavenly country, to be very much on our guard. It is deeply charged with unthankfulness and ingratitude ; and needs to be watched against the more, because it may be thus nourished within, and seen there of God, while it is concealed from every human eye.

Not in this, but in quite another spirit God meant that we should walk when He called, and calling brought us out of the spiritual Egypt. It was that we, as the literal Israel of old, might show forth the praises of Him that hath brought us out of darkness into his marvellous light, that we might be his witnesses, doing all things without murmurings and disputings, the sons of God without rebuke, blameless and harmless, shining as lights in the world, and holding forth to others that word of life which we had received into our own hearts.

5

SERMON X.

THE PRODIGALITIES OF LOVE.[*]

To what purpose is this waste ?—MATT. xxvi. 8.

IT is indeed very worthy of notice that, whatever God's servants may do, the world is ever ready, ever on the watch, to pick a quarrel with it. There is always something wrong in it, some side or other on which a fault will be found, an offence taken. · Elijah is a troubler of Israel; Ezekiel a speaker in dark and obscure parables; Jeremiah causes the heart of the people to fail; Moses lets the people from their burdens; Paul and Silas turn the world upside down; David behaves himself unseemly, and makes himself vile when he dances in holy exultation before the Ark; the austere Baptist, withdrawing from the world, "hath a devil;" the gracious Saviour, mingling with the world, is "a gluttonous man and a wine-bibber, a friend of publicans and sinners." And thus is it ever. The world can always find something wrong in that which God's servants do; or if it be manifestly lifted

* Preached on the first Sunday after the Consecration of All Saints', Marylebone, May 29, 1859. I have not thought it needful for the sake of this single Sermon, not preached in the Abbey, to alter the title of this volume.

above all reproach, then, if not in the matter, yet in the manner; in the degree of the thing, if not in the thing itself. The good work which that holy woman wrought on the person of the Lord did not escape this universal law of reproach. It was too lavishly, too prodigally done. "To what purpose is this waste?"

You remember, doubtless, my brethren, who it was that spoke these words, and on what occasion He spoke them. The Lord Jesus, some very few days before his Passion, was sitting in the house of Simon,—of "Simon the leper," as he is still called, for the recent healing which he had received at the Lord's hands had not abolished his old name. Another and still more eminent trophy of Christ's power and grace was sitting at the same table,—Lazarus, whom He had recalled from the grave; the Lord, it may be, was sitting between these two. But while He thus sat at meat, there came a woman,—St. Matthew does not name her by name, but from St. John we learn that it was no other than Mary, the sister of Lazarus,—one, therefore, who owed, and felt that she owed, everything to Jesus. She owed Him herself, for, sitting at his feet she had heard words of eternal life; she owed Him her brother, rescued from the jaws of death which had already closed upon him, and given back to her love. This Mary, owing, and feeling that she owed, everything to the Lord, came, not indeed "behind Him weeping," as that other poor contrite sinner had done;* but with holy boldness, with the lavish prodigalities of grateful affection,

* Luke vii. 38.

taking no account of the more or the less, but counting that the most was all too slight an utterance of her thankful heart, and "having an alabaster box of very precious ointment, poured it on his head;" nor yet content with this, anointed also the feet of Jesus with the ointment, till the whole house where the guests were assembled was filled with the odor of the ointment; and the word of the Bride in the Canticles was fulfilled, "While the King sitteth at his table, my spikenard sendeth forth the smell thereof."

And yet this savor, sweet as it was, was not a sweet savor to all; there was one indeed to whom, so far from being a *sweet* savor, a savor of life unto life, it was a savor rather of death unto death. In St. Matthew and St. Mark we are told generally, that some, and these some even disciples, when they saw it, had indignation within themselves, and said, "Why was this waste of the ointment made?" A perplexing statement enough, that any who were disciples should grudge the honor due to their Master, or count any honor too great for Him; a most perplexing statement, if it were not completed by the statement of St. John, from which we learn that this was not the thought of their *own* hearts, had not its birth there, but only that they were drawn away too easily by the fair speeches, that they fell in too easily with the plausible indignation, of the traitor; who indeed grudged this or any other honor to Him; and who led them in their guilelessness and simplicity to share for a passing moment in his own murmurings and discontent.

The words themselves, and the rebuke which they

call out, "Why trouble ye the woman? for she hath wrought a good work upon me," reach very far; they find their application again and again. For indeed this is the wonderful character of Scripture, above all of the incidents in the life of our Lord, that every thing there, however unpretending in its outward form, yet touches the central heart of things, and therefore is never old, never out of date; having found a thousand fulfilments in time past, is prepared to find in the future a thousand more.

"To what purpose is this waste?" How do these words emerge again and again from the deep of men's hearts, find utterance more or less distinct from their lips! Sometimes they are words of disciples, and spoken by them in simplicity and good faith, with no malice in those who uttered them, whatever malice there may have been in those who first suggested them to their minds. Sometimes they spring out of a far bitterer root, as in the case of that unhappy one who played the foremost part among the murmurers here, himself a false disciple, and a foe in the disguise of a friend. Sometimes, I say, they are thus the voice and utterance of the world, as it *is*, however it may not avow itself as such, the foe of God, the foe of Christ; and which, being this, can ill endure that He should be made much of, that He should be honored, that to Him should be rendered the unstinted devotedness of hearts and hands, and of whatever these hearts and hands can bring and dedicate to his service.

How much *time*, for example, the Christian man must seem to the votary of this world to be throwing away in meditation and prayer! What do these people mean, it says, or, if it does not say, it thinks, by being always at church, so often at sacraments, setting apart such portions of the day for secret devotions, for study and meditation in the Scripture? What comes of it? What return does it bring? Why cannot they be content with a few minutes of prayer in the morning, and a few minutes of prayer at night, and an occasional chapter in the Bible, and church upon Sunday, once, or if they choose it, twice, as others were before them? "To what purpose is this waste?"

Once more, the world grudges and resents any signal outbursts of feeling and passion, any manifest warmth or heat of the affections, in any of the services offered to God. For if God is a jealous God, and will not give his glory to another, it is quite as true that the world is a jealous world, and can ill endure to see any eagerly and passionately served but itself. That there should be, what one of the old Fathers has called "martyrs of the devil," who run to hell with the same eagerness wherewith some of God's saints have run to heaven, who serve the world with their whole heart and mind and soul and strength, this seems quite according to rule with it; but that any should be martyrs of God, their life seems folly, and their end madness. And all lower degrees of the same passion which has led some to snatch and seize the martyr's crown, are, in their degree, offensive to it no less. It cannot understand that fine madness which from time to time possesses those whom the Spirit of God has laid hold of with power. To be drunk with wine, it can understand and pardon; but not to be "filled with the Spirit." David dancing before the Ark is as one of the shameless fellows in the eyes of a cold and mocking Michal. The height, the strength, the exorbitancy of the love with which some have loved Christ their Lord, this is a rank offence in the eyes of them, the Simons, who, loving Him little, in fact love Him not all. Cold formal homage and lip-service they can bear with; but that any should praise Him out of the great deep, should testify of Him that He giveth songs in the night, should glorify Him in the midst of the fires, this they cannot endure. "What is thy Beloved more than another beloved?" Why render to Him, as invisible Lord, the author of a remote invisible good, if indeed He be the author of any, that love, those affections, which might find their fitter object in some nearer and more satisfying good? "To what purpose is this waste?"

And not otherwise is it when this inner devotion of heart finds utterance in some costly offering of the hands; when any thing that at all transcends the common rate is rendered back to Him from whom all things proceed, and to whom all things belong. The world will allow and praise any prodigality which is bestowed upon itself; but when it is for God and for Christ, when the costly cedar is overlaid with the pure gold in the temple of the Lord, when the alabaster box of precious ointment is broken above the head of Christ, and no drop reserved, but all poured out, and not on his head only, but on his feet, even then, while the whole house of the church is filled with the odor of the ointment, there will not be wanting some to exclaim, "To what purpose is this waste?"

But see, my dear brethren, on the first occasion when these words, so often since repeated, were uttered, how the Lord silences the murmurers, allows and accepts the gift, and takes her that brought it under his shelter, and throws over her, dashed and abashed as no doubt for a moment she was to find her good thus evil spoken of, the shield of his protecting love. "Why trouble ye the woman? for she hath wrought a good work upon me." And these words also reach very far. I see in them, setting as they did the seal of Christ's approval on that costly service just done to Him, disallowing as they did the plea that the money expended upon it might have been more usefully expended in some other way, the allowance, the authority, the justification for very much which has since found place in his church. No cold utilitarianism is to reign there, no niggard calculation of the cheapest rate at which He may be served. The best which any man can bring to Him is not too good, the richest and the rarest is not too rich and rare, for Him. All things are to serve Him. The kings of the earth should bring their glory and honor into his temple; and not merely the kings who sit on visible thrones; but they who reign as kings in the spirits of men, the mighty in science, the mighty in art, the mighty in song, they are then doing their best, they are then fulfilling most truly the ends for which these transcendant gifts were imparted to them, when they consecrate all without reserve to Him, when they count all their science, their art, their song, only then to have reached their highest consummation and end, while they wait as ministering handmaids upon Him, setting forward the beauty of his service, the spread of his truth, the glory of his name.

Thus, if any should ask concerning this beautiful house in which we are worshipping to-night, "To what purpose is this waste?" we answer, in the words of Christ, that it is a good work which has here been wrought for Him; nor shall we be led astray even though some should remind us how ten or twenty churches for the poor might have been erected for the cost of this one. I honor those who, serving in the spirit and not in the letter, have, in some great famine or distress, sold the very sacramental vessels themselves, that with the price they might feed the poor or redeem the captive; but let us honor her also, for Christ honored her, and declared that her praise should be in all the churches, she too serving in the spirit, and not in the letter, who broke the alabaster box of ointment, very precious, over the Saviour's head, which "might have been sold for much, and given to the poor;" let us honor her, and all who have since trodden in her steps. Short-sighted indeed, even from their own point of view, I believe the alternative course suggested by the objectors would prove. "Deep calleth unto deep." One signal act of self-sacrifice calls out many more; and if ever there are to be churches for all the poor in the land, such good works as this which we here behold do not stand in the way of such a consummation, but are rather the very deeds which are likeliest to provoke it.

We put back, therefore, the charge, "To what pur-

5*

pose is this waste?" We feel that it touches not us, who rejoice in this goodly house; that it touches as little them whose munificence designed and accomplished it. Nay, we retort these words on the world, and on the world's votaries. "To what purpose is this waste?" this your lavish expenditure of thought, of labor, of time, of affections, of all precious things, upon unworthy objects, this wearying of yourselves for very vanity, this toiling for that which satisfieth not, this laboring only for the meat which perisheth; this hugging to your bosom of a world which pierceth you through with many sorrows; while you meanwhile, like that desperate king of Israel, make altars to the gods that smote you, and, though wounded in the house of your friends, wounded a thousand times in the house of your false friends, yet trust and believe in them still? May we not ask you, children and votaries of this world, who are working all for time, nothing for eternity, who are working all for the flesh, nothing for the spirit, whose sowing can be followed by no reaping, whose scattering can be crowned by no gathering, who are making so much of the inn where you lodged for a single night, furnishing and adorning *it*, while you leave meanwhile empty and unfurnished and desolate the house where you must continue for ever,—may we not turn the tables, and ask of you, "To what purpose is this waste" of the priceless treasure of a heart which was made for God, but is wasted on the world; of a life which might have been laid out for the highest, but is squandered on the meanest, objects and aims?

But you, brethren beloved of the Lord, who will worship from day to day, and from year to year, in the courts of this house, you will give all diligence that, great as is the outward glory which it wears, it may have another and a higher glory still. " The king's daughter is all glorious *within*." Her apparel may be of wrought gold ; but this is nothing. Faith and hope and love, it is these which make her glorious indeed. Truth and beauty, it is well when these two are wedded, as they are wedded here—truth in doctrine and discipline, beauty in form and outward service ; but if ever these should be divorced, as divorced by evil accident in some ages of the church they have been, let us pray God that we may have grace to cleave to the truth, and to let the beauty go. For better the sternest, the ruggedest, the most unattractive presentation of the faith, which has yet fast hold of the central truth, than the fairest and the loveliest, which has allowed any vital portion of this to escape.

So too with these houses of God. Christ in the midst of his church, his presence and his power, these have turned many a rude upper chamber, or darksome crypt, or narrow catacomb, into the very gate of heaven, with angels ascending and descending upon the Son of Man ; while his absence, the putting of any other before Him, or instead of Him, or beside Him, this would empty even such a house as this of its glory altogether, would leave it a husk without a kernel, the mausoleum of a dead faith instead of the temple of a living. Oh, then, let us pray earnestly that not now only, but so long as this house endures, long after we have passed away, Christ may be here preached, in the freeness of his grace, in the power of his sacraments, in the fullness of his redeeming love, in all his readiness to heal, in all his mightiness to save. Let us pray that careless hearts may be here aroused, and weary may find rest, and wounded may find healing ; that Christ on his cross, Christ set forth evidently crucified among you, may draw many to Him, many, as the doves to their windows, to find their refuge and their shelter in his wounded side, even in the clefts of that Rock that was cleft and smitten for them. So, when the Lord writeth up the number of his people, it shall be said of this man and of that, yea, of no mean number added to the multitude of the white-robed and palm-bearing who stand before the throne, that they were born here, that this was as the Beautiful gate to the heavenly Temple ; in which, by the name of the Lord Jesus, and through faith in his name, they were healed ;* and by which they entered that Temple not made with hands, eternal in the heavens, of which all the fairest and brightest which we here behold is but the faintest type and the dimmest shadow. We wish you good luck in the name of the Lord.

* Acts iii. 6.

SERMON XI.

THE WATCH AGAINST SINS OF THE TONGUE.

I said, I will take heed to my ways, that I sin not with my tongue.
—Psalm xxxix. 1.

HOW many, my brethren, have *said* this, and yet have failed to *do* it; and unless they have said something *more* than this, they have assuredly failed; unless, that is, they have added to this good resolution of their own, earnest prayer to God that *He* would assist them in keeping their good resolution; unless they have also said with the Psalmist, "Set a watch, O Lord, at the door of my lips." If they have neglected to ask for God's watch, for Him by his grace to stand sentinel there, their own purposes of not offending with the tongue, however honest, however sincere at the moment, will have been continually baffled and defeated. We have the sure word of Scripture for this which we assert. "The tongue," it is said there, "can no man tame;" no *man* can tame it, but only the grace of God. It is the best member which we have; but, as the corruption of the best proves ever the worst, it, being the best, *may*, and if misemployed *will*, prove the worst member which we have. For, indeed, is it not so? With it, as St. James reminds us, we may bless God, and with it we may curse men made in the similitude

(109)

of God. With it we may pour oil and wine of consolation into the bleeding wounds of our brethren, or with it we may rub in biting salt to exasperate those wounds the more. With it we may defend the truth; with it we may make specious and plausible a lie. With it we may provoke one another to love and good works; with it we may provoke one another to envy, strife, and debate. There is no instrument so potent for good and for evil. "Life and death," as the wise king said, "are in the power of the tongue." It may be a tree of life, or a root of bitterness and death; and this or that at once to ourselves and others.

But if these things are so, what reason is there that we should fall in with that holy purpose of David, and say with him, "I will take heed to my ways, that I offend not with my tongue." What reason, if we mean to keep this purpose, that we should further pray with him, "Set a watch, O Lord, at the door of my lips." Nor shall I, I am sure, occupy your time in vain, if I can suggest to you a few considerations which should the more earnestly move you to all this.

And this first,—how important it is that we should seek to order our speech aright, seeing that our words are the outcoming of our inmost heart, the revelation of the deepest, most hidden things which are there. Christ Himself has declared as much: "Out of the abundance of the heart the mouth speaketh." It is, indeed, quite true that a man may speak other things than those which are in his heart, for a little while, and so long as he is on the watch. But no one can be always on the watch. Every man lays aside his masks and disguises sometimes ; or if not, yet sudden temptations, unlooked-for provocations, or any of the thousand unexpected accidents of life, will strip them from him. In one way or other he will be often off his guard ; and then the proud man will speak proud things, and the covetous man will speak covetous, and the malicious man will speak malicious, and the unclean will speak unclean. That which has always been the voice of his heart will be now the voice of his lips. He will bring out of the evil treasure-house of his heart the evil things which may have long been hidden there, but which now he either no longer cares to conceal, or is no longer able to conceal, therein.

And would we know our own selves, the deepest folds, the most intricate windings of our own hearts, let us consider what our words have been, or what they now are, not when we are on our good behavior, not when we are in the company of those who keep us in a certain restraint and awe—parents, employers, superiors, those older and better than ourselves, those to whom we wish to present ourselves in a favorable light, it may be, a far more favorable light than we deserve ; but let us consider in what channels our speech runs when we are with our familiars, with those in whose company we are quite at our ease, who keep us in no sort of awe, before whom we lay aside all those troublesome masks which were worn in the presence of others. Is our speech at such times malignant, detracting, backbiting ? or, again, is it vaunting, proud, boastful ? or, once more, is it gross, carnal, sensual, calling the proud happy, speaking good of the covetous whom God abhorreth? We may be quite sure that as our speech is, so we are; that what our speech is, that is what we are ourselves. It is just the running over of the heart; and as a vessel filled with wine, and then overfilled, would run over with wine, or a vessel filled with gall would run over with gall, must run over with that, and could not run over with any thing else; so what the heart is filled with, with that it will run over. Surely, then, if pure lips are thus the only index of a pure heart, and impure lips the certain index of an impure heart, if unkind words on the lips give sure evidence that no law of kindness reigns in the heart, and so on with the rest, there is ample cause why we should make David's resolution, why we should pray David's prayer.

But, secondly, how important it is that we should seek to order our speech aright, seeing that words reach so far, exercise so vast an influence. They have been sometimes called "winged;" and so they are, travelling far and fast by paths of their own. And this power of theirs, how mighty is it both for good and for evil. How mighty for good! "The words of the wise," says Solomon, "are as goads," as such, inciting, urging, prompting to good; "and as nails fastened by the masters of assemblies," which, therefore, where they were fixed shall remain. Nor is this peculiar to good works only. Others too may be goads, but goads to evil, and nails which are fastened only too well. How easily, without positively intending any mischief, we may by some single word be lowering the whole tone of another man's mind, the whole future standard of another man's life! We did not mean to do him any positive wrong, and yet we have done him the greatest. He has heard us allowing ourselves in free, unrestrained speech about others, and he has been emboldened to allow himself in the same. He has heard some low, worldly, selfish maxim drop from our lips, and he has taken it up, and made it henceforth the rule of his life. And we can never say where this mischief will end. We may have infected but one, while yet he in his turn may have infected many ; and the wrong we do is such as in this way may long survive the natural term of our lives. How many are there now in their graves, some it may be for centuries turned to their dust, but whose wicked words, through the pen and through the press, have obtained a dreadful immortality, and have taken wings over all the earth! Of these too, as well as of the righteous, it is true, being dead, they yet speak. The wanton poet or novelist, the unholy fires in whose own heart have long since been raked into dust and ashes, he can still with his words awaken impure thoughts and imaginations in others, setting on fire with sparks as from hell the whole course of nature. The witty scoffer against God, against his providence, his word, his laws, his love, may have past long since to his account ; but the words of scorn and unbelief live on, undermining in many hearts their faith in God, and in his loving and righteous government of the world. And who shall dare to limit the effect of any evil word which is spoken, or pretend to say how long it may survive as this sinful tradition, passing from mouth to mouth, and that whereby many shall be defiled? This then, namely, the *far*-reaching and *wide*-reaching mischief which our words may effect, is a second consideration that might well move us to pray with David, "Set a watch, O Lord, at the door of my lips."

But then, thirdly, we might well pray this prayer, having regard to the difficulty of the duty which we here propose to ourselves; a difficulty so great, that St. James could say, "If any man offend not in word, the same is a perfect man, and able also to bridle the whole body." We may seriously mean and purpose not to offend with our tongue, and yet in our actual intercourse with the world the keeping of this resolution proves not easy, but hard; and we are only too soon overtaken with this fault, moved to speak unadvisedly with our lips. We are masters and employers perhaps, and on occasion of slight neglects or omission rebuke harshly and severely those placed under us, unmindful of all the hearty and zealous service which at other times they may have rendered; or we are servants, and if ever so little a fault is found with us, if we are blamed ever so slightly, we forget the apostolic admonition, "not answering again," and reply with petulance to those whom we are bound to honor and respect. We are parents, and our children's faults are noted hastily and passionately, as offences against us, not offences against God; or we are children, and being reproved, we answer again as those who will not endure to be checked and corrected. We are buyers, or we are sellers, and we have spoken something to our own gain or our neighbor's loss, for which our hearts afterwards condemn us; words which perhaps might pass, weighed in the coarse scales of this world, but which would be found wanting if tried in the finer balances of the sanctuary. We have committed one fault, and almost before we are aware, have made the one fault two by some palliation of it, or excuses for it, that are not consistent with perfect sincerity and truth. We leave some company, and feel that a brother's character has suffered at our hands. What we said of him, perhaps, was true, but it was not kind; there was no need to have said it; no call upon us to utter it; to draw it from that forgotten past in which we should have left it buried, if the law of a perfect charity had ruled in our hearts, or of a perfect kindness on our lips. But if in any of these ways we have been, or are in danger of being, overtaken with a fault, of slipping with the tongue, what additional reason is there here why we should keep our watch, and ask of God that He would keep his watch no less, over this unruly member, which, left to itself, will soon entangle us in sin.

But, once more, we may fitly ask this, and ask it earnestly, while we consider the strict judgment and account to which God will call us for our use of this excellent talent of speech. "By thy words thou shalt be justified, and by thy words thou shalt be condemned;" and from other sayings of Christ our Lord, it is to be feared that many a light word, as it seems now, will prove heavy enough at the day of judgment; many a word lightly spoken now will have to be heavily accounted for then. For, indeed, how can our words do otherwise than play an important part, how can they escape being brought into prominent consideration on that day, if what was just now spoken be true, namely, that they are the index and evidence, the coming out of the inmost things of our hearts, of the deepest things which are there ; if it is out of the heart's abundance that the mouth speaketh ? Or again, if God shall judge men in that day according to their works, are not our words our works just as truly as anything else which we do, the works of our lips as our other doings may be works of our hands, only differing from others in that they are a truer index of our character, have a deeper significance, and oftentimes act in a far larger circle for good or for evil ?

Does it seem strange to us, then, my brethren, that when Isaiah the prophet stood of a sudden in the presence of God, and saw his glory, the first words of confession which he uttered for himself and for his people were these, "Woe is me, for I am undone"? and why "undone"?—"because I am a man of unclean lips, and I dwell in the midst of a people of unclean lips."* Shall we wonder that not till a live coal from the altar had touched those lips it could be said, "Thine iniquity is taken away, and thy sin purged"? Who needs not a like cleansing? to be cleansed by Christ's blood and Christ's spirit, by the sprinkling of his blood, by the effectual working of his spirit, from all idle, excessive, untruthful, unkind, malicious, flattering, provoking words, that I speak not of worse, which he has ever

---

* Isaiah vi.

uttered ; to be cleansed from their guilt, to be delivered by the grace and power of God from the recurring temptation to fall into those same sins of the tongue which have betrayed him in the time past ?

And yet one word here in conclusion. In praying against sins of the lips, let us in every case go to the root of the mischief and pray against those sins of the heart out of which these others spring ; else we may make more accomplished hypocrites of ourselves, but not more perfect Christians. We pray that we may not *speak* uncharitably ; but oh! let us pray that we may not *think* uncharitably, that the law of love may not be on our lips only, but in our hearts. There are some cautious persons who exercise much self-restraint upon themselves in not *speaking* unkindly of others, because they feel that in so doing they should blemish their Christian reputation ; but they make up for it by hard, cruel, uncharitable thoughts, which they keep to themselves in the deep of their heart. We pray that we may not speak proud things with our lips ; but if we confine ourselves to this, it may really be only a prayer that we may not ourselves come to any open shame, lowering ourselves by vaunting, vainglorious speeches in the estimation of others. But he who is rightly praying to be delivered from lips of pride, as sinful before God, will at the same time make his prayer to be delivered from the heart of pride. His desire will not be, to *seem* humble, which is only a subtler pride, but to *be* humble ; to be a man of humble speech, because he is first a man of humble thoughts ; to be clothed with the garment of humility within as

well as without.   So, again, every Christian will needs
hate impure lips ; he will pray that at no unguarded
moment of his life any word may escape him, growing
out of the corruption which is in the world through
lust.   But what is this unless he is also asking for a
clean heart ? What were he who should be content if
only his words were pure words, and should at the
same time entertain, or even invite, thoughts and
imaginations of impurity and uncleanness ? what, indeed, but a whited sepulchre, decent indeed and fair
without, but full of all filth and rottenness within ?
Seek, then, I beseech you, to make thorough work here.
Strive, pray, cry, that in this, as in everything else,
the root of the matter may be in you.   If you pray,
" Set a watch, O Lord, at the door of my lips," or,
" Deliver me, O God, from lying lips and a deceitful
tongue," remember that behind each and every such
prayer there should lie another prayer, which is this,
" Make me *a clean heart*, O God, and renew a right
spirit within me."

SERMON XII.

COUNTING THE COST.

Which of you, intending to build a tower, sitteth not down first, and counteth the cost, whether he have sufficient to finish it? Lest haply after he hath laid the foundation, and is not able to finish it, all that behold it begin to mock him saying, This man began to build, and was not able to finish. Or what king, going to make war against another king, sitteth not down first, and consulteth whether he be able with ten thousand to meet him that cometh against him with twenty thousand? Or else, while the other is yet a great way off, he sendeth an ambassage, and desireth conditions of peace. So likewise, whosoever he be of you that forsaketh not all that he hath, he cannot be my disciple.—LUKE xiv. 28-33.

THERE is an interpretation, I may call it the ordinary one, of this passage which is encumbered with considerable difficulties—difficulties which, I dare say, have been more or less felt by many. That interpretation, as I take it, is as follows: Christ here admonishes those who were offering themselves as candidates for his discipleship, that before they came after Him they should seriously consider and ask themselves, whether they had strength and resolution sufficient to carry them through with that which they undertook; and if, on a sober calculation, they found they had not, that they would do wisely not to undertake his discipleship; this rather than, having undertaken, afterwards to abandon it, so exposing themselves, and with themselves the holy interests of the truth itself, to the world's mockery and scorn. And even this would not be the whole of the mischief; for they would thus bring upon themselves, as the second comparison would imply, an increased wrath and malice of their great adversary, the devil, by that impotent challenge of him to a conflict.

Such is the usual explanation ; but encumbered, as I have said, with serious difficulties. For, while we can quite understand that the Lord should advise such a calculation as this, prudence and foresight being eminently features of the Christian character, we cannot at all understand how He should give that further counsel which the words thus explained make Him to give ; namely, that when the means for carrying up the tower of the spiritual life are found insufficient, the intending builder should then desist from the attempt to build at all ; or that, when the forces of him who would fain challenge to battle the great adversary are found too feeble and too few, he should thereupon desire of him shameful conditions of peace.

Surely the gracious Lord's counsels to him about to build would be different from these—would be, that, discovering the scantiness of his own resources and the largeness of the cost, he should desist, not from his purpose itself, but from the attempt to carry it through in the manner that he had hitherto proposed ; that, instead of this, he should furnish himself more abundantly for the necessary costs out of that inexhausted and inexhaustible treasure-house of God, upon which he and all might draw without stint and without limit.

Surely his advice to him meditating a war with sin and Satan would be, not that, being convinced of the power and predominance of his spiritual adversary, he should make terms with that enemy, whom to defy to the uttermost is his first duty and only safety; but rather that he should seek to multiply his ten thousand, to seek more grace, more faith, more of God's Holy Spirit, till from weak he had grown strong, till his forces exceeded many times even the twenty thousand which the enemy could bring against him.

And then, even if these embarrassments were got over, how does this passage, interpreted as commonly it is, fit in with what has gone before, and, which is still more difficult to answer, with what follows after? For there is the praise, not of spiritual wealth, but of spiritual poverty; there the Lord counts him happy, not who discovers that he has much, but who discovers that he has nothing; who renounces, or forsakes, or bids farewell to, all that he hath. And I feel very confident that this too is what the Lord is urging in these two similitudes. He will teach those who would fain undertake his discipleship that they must begin, not as a proud man supposes (proud even after he has taken up the profession of humility); not, that is, by counting up their riches, but by making discovery of their poverty; not by affecting to be something even face to face with God, but by acknowledging themselves nothing. "There went," we are told, "great multitudes with Him;" but they were those who knew not what this going with Him meant: they fancied that they could build up the tower of the Christian life at their own cost, instead of confessing that they had not, and never could have, more than enough to make a weak and impotent beginning. He saw them preparing to enter on the warfare of the Christian life with none of that true emptiness of self which is the only secret for obtaining the fulness of God; dreaming that they could hold their own even against Him, when He came, searching, trying, tempting, chastening, bringing into judgment, instead of evermore casting themselves down before Him, throwing themselves merely and simply on his mercy, and asking of Him, while it was yet time, conditions of peace.

Christ saw this, and sought to set before them, by the help of two examples derived from this world's affairs, the mockery and the defeat which would thus be their portion; and at the same time to warn them in what way, and by what means, that mockery and that defeat, with, indeed, the failure and shipwreck of their whole spiritual life, might still be averted. To the end that they may understand something of the difficulty of that discipleship which they were ready so lightly to assume, He compares it to two important enterprises; one the building of a tower, arduous for a private person; the other the carrying on of a war, arduous, and full of doubtful and dangerous issues, even for a king.

He is not, in our Lord's estimation, the true spiritual builder, such as will bring his work to a successful end, who, counting the cost, finds that he *has* enough, as he supposes, to finish the building which he has begun; but the wise and happy builder is he who counts and discovers that he has *not* enough, that the work far exceeds any resources at his command, and who thereupon forsakes all that he has, all vain imagination of a spiritual wealth of his own : and thenceforth proceeds to build, not at his own charges at all, but altogether at the charges of God, waiting upon Him day by day for new supplies of strength. He, on the other hand, who counts the cost, and finds that, according to his estimate, he *has* enough, is the foolish builder, whose calculations will all be defeated, who will presently have run through and exhausted the slender stock upon which he began ; and will then leave the spiritual building unfinished, having discovered to his infinite loss that to rear the fabric of the Christian life is a far costlier work than he had anticipated, and to be carried to an end in a far other strength than that on which he had proposed to draw.

Christ does not, you will observe, deny that such a one may begin, that he may lay the foundation ; only He affirms that he will bring nothing to perfection. For we must not pass too slightly over those words, "after he hath laid the foundation," but rather give them their full weight, containing as they do a very important truth, and no less solemn warning. The spiritual builder here, who leaves off after a while, *has* laid the foundation, and the right one, for there is no fault found with him on this point ; but, just as in another place* we are taught that the one right foundation may be laid, and yet untrustworthy materials, " wood,

---

* 1 Cor. iii. 12–15.

hay, stubble," may be built even upon that, so here we learn that the one right foundation may be laid, and yet the building stand still at that point, and never go on to completion.

And what then? "All that behold it begin to mock him, saying, This man began to build, and was not able to finish." The introduction of the mockery is borrowed from the life. There is nothing in this world which so provokes scorn as the utterly wasted expenditure on some proud building, which, after a vast outlay, he who planned it, having totally miscalculated his means, is compelled to leave unfinished, open to the winds and rains of heaven; a ruin from the beginning, a monument of his folly that began it. We know indeed how this scorn will often embody itself in a name given to the unfinished structure. It is called this man's or that man's 'folly;' and the name of the foolish builder is thus kept alive for long after-years on the lips of men. The same mockery will be the portion of those who have spiritually undertaken a work, which presently they lack the right ability to go through with. The world cannot help respecting earnest, entire Christians. It has only scorn for the half-hearted; for those who halt in the middle of their career; who lay their foundations as though they would scale heaven, but this done, presently leave off, so that nothing but a deformed, shapeless heap of bricks marks the Babel they would have reared. The world has itself perhaps bid them to leave off; but it does not the less despise them when they obey. The scorn which it feels for them may clothe itself in the language of praise. The world may receive back *its* prodigals as with open arms, may profess to make festivals for their return. The man, it may say, has grown wiser; he has left off that foolish scheme of his, impossible to carry out, and needless even if it had been possible; he has come to his right mind; we may now receive him as one of ourselves. But behind all these fair words and welcomes there is scorn for this man who began what he had not strength to go through with, a scorn which pierces through the words of our text: "This man began to build, and was not able to finish."

Such is the first comparison by which our Lord warns his disciples of the need of counting the cost, and confessing their own utter bankruptcy from the beginning, that so, being empty of self, they may be full of God. But it is very characteristic of our Lord's gracious manner of teaching to set forth an important truth under a double aspect, by the aid not merely of one similitude, but of two; having presented it upon one side, then to present it upon another. He does so here. Having presented the Christian life as the building of a tower, He proceeds now to present it as a conflict and shock of arms. This comparison is in advance upon the other; sets forth the gravity and seriousness of the matter in hand still more clearly. Weighty as for a private man is the building of some great tower, weightier, more hazardous, and that even for a king, is the provoking of a war. Many a king has in this way pulled down ruin on his head. Deceived by the lying oracles of a greedy, presumptuous heart, hoping to overthrow a kingdom, he has indeed overthrown one, but it has been his own. Even good king Josiah failed here. Challenging to unequal battle Pharaoh and the armies of Egypt, he lost on the plains of Megiddo his own life and his kingdom's independence.* Not, therefore, for nothing had the Wise man said, " With good advice make war ; " † and the conduct of Hezekiah was only prudent, when having provoked the mighty king of Assyria, on maturer counsel he sent to him while he was yet a great way off, saying, " I have offended ; return from me ; that which thou puttest on me will I bear. ‡ Better thus, even at the cost of some humiliation, to desire conditions of peace, than to advance in blind presumption, and overmatched and outnumbered, to be shattered at the first shock with a too prevailing foe.

Transfer all this to spiritual things ; never, I would entreat you, forgetting that any interpretation which makes the king who comes against us with twenty thousand to be the devil, involves the whole passage in inextricable confusion. For what can be the meaning of sending an ambassage to him, and desiring conditions of peace from him, with whom we are bound to wage war to the death, and under no circumstances to believe that we are overmatched by him, but to believe evermore that greater is He who is on our side than he which is against us ? It is quite impossible to conceive that such counsels of unworthy compromise, of peace with him who is to be defied to the uttermost, should

* 2 Kings xxiii. 29.　　† Prov. xx. 18.　　‡ 2 Kings xviii. 14.

ever have proceeded from the lips of that Lord who came, by Himself and by his servants, to destroy the works of the devil. But all is comparatively easy, and every thing here spoken falls into its place, is in perfect harmony with all which the Lord has spoken elsewhere, so soon as we acknowledge in Him who cometh against us with his twenty thousand no other than the Lord God Almighty Himself. How many passages in the book of Job are explained by the parable thus understood, and in their turn help to explain it; as this, "If God will contend with him," that is, with the sinner, "he cannot answer Him one of a thousand;"* or again, "Behold God findeth occasions against me; He counteth me as an enemy." What light is here thrown on that mysterious scene by the brook Jabbok, where Jacob wrestled with the angel all the night; what light on that still more mysterious scene in the inn, where God met Moses by the way and sought to kill him.† It is, of course, on God's part only a *seeming* to come against us with the army of his temptations, his judgments, and his terrors; or rather, it is only a being against us for a time, that so He may be with us for ever. So long as we think to hold our own before Him, to be any thing in his sight, to plead and maintain our own cause, saying, with the sons of Zebedee, "We are able," so long we are as some foolish king who should think with his ten thousand to resist the far mightier king who came against him with his twenty thousand.

---

* Job. ix. 3.　　　　　　† Exodus iv. 24.

You will observe that, with a certain irony, the Lord so far falls in with the exaggerated estimate which men form of their own resources, so far adopts their language, as to speak of the ten thousand which they bring against God's twenty thousand, as though they were only overmatched by Him as one to two; when, indeed, it is true, as between God and the holiest saint, if God will contend with him, he cannot answer Him one in a thousand. What, then, is the true wisdom of him who has learned the blessed lesson that he is thus overmatched, that he cannot stand upon equal terms in this conflict, that nature cannot stand, no, nor yet grace itself, in so far as it is *our* grace, so as to measure its strength with Him? The Lord Himself shall declare what this wisdom is: "While the other is yet a great way off, he sendeth ambassage, and desireth conditions of peace. The man does not wait till, having lifted himself against God, he has learned by some shameful fall the disparity of *his* forces, and those with which God will try him, and will convince him of his pride and his presumption; but, while all this is yet at a distance, he sends the ambassage of his submission, and will walk humbly with his God. He does not clothe himself in any righteousness of his own, in the righteousness of the natural man, like the young ruler, who said of the commandments of God, "All these have I kept from my youth up,"—no, nor yet in the righteousness which God's Spirit has wrought in him,—and propose in this to outface the righteousness of God. He knows it at the very best a garment too narrow to wrap himself withal, armor in which if he has trusted, God will take it from him, and leave him shamed and naked before his foes.

If there were the slightest doubt or misgiving in the minds of any in regard of this being the right interpretation of these most pregnant words, it must, I think, be removed by the concluding words: "So likewise whosoever he be of you that forsaketh not all that he hath, he cannot be my disciple." For this forsaking all that he hath on the part of every disciple of Christ, what exactly may it mean? As Christ certainly did not intend to resolve his whole church into a mendicant Order, as He had far higher counsels of perfection for it than this, the words must express the loosening of ourselves in will and affection, in trust and confidence, from the creature, and from all reliance on the creature; and this, whether in ourselves or in the world;—with, indeed, the preparedness to renounce in outward act what has been already renounced in will, if the allegiance which we owe to Christ should at any time demand this at our hands. At the same time, it is a very shallow interpretation of Christ's words, to restrict "all that he hath" to a man's outward faculties and possessions. Barnabas, indeed, may have most truly fulfilled this commandment, when, "having land he sold it, and brought the money, and laid it at the apostle's feet;" but I am sure St. Paul was in a far deeper sense forsaking all that he had, all which had grown and incorporated itself with him, which had become a part of his very self, that too which cost him a far greater struggle to renounce, when he counted all things in which hitherto he had gloried but loss, that so he might be found in Christ, not having his own righteousness, but the righteousness which is of God by faith.

Here was one, my brethren, who thought not to build the tower of the Christian life at his own charges, yet did not therefore give over the attempt to build it, but only went on to build it at the charges of another. Here was one who did not count that *he* could stand, when God should set his armies, the armies of his righteousness, of his terrors, of his law, in battle-array against him ; and who sought therefore a blessed peace with God, rather than a miserable and desperate war. But how is it with us? Have we renounced to build at our charges, that so we may build at God's? Have we counted up our forces, and found them too few to stand against those of the Almighty and the All-holy, and finding this, cast ourselves merely and only on the riches of God's grace, desiring of Him the true conditions of an everlasting peace, of that covenant of peace which He has ordered and made sure in the blood of his dear Son? This is the question of questions, which concerns us more nearly than every other question in the world.

SERMON XIII.

RESIST THE DEVIL, AND HE WILL FLEE FROM YOU.

Resist the devil, and he will flee from you.—JAMES iv. 7.

HERE is first a duty, "Resist the devil," and then a promise linked with the fulfilment of that duty, "he will flee from you." I shall occupy your attention to-day first and chiefly with the duty and the ways in which we may best fulfil it; at the same time not leaving wholly untouched the second portion of my subject, —the blessed promise which is connected with that duty, and whereby we are encouraged to an earnest and persevering and manful fulfilment of it.

And first the duty, "Resist the devil." Now, the adversary whom we are here bidden to resist is only known to us *through* his temptations, through the evil suggestions which he causes to rise up out of the deep of our hearts, through the fiery darts with which he seeks to set on fire in us the whole course of nature. *Him* we are not brought into personal immediate contact with, as was our Lord when He was tempted of the devil in the wilderness. Temptations, suggestions of evil, solicitations *to* evil, these are the signs and tokens of that mighty though fallen Spirit's presence and power and working among us; so that for all practical purposes the words of St. James might be translated into such language as this : Strive manfully against temptations, and you have God's promise and pledge that these, instead of overcoming *you*, shall be overcome *by* you. And I do not think that we shall ill employ our time this morning if we a little consider some of the means and methods by which we may best fulfil that command, and inherit this promise. For, indeed, occupying ourselves with this matter, we shall occupy ourselves with one which concerns most nearly every one of us. All of us are tempted. Our temptations may be of the most infinitely different kinds, but the fact of temptation is common to us all. There is not one of us, young or old, rich or poor, learned or simple, whose whole life is not, in one shape or another, and whether he will acknowledge it or no, one long temptation. There are temptations in adversity, temptations in prosperity ; temptations in sickness, and temptations in health ; temptations for the poor, and temptations for the rich ; temptations for the young, and temptations for the old ; things pleasant to the flesh seeking to allure and entice us from our allegiance to God, and things painful seeking to terrify us from that allegiance ; the adversary trying with us, as with our Lord, now the door of desire, and now that of fear.

If, then, we would resist him, what shall be our first wisdom? Plainly this, to resist him in the only strength in which he can be effectually resisted, in the strength of Him who has said, " My strength is sufficient for thee ;" putting on the armor of God. How often we forget this ; not altogether perhaps, but in part; relying on some strength of our own; wielding weapons which *are* carnal; acting as foolishly herein as David would have acted, if, going to fight with the Philistine, he had encased and encumbered himself with the unserviceable armor of Saul. In all human likelihood this would have proved fatal to him. He would have forfeited and foregone the secret of his strength, that strength lying in the weakness which caused him to lean upon God, and thus to become partaker of a heavenly strength. So, too, let our strength be a strength in God and from God; a strength gotten in prayer, gotten from the Word, gotten through sacraments; a strength not such as that which the rude boisterous Esaus of this world may boast of, but such as the Jacobs know, who have wrestled with God's angel and have prevailed. And how prevailed? with tears and supplications, which are the only prevailing arms of man with God, refusing to let Him go until He bless them. For of this let us be sure, that, if we lean upon any strength of our own, or trust in our own hearts, there is no temptation so weak but it may prove too strong for us; while, on the other hand, if we lean upon the strength of God, put on his armor, seek his grace, there is no temptation so strong but that we may and shall prove stronger than it.

But, secondly, let it be ours to resist temptations at the beginning, when they first display themselves as such. This is the only wisdom. Then the temptation is comparatively weak, and you are strong. But if you let it grow, dally with it, entertain it ever so little, the positions will be reversed, and *it* will be strong, and you weak. Now it is a dwarf; do not wait to engage in a death-struggle with it till it has grown to be a giant. The darts of Satan, that is, the temptations which he injects into our hearts, are called "fiery darts" by St. Paul, with allusion to a practice in ancient warfare of shooting darts or arrows wrapped round with lighted tow into a besieged city, that these, kindling a flame where they lighted, might presently set all in a blaze. Nothing could have availed to hinder this catastrophe but extreme watchfulness on the part of the besieged, treading out, or otherwise extinguishing, these fiery missiles as fast as they fell. Now temptations are exactly in this same way "fiery darts," the messengers of mischief, which our ghostly enemy launches against us. He means that where they light upon our hearts they should kindle there ; and with so much in us all which is akin to the temptation, nothing will hinder this except the utmost vigilance on our parts, and a treading out of these sparks of hell before they have burst into a blaze. That memorable fire which two centuries ago laid nearly one half of this city in ashes, which defied for days and days the efforts of thousands of men, there was no doubt a moment when a pitcher of water in the hands of a little child might have quenched it. So, too, the sin which has now grown to such a fearful mastery over a man that it is the tyrant of his life, it was once but a wandering temptation, a vague floating suggestion to evil, against which, if he had resolutely shut the door of his heart when it first presented itself for admission, he might perhaps never have heard of it again. That verse of the Psalmist has perplexed many, "Blessed shall be he who taketh thy children, and dasheth them against the stones;" but it need perplex none as applied to the brood of Satan, sinful thoughts and sinful desires, which cannot be too early dashed against the stones of God's law. If David, on that occasion known too well, had made a covenant with his eyes, and withdrawn them at once, what a blurred and blotted page in his history might have been spared.

Yet it must be owned that this which I spoke of just now, namely, of temptations small at the beginning, and only great through neglect, though the general, is not the invariable, rule with them; for sometimes they present themselves full grown at the first, challenging the very utmost strength which we have, if we are not to be overmastered by them. And therefore I would urge, as another branch of Christian prudence in the resisting of evil, that we do not wait till the temptation comes, and then begin our preparations against it. Arm yourself against it beforehand. What were he for a soldier who only when the signal of battle had been already given, and when he stood face to face with his foe, began to rivet the joints of his armor, and to put a sharper edge on his sword? Or how would that nation fare which should be providing for the first time fleets and armies and arsenals, when it was already committed to deadly strife with another people as mighty as itself? The conflict is a time for *using* weapons, not for *preparing* them. And who can say how suddenly, how fiercely, from what unlooked-for side, a temptation may assail him? How, think you, would it have fared with Joseph, if, cast suddenly as he was into that fiery furnace of temptation, his wanton mistress seeking to entice him to sin, he had not already, and by many prayers going before, sought and obtained the gift and grace of chastity from God? Do we not feel sure, if he had needed then for the first time to seek this grace, he would not have sought, he would not have obtained it, but have been in that fierce furnace scorched and utterly consumed? Say then often to yourself: I am in a world full of temptation, the fiery darts of the wicked one are flying thick and fast about me; if one lights not on my heart to-day, it will light to-morrow or the next day; my wisdom, my safety, is to seek betimes that grace which sooner or later I must need. It will be too late then first to seek it when the need of it has actually arrived. Neither content yourself with *saying* this, but actually seek it, and store it against the evil time which is coming, that you may be able to stand in that evil time, and, having done all, to stand.

But once more, while we desire to arm ourselves against the whole circle of temptations, known and unknown, future as well as present, it will be our wisdom to make especially strong our defences against the temptations which are the most threatening to our own spiritual life. You remember the Apostle speaks to the Hebrews of the sin which so easily besets them; and we have learned from those words of his to speak of men's "besetting sin." Whether what we mean by "besetting sin" did lie in his intention may be doubtful; but the phrase itself is a most valuable one, does express a most important truth in the spiritual life of each one among us. We have every one of us besetting sins. I use the plural, for they are sometimes, alas! not one but many; sins, that is, which more easily get advantage over us than others, to which we have a mournful proclivity, an especial predisposition; it may be through natural temperament, it may be through faults in our education, it may be through circumstances in which we are placed, it may be through having given way to them in times past, and thus broken down on their side more than on any other the moral defences of our soul; the soul in this resembling paper, which, where it has been blotted once, however careful the erasure of the blot may have been, there more easily blots and runs anew than elsewhere. It is, then, a point of obvious prudence to strengthen the defences of the city of the soul there where they are felt and known to be weakest—where *that* is, every one who has kept any close record of the sad secrets of his own spiritual life, will in his own case abundantly know—to watch and pray against *all* sin, but above all, and with especial emphasis and earnestness, against the sin which most easily besets us.

And yet this must not be to the neglect of the other avenues by which temptation may find an entrance into the fortress of our hearts. If many a city has been taken on its weakest side, it is also true that many a city has been taken on its strongest side; which was counted so strong that no watch was kept, even as no danger was dreaded there. As regards the spiritual life of men, we are not without solemn warnings and proofs in Scripture that this may easily come to pass. Who so wise as Solomon? and yet this wisest king is betrayed into the gross folly of idolatry. What man braver and bolder by nature than Peter ever walked this earth? and yet the taunt of a maid-servant is sufficient to terrify him, and to cause him to deny his faith and his Lord. We think that we are not exposed to one particular form of temptation. Let none be too sure of this; and in resisting one form of evil, never let us forget that there are others in the world. Fleshly sins may be watched against, and yet room may be given in the heart for spiritual wickedness, pride, self-righteousness, and the like. Yea, the victories gained over the lusts of the flesh may themselves minister to those subtler mischiefs of the spirit; and our fate may be like that of the hero in the Maccabees,* who was crushed by the falling elephant which himself had slain. There is a white devil of spiritual pride as well as a black devil of fleshly lusts. Satan can transform himself, where need is, into an angel of light. If only he can ruin us, it is all the same to him by what engines he does it; all are fish for his net, profligate publicans and proud Pharisees; it is small matter to him whether we go down into hell as gross carnal sinners, or as elated self-righteous saints; nay, surely he must be best pleased in the latter case, for these last are twofold more the children of hell than the others. Set a watch, therefore, I would say, all round your heart; not on one side only, but on all; for you can

---

* 1 Macc. vi. 46.

be never sure on which side temptation will assail.
"Walk circumspectly," says the apostle, which means
looking all round about you, having eyes, so to speak,
in the back of your head.

But one counsel of Christian prudence more. Never
count a temptation so triumphed over, so beaten off,
that it will never assault you any more. Satan has
been called Beelzebub, or the god of flies, some tell us,
because he will not take a repulse, because he comes
back again and again, because it is impossible so to
drive him away that he will not return. Consider the
Lord of Glory Himself. When the Tempter, thrice
encountered and thrice defeated in the wilderness, left
Him, it was only, as we are expressly told, "for a
season." There were other hours and powers of darkness still to come, when the Prince of this world should
make further proof in the garden whether there was
not something which he could claim for his own even
in that Lord who had so foiled and baffled him in the
desert. And shall we think that when he departs from
us it is more than for a season? Never, so long as
you bear about these sinful bodies, count any corruption to be so dead in you that you are perfectly safe
from it henceforth, that it can never stir or trouble
you again. How much that seems dead, by a sad experience will be shown to have been only sleeping;
like snakes, which, frozen in winter, lose for a while
their power to harm, appear as though there were no
life in them, but, brought to the warmth, can hiss and
sting again. How many an old corruption is perhaps
at this present moment thus torpid and inactive in us,

6*

which yet only waits the returning warmth of a suitable temptation to revive in all its malignant strength anew.

When you seem to have got the better in the struggle with some sin, let not this content you, namely, to have beaten off and repulsed the foe. Be not contented to have just escaped defeat, nor say, like some timid commander who knows not how to use success, that this victory is enough; but rather follow up the victory, make the most of it, hang as upon the rear of the broken foe, seek to break his power, not for the moment only, but for ever. In the struggles of this world it sometimes may be, it often is, a point of generosity, or even of wisdom, to spare a conquered foe, but in the conflicts of the soul never. We are only too ready to spare a lust. We do not, perhaps, desire that it should get dominion over us; but there is something in us which so takes its part that we shrink back from inflicting any thing like a deathblow upon it. And yet be sure that such pity. such mercy, is as ill-timed and misplaced, as much displeasing to God, as the self-interested pity of Saul when he spared Agag, as the weak pity of Ahab when he let go out of his hand Benhadad—"Benhadad, *my brother*," as he called him,* but a man whom God had appointed to utter destruction, and Ahab to execute the doom upon him. Our lusts, our sins, God has in like manner appointed them to utter destruction, and us to destroy them; but if we spare them, or if we are satisfied with just so much tri-

---

* 1 Kings xx. 32.

umph over them as shall prevent them from altogether triumphing over us, and this done, suffer them to live and move, what can we expect? What but that which the children of Israel found, when they would not obey God's commands, and, root and branch, extirpate the wicked inhabitants of Canaan? They were content if only they could just find room for themselves in a land which had been wholly given them; but that of driving out the Canaanites altogether, it was too toilsome, too painful a task for them to undertake; it would have deprived them, moreover, of serviceable vassals. The Canaanite would dwell in the land; and they suffered him there, leaving half their commission unfulfilled. But with what results? Those whom they spared were traps in their way and thorns in their side; yea, from time to time taking advantage of their weakness, rose up in strength, and brought them into bitter bondage again. I leave the application to yourselves; for the very few words which I can add must refer, not to the duty, "Resist the devil," but to the promise annexed to the duty, "he will flee from you."

I can conceive some thoughtful hearer saying in his heart, How does this promise agree with what has just been spoken, and what, indeed, our own experience bears out, namely, that temptations, though beaten off, will return again and again, that we may never dare to count a corruption to be so absolutely dead as that it can never revive, never trouble us again? Is this consistent with the promise, "Resist the devil, and he will flee from you"? We are quite sure that it must be, and a little consideration will show us in what way it actually is. The words cannot mean, that after one earnest and successful struggle against temptation, or the devil who is the author of temptation, he will so leave us as never to return and vex us any more. To give such a latitude to the words would be absurd. This was not true even of Christ Himself. But the words of the promise do meet a very crying need and necessity of the heart; and there are times when they have an exceeding preciousness for the soul. Take some poor, perplexed, tempted man: he is in the fires of some fierce temptation; hitherto he has not been scorched and consumed by them, but he feels as if they must soon kindle upon him. Satan is lying in wait for his soul; he has escaped hitherto, but it seems to him as by miracle; and he says in his heart, as David said at last, "I shall now perish by the hand of Saul." Some hideous suggestion of the Evil One presents itself again and again to his soul, and he asks himself, almost in despair, Must it be ever thus? must I feel at each moment of my spiritual life that there is but a step between me and death? must I go on through my whole life in this never-ceasing struggle with impure, defiling, hateful, blasphemous thoughts?

The words of the promise of my text say, No; this is not thy portion, this is not the portion of any faithful servant of the Lord. Thou shalt, indeed, always need to stand upon thy guard; from time to time, during thy whole life, thou shalt have to do most strong and earnest battle against thy foes; but this temptation, the devil in the shape he now wears, resist him by faith, and he will flee from thee presently.

Whatever else may hereafter come, the stress of the present temptation will pass away from thee, even as the stress of a mightier passed away from thy Lord; and thou too shalt know something of the joy of a temptation met and overcome, something of the joy which thy Lord and Saviour knew, when, after He had fought and conquered for thee, angels came in the wilderness and ministered unto Him.

SERMON XIV.

LOST OPPORTUNITIES.

And He came and found them asleep again: for their eyes were heavy.
  And He left them, and went away again, and prayed the third time,
  saying the same words.   Then cometh He to his disciples, and saith
  unto them, Sleep on now, and take your rest: behold, the hour is at
  hand, and the Son of man is betrayed into the hands of sinners.—
  MATT. xxvi. 43–45.

THERE is nothing, perhaps, in the whole history of
our Lord's sufferings which so brings home to us
the depth and reality of those sufferings as the Agony
in the Garden of Gethsemane ; not the cruel mockings,
not the forlorn masquerade of royalty, not the scourg-
ing with Roman rods, no, nor yet the shame and the
bitterness of the cross itself.   All' these were borne
with such meekness and such majesty, such calm en-
durance, such a steadfast will, He who endured them
had so set his face like a flint, that we might be
tempted to a secret thought as though He felt not as
other men ; we might suspect that, being He was God,
these insults, these outrages, these pains, touched not
Him to the quick as they would have touched another ;
that their bitterness was not to Him as it would have
been to the other children of Adam.   Such thoughts
might easily rise in our hearts ; thoughts no less dis-
honoring to Him than injurious to our own spiritual

life, separating, as they would, Christ from us, and us from Christ: they might, I say, arise, if we had not these strong cryings and tears and prayers to tell us how that hour of Passion, as it drew near, presented itself to his mind; if we had not, of God's infinite condescension and grace, been permitted to behold Him in his weakness (I may venture to use this language) as well as in his strength; if the veil had not thus been drawn back, and we admitted to see all, even the awful and innermost secrets of his soul's preparation for that hour of extremest trial.

And these leave no doubt that we have a *human* sufferer in Him,—the augustest, indeed, that ever shared our flesh and blood, but still most truly a sharer in it, as in every thing which belongs to man, except, indeed, his sin. And wonderful is the *human* character of all his feelings at this hour. We all know how men in some deep anguish or desolation of spirit shrink from utter loneliness. The friend that is made for adversity, whose very silence is better than the world's loudest consolations, whose mere presence is itself strength, such a friend is precious then; and that which would have been precious to other men was precious also to Him in whom all which is truly human was perfectly fulfilled. He too had chosen friends from among men; and now, when his soul was exceeding sorrowful, even unto death, He would have them to tarry near and to watch with Him. There were three, and these three the flower and crown of the apostolic band, whom He selected for this; Peter, the first who had confessed Him as the Christ, the Son of the living God; and John, among many loved, the best beloved of all; and James, who, earliest among the apostles, should drink to the full of his Lord's cup of pain, and be baptized with his Lord's baptism of blood.

They might not, indeed, even these three, be close by his side; for none might be actually present at those mysterious pleadings of the Son with the Father, when even He seemed to stagger for a moment under the weight of the world's sin. But still they should not be far off. When He said, "Tarry ye here, and watch with Me," it was only a little further, about a stone's cast, that He was withdrawn from them;* and they in this nearness were to watch with Him and to pray, to pray for themselves that they might not enter into temptation, that they might draw out the full blessing of that awful hour; and also, as we cannot doubt, they were meant to help Him with their prayers.

This was *his* meaning; but it had been appointed otherwise of his Father. He who appointed all for the glory of his Son, had appointed that He should tread the wine-press alone, even the wine-press of this mortal agony, and of the people there should be none to help Him. These Apostles were men, they were flesh and blood, and they failed Him. While He was praying they were sleeping. Once before the same had befallen them. At the Transfiguration they had been as little able to bear the weight of glory, as now they were able to bear the weight of this exceeding sorrow; and

* Luke xxii. 41.

there, too, their eyes had been heavy with sleep. But now the leaden weights of a still more untimely slumber lay heavy upon them. Thrice He returned to them, and thrice sought to arouse them from their lethargy at once of body and of soul, but in vain. If anything could have done this, we might suppose that mournful, reproachful appeal, " What, could ye not watch with Me one hour?" would have been effectual for it. But no, it is the hour and power of darkness; there is no help, and little comfort, in them. They might have shared with the angel the inconceivable honor of strengthening the Son of God ; and of Him who had been, and should be, their Helper always, they might have been the helpers once. But they would not ; and at length the hour is past, the opportunity is gone, the struggle is over ; and He comes to them now, not saying any longer, " Watch with Me," not bidding them any more to watch and pray ; but his words have a sadder, a far sadder import than this, " Sleep on now, and take your rest ; behold the hour is at hand, and the Son of Man is betrayed into the hands of sinners.

What a melancholy meaning that " Sleep on now " has, if only we understand it aright. It is not that He was now approving or allowing that drowsiness of spirit in which they were holden still ; far from it. But the import of the words we may take to have been this : The opportunity is past and gone. Even if you should at length shake off this clinging sloth, yet now it would profit nothing in this matter. Other opportunities of service may indeed occur, but this one is gone, and for ever ; the moment, with all its rich possibilities of service, the golden moment, has fled ; the battle has been fought without you ; the victory has been won without you. You may sleep on now, and take your rest, for the time when your watching and waking would have profited has passed away.

Ah, brethren, how bitterly must the three Apostles, fervent lovers of their Lord, although greatly wanting now, have subsequently mourned that they should have failed their Lord in such a moment as that, a moment which never in the history of their lives, which never in the history of the world, could return again ; how must they have resolved not to slight, but to make much of, every future occasion of high devotion to Him which should present itself to them, lest that too, by a carnal drowsiness, through the same unreadiness of spirit, should slip by and escape them for ever. And my desire is, that we should take this lesson home with us to-day, namely, that special occasions for serving God and his church, for bringing glory to Him, are in their very nature swift of passage, and, when they are past, often irrecoverable ; that, if we are wanting in watchfulness to recognize them, and in what I may call the grace of Christian promptitude to seize them and make them our own at once, we cannot afterwards recall them, we cannot, by any self-willed efforts of our own, reproduce the combination of circumstances under which they offered themselves to us. Does not this, at every turn of our lives, approve itself true ?

How often, for instance, in our daily life, in the social intercourse which we hold with our fellow-men, if we will not bear witness for Christ on the moment, we cannot do so at all. If we will not throw ourselves into the gap at the instant, then, while we are delib- crating, while we are mustering our tardy forces, the gap is closed, and it becomes impossible for us to do at all what we would not do at once. The stream of conversation flows on, and cannot be brought back to the point where it then was. The pernicious maxim was left unreproved, the word dishonorable to God, or injurious to his servants, to his truth, was suffered to pass by unrebuked; and it must continue so now, for that word which we would not speak at once, we cannot now speak at all. We may sleep on, and take our rest; for the time when we might have served God and the cause of his truth in this matter is past.

Nor does it fare otherwise with acts of kindness and deeds of love. It is, indeed, quite true of these, that, in one shape or another, they may always be done by those who have any mind or affection to them. In a world of woe like ours, the stripped and wounded traveller lies ever in the way, if only there be the good Samaritan to see him and to help him. But it is not the less true that many precious opportunities of bind- ing up wounds, strengthening the weak, comforting the mourner, may escape us unimproved, and, having once escaped, may have passed from us for ever; for they are as guests from another world, whom, if we do not invite to turn in upon the instant when they show themselves to us, we may afterwards follow, but we shall not over- take them, least of all shall we persuade to turn back again at our bidding. The need which we might have helped, but did not, another has helped in our stead;

or it has outgrown all human help, because we would not help it in time. The prayers which we might have offered for a suffering brother in the hour of his sore temptation or his pain, with which we might have helped him, he has struggled through without them, or has passed. it may be, into a world where they cannot reach to aid him.

Nor will it fare otherwise in regard of our own spiritual life. We have great need of watchfulness to turn to present and immediate account God's manifold dealings with us. When the heart is deeply stirred by feelings of gratitude and joy, we must seek to direct those feelings into their due channel at once, or else they will run to waste, and the blessing which they might have brought will escape us altogether. We must seek to embody them at the time in some distinct act of thanksgiving and praise, in the dedication, it may be, of some special portion of our substance to the service of God, or to the needs of his saints; or else, if we do not give diligence to embody our gratitude at once, we scarcely shall do so at a later day, when, in the very necessity of things, the high tides of our grateful thanksgiving shall have somewhat ebbed and abated.

And if this behoves in the time of a great joy, it behoves still more in the time of a great sorrow, which, as such, ought also to be the time of a great holiness. The fruits of such a time, the peaceable fruits of rightousness which that season was intended to bear for us, must be gathered at once; or if they are not thus gathered by us at once, they will not be at all. The mere onward course of time, the succession of events, the business of the world, will inevitably rob us of that sorrow, deaden at least the quickness and liveliness of it. If, then, when that sorrow was fresh and new, we did not use it, we did not compel it to yield up its blessing to us, the sweet which it had as well as the bitter, at a later day we shall seek in vain to extract from it that spiritual profit with which once it was charged for us to the full.

In like manner, how many a man mourns during his whole after-life the idleness and wasted opportunities of his school-days or his college-days. Mourning this, he repairs perhaps in part, but he can never repair entirely, the negligences and omissions of that particular period of his life. There is a deficiency, a weakness, an imperfection, which he can never quite get rid of, which no after-toil, though many times larger in amount than what then would have been needed, avails to remove; and this because there were certain things, according to the constitution of his moral and mental nature, which were intended to be learned then, and which can never be so well or so effectually learned at any other time.

And apply, I would beseech you, all this which has been said to the present season of Lent, to this week of Passion above all, which, though fast running out, is still partly ours. If this holy season slips by us un-improved, if *we* will not watch our one hour with Christ, if we will not enter into his sufferings as at this time so vividly brought before us, if those solemn words of the Litany, "by thine agony and bloody sweat. by thy cross and passion," have no deeper meaning for us at this time than at another, then, indeed, other like times may come round to us; another year, should we be permitted to see it, may bring with it its own opportunities, its own holy seasons, its fasts and its festivals, its Lent and its Easter, but the blessing of this present time will have been missed, and that without recovery. We cannot later in the year, even if we should desire it, go back for it and find it; we cannot in Pentecost obtain the blessing of Lent. We may, indeed, obtain the Pentecostal blessing, though in stinted measure as compared to what it might have been, but the Lent one is gone; we cannot, by arbitrary and self-willed efforts of our own, recall or reproduce a time which, in the natural course of things, came to us, and which we then refused to entertain, any more than we could hope to gather spring flowers in the season of autumn fruits.

My Christian brethren, what a motive and argument is here for making much of each holy time, each precious occasion which, in the course of our Christian year, is brought near us for some special service of the Lord our God; this motive, I mean, that each is in its very nature irrevocable. How often we are satisfied with saying, I have not prayed well to-day; I have not shut the door of my heart, that door by which vain thoughts find entrance there; but I will pray better, with more collection of spirit, to-morrow. I have been inattentive to-day in God's house; I have drawn near to the table of the Lord with a cold and careless heart; but I will be a more earnest worshipper, a more devout partaker, when I tread those courts, when I approach that table again. I have left undone this labor of love which God put in my way: but the next shall not escape me in like manner; the good works which He has prepared for me to perform, I will not fail to perform them then; the good words which He would have me speak, I will not leave them unspoken again.. And so time creeps on with us: we are ever going to be earnest, devoted Christians, but never being such; ever missing a present benefit and blessing, and ever consoling ourselves with the expectation of reaping a future. But how unlikely it is that we shall do so; how much more probable that the negligence of to-day will be followed up, yea, will be punished, by the worse negligence of to-morrow.

And even if that unwarranted expectation, that what we miss to-day we shall not miss equally to-morrow, should, against all likelihood, be fulfilled, is this enough? shall we thus recover and get back the lost? We may thus, indeed, arrest our steps in that downward course of spiritual declension and decay which it is only too easy to tread; but we are very far from replacing ourselves where, but for these negligences and omissions, we might have been. Surely we are not so strong that we can afford to lose the returns of any one prayer, the strength of any one communion, the grace of any one holy ordinance of our faith? Do we not, in our own utter weakness and helplessness, need them all, the strength, the grace, the consecration which each several one was ordained to impart to us?

Apply all this to the present time. Christ has been saying to you now, as He said to the three disciples

7*

of old, Watch with Me one hour, watch with Me in the garden, wait on Me at the Cross. Help the sufferings, if not of my natural body, yet of my spiritual body, the church, by your prayers, by your intercessions, by your active ministrations of love. But what if, instead of this, your eyes have been heavy; what if there has been no shaking off the drowsiness of your spirits, no girding up of the loins of your minds to active well-doing, if your hearts have been overcharged during all this time with the cares and pleasures of this world; if it has been thus with you, what words can you, then, look to hear from your Lord but words of a sad rebuke, such as those which the three disciples heard? When this season is past, when it is gone, and belongs to the things which never can be again, He will say to you, and the words will sound sadly in your ears, Sleep on now, and take your rest; you might have helped Me, but you did not; you might have won the blessing of this Lent, but it has escaped you. Other blessings may be in store for you still, though this is less likely than it was; other gifts and graces you may still make your own; but what this season would have yielded, of strength to serve Me, of closer fellowship with my sufferings, and of the holiness consequent on this, of nearer acquaintance with my Cross, and of higher peace derived from that acquaintance, and from the blood of that Cross sprinkled by faith anew upon your souls, this you must be contented to forego. If words like these would have a mournful sound in our ears, let us so watch and pray that they may never be spoken unto us.

SERMON XV.

CHRIST THE LAMB OF GOD.[*]

The next day John seeth Jesus coming unto him, and saith, Behold the Lamb of God, which taketh away the sin of the world.—JOHN i. 29.

IT has been sometimes asked and debated, to which of the lambs of sacrifice, ordained in the Old Testament, did the Baptist here refer; with which did he liken that immaculate Lamb, who, being without spot and stain, should take away our spots and stains, and bear the collective sin of the world. Did St. John allude to the daily lamb of the morning and evening sacrifice? or was it to the lamb of the passover, commemorating the old deliverance from Egypt? or was it to some other of the many lambs which were prescribed in the law of Moses, as a portion of the ritual of sacrifice appointed there? The question is surely a superfluous one. The reference is not special, but comprehensive. It is to none of these in particular,

---

[*] This sermon, preached at Cambridge before it was preached in the Abbey, has been already published in a small volume of Academical Sermons. The limited circulation to which such volumes are doomed, together with the exceeding importance of the subject it treats of, must be my apology for reprinting it here.

(155)

being indeed to them all. They severally set forth in type and in figure some part of that which He fulfilled in substance and in life ; in Him, not now a lamb of men, but the Lamb of God, being at length fulfilled to the uttermost the significant word of Abraham, " God will provide Himself a lamb."

The disciples of John understand the intention with which he thus designated Jesus unto them ; they understand it, if not at the first designation, yet at the second ; and as the Evangelist tells us (he probably was himself one of the two disciples, Andrew being the other), they " heard him speak, and they followed Jesus." They quitted one master, and joined themselves to another. There was a drawing, attractive power in that word about the Lamb, the taker away of the world's sin, which no other word possessed or could possess. At a later day, Christ Himself declared, " I, if I be lifted up, will draw all men unto Me." Already this potent drawing had begun ; and set between two magnets, the disciples showed at once which was the mightier of the two. The Baptist, indeed, had met and had satisfied many needs of men's spirits,— their need of repentance, of confession of sin, of amendment of life ; but there were other needs which he could not meet. The spirit of man cries out for something deeper even than these, something which shall reach farther back ; which shall not be clogged with sinful infirmities, as his own repentance even at the very best must be. Men cry for some work to rest upon which shall not be *their* work, and thus underlying the weaknesses of every thing human, but which shall be God's;

perfect, complete, to which nothing need be added, from which nothing can be taken away. They feel that behind and beyond their repentance, even though that repentance be wrought by the Spirit of God, there must be something which God has not so much wrought *in* them, as *for* them ; and that on this they must rest, if they are to find abiding peace for the soul ; a rock to flee to, which is higher than they ; higher than their repentance, than their faith, than their obedience, even than their new life in the Spirit. Now this Rock is Christ ; and John pointed to this Rock, and the two at once understood him. They had longed after amendment of life, and John had helped them thus far ; but they yearned for more than this, for atonement, propitiation, ransom, a conscience purged from dead works by the blood of sprinkling, and John could not help them here ; except, indeed, by directing them to Jesus, as in these memorable words he did, "Behold the Lamb of God, which taketh away the sin of the world."

It is impossible to estimate too highly the significance of these words, or the place which, in a true scheme of Christian doctrine, they must assume. As the church understands them, they set forth our Lord in his central function and office, as the one perfect sacrifice ; they set forth the effectual operation of his sacrifice of Himself, as a bearing, and a bearing away, of the world's sin. They may therefore fitly constitute our starting-point from which to consider what the church's doctrine of the atonement, or of the sacrifice of the death of Christ, and of the consequences which

follow thereupon, may be; and this, with especial reference to objections brought against this doctrine, as
failing to commend itself to the conscience, as indeed
outraging that sense of right, that revelation anterior
to all other revelations, which God has planted in the
heart; as a doctrine therefore, which, however it may
seem to be in Scripture, however a superficial interpretation of certain passages may favor this impression,
it is impossible can be truly there.

The gravity of the matter thus brought to issue none
can deny, nor yet the very serious and far-reaching
consequences which must follow, if, while the word
'sacrifice' should indeed be left us, all wherein the es-
sence of sacrifice consisted, as mainly its *vicarious* and
satisfactory character, were to be exploded from the
New Testament. One of the first of these consequences
would be a loosening, that I say not a dissolution, of
the bonds between the Old Testament and the New.
There can be no question that in the Old, the doctrine
of sacrifice, of the vicarious suffering of one for another,
of satisfaction resulting thereupon, everywhere pre-
vails. If there is nothing of this in the New, if this is
Jewish only, and not Christian as well, if Christ, for
instance, is only the Lamb of God because of his innocence and purity, and not because of his sacrificial
death, if He takes away the sin of the world only in
the way of summoning and enabling men to leave off
their sins, all bonds between the New Testament, and
at least the Levitical sacrifices of the Old, are broken.
These last point to nothing. They are a huge husk
without a kernel; types without their antitype; shad-

ows, but not 'shadows of the true,' and thus with no substance following ; a promise without performance ; an elaborate and enormous machinery for the effecting of nothing.

That which hitherto has ennobled those sacrifices in our eyes, was the truth which they foreshowed. Let them have foreshowed nothing of the kind, and they sink down at once to a level with the heathen sacrifices ; nay, not merely to a level with those, as those have hitherto been regarded by us, but they drag down to a far lower depth the heathen and themselves together. Hitherto the heathen sacrifices, hideous distortions of the true as they so often were, yet were not without a certain terrible grandeur of their own. A ray of the glory of Calvary fell upon them, and, dark as they remained, yet did not leave them altogether dark. They were blind feelings after the Cross of Christ, passionate outcries for it ; they were lies indeed, yet lies which cried after the truth. But take from Christ's Cross its character of an altar, and from his death its character of a sacrifice, and at once the Levitical sacrifices no longer remain as shadows of the true, and the heathen cease to be remote resemblances of the same. Let the doctrine of Christ's death as being a vicarious atonement and satisfaction be dismissed from the New Testament, on the ground of its contradiction to the righteous moral instincts of humanity, and it is impossible consistently to maintain the divine character of large portions of the Old.

But let us a little consider what the objections are, which are now being made to the church's doctrine of the atonement, and what the answers which they seem to demand. And first, in regard to this discussion, it may be generally observed, that it is *not* sufficient to reply to these objections out of Scripture ; the very argument of the objectors being, that the meaning we attach to our Scripture proof cannot be the right one, revolting as it does that sense of righteousness and justice which is God's gift to men anterior to all other gifts, that earliest revelation of Himself which no later one can ever gainsay or set aside, but into harmony with which each later must be brought. We must seek our arguments elsewhere. We must endeavor first to show,—and confined within the narrow bounds of a single discourse, I shall limit myself to this,—how that truth, which we affirm, does not offend, but indeed commends itself to, the moral sense ; by manifestation of the truth commending ourselves and it to the consciences of men.

The objection, then, as I take it, to Christ's *vicarious* offering,—for I will first deal with this,—to the assertion that He died not merely for the good of, but in the room and in the stead of, others, tasted death *for* them, commonly assumes this form. Must not righteousness, it is asked, be the law of all God's dealings? Most of all, must we not expect to find consistent with highest righteousness that which is the most solemn and awful of all God's dealings with his creatures? But how is it agreeable with this, how can it be called just, nay, how can it be acquitted of extremest injustice, to lay on one man the penalties of others, so that he pays the things which he never took, so that they sin and he is punished, on him being laid the iniquities of them all? What have we here, an adversary will insist, but in the awfullest sphere of all, and in matters the most tremendous, the same injustice which, even in least things, provokes our indignation; as, for instance, when some playfellow of a young prince is constituted, as we may sometimes have read of, to suffer the consequences of *his* idleness; so that one neglects his tasks, and another is chastised; one plays the truant, and another bears the smart?

But the case is not in point: and, since it has been started, it might be worth our while to make it in point, and then to consider whether it presents itself in any aspect so monstrous and absurd. To make it in point, the parts which the several persons sustain must, in the first place, be reversed. It must be that the young prince suffers for his humbler truant companions, not one of them for him; it must be that he does it, not of compulsion or constraint, but of his own free will; it must be that only such an act as this would overcome their perversity and idleness; that he offers himself to this correction, knowing that nothing else would overcome it, and that this would be effectual to do so. A submission with this knowledge to the punishment of their faults and negligences and shortcomings might be strange, even as all acts of condescending self-offering love are strange in a world of selfishness and pride; but surely there would be nothing in it either monstrous or ridiculous.

And exactly in the same way, when we hear it urged, How can it be righteous to lay on one man the penalties of others? surely we must feel that the question, to be effectually answered, needs only to be more accurately put; that the form which it ought to assume is this, How can it be righteous for one man *to take upon himself* the penalties of others? and none who remember the " Lo! I come" of the Saviour, the willing sacrifice of our Isaac, prefigured by his who climbed so meekly in his father's company the hill of Moriah— none, I say, who remember this, will deny our right to make this change; while surely the whole aspect of the question is now by this little change altered altogether. For how many an act of heroic self-sacrifice, which it would be most unrighteous for others to demand from, or to force on, one reluctant, which indeed would cease to be heroism or sacrifice at all, unless wholly self-imposed, is yet most glorious when one has freely offered himself thereunto; is only *not* righteous, because it is so much better than righteous, because it moves in that higher region where law is no more known, but only known no more because it has been transfigured into love. Wherein else is the chief glory of history but in those deeds of self-devotion, of heroic self-offering, which, like trumpet tones sounding from the depths of the past, rouse us, at least for a while, from the selfish dream of life to a nobler existence; and of which if the mention has become trite and common now, it has only become so because the grandeur of them has caused them to be evermore in the hearts and on the lips of men.

Vicarious suffering, it is strange to hear the mighty uproar which is made about it; when indeed in lower forms,—not low in themselves, though low as compared with the highest,—it is everywhere, where love is at all. For indeed is not this, of one freely taking on himself the consequences of others' faults, and thus averting from those others at least in part the penalties of the same, building what others have thrown down, gathering what others have scattered, bearing the burdens which others have wrapped together, healing the wounds which others have inflicted, paying the things which he never took, smarting for sins which he never committed ; is not this, I say, the law and the condition of all highest nobleness in the world? is it not that which God is continually demanding of his elect, they approving themselves his elect, as they do not shrink from this demand, as they freely own themselves the debtors of love to the last penny of the requirements which it makes? And if these things are so, shall we question the right of God Himself to display this nobleness which He demands of his creatures? Shall we wish to rob Him of the opportunity, or think to honor Him who is highest love, by denying Him the right to display it?

But the sufferings and death of Christ were not merely vicarious ; they were also satisfactory ; and thus atoning or setting *at one*, bringing together the Holy and the unholy, who could not have been reconciled in any other way. When we speak thus, we are sometimes taunted at the outset with the fact that the word 'satisfaction,' as applied to the death of Christ and its results, nowhere occurs in Scripture ; so belongs to the later Latin theology, (Anselm being the first to employ it,) that the Greek theology does not so much as possess the word,—I mean of course any Greek equivalent for it. This is true; but though the *word* 'satisfaction' is not in Scripture, the *thing* is everywhere there, and we are contending not about words, but things; the idea of it is inherent in ransom, in redemption, in propitiation, in scriptural words and phrases and images out of number; and just as in the Arian controversy, the church had a perfect right to the 'homoousion,' careless whether the *word* were in Scripture or no, so here to 'satisfaction,' seeing that this best expresses and sums up the truth which in this matter she holds.

But, not to tarry longer with this objection at the threshold, how, it is further urged, could God be well pleased with the sufferings of the innocent and the holy? What 'satisfaction,' since we will have this word, could He find in these? Here, as so often, the faith of the church is first caricatured, that so it may be more easily brought into question. Could God have pleasure in the sufferings of the innocent and the holy, and that innocent and holy his own Son? Assuredly not; but He could have pleasure, nay, according to the moral necessities of his own being, He must have pleasure, yea, the highest joy, satisfaction, and delight in the love, the patience, the obedience, which those sufferings gave Him the opportunity of displaying, which but for those He could never have displayed; above all, He must have rejoiced in these as manifested in his own Son. For even we ourselves, when we read in story of those who for the love of their fellows have made their lives one long patient martyrdom, or who, witnessing for the truth, have been borne from earth in the fire-chariot of some shorter but sharper agony, do we not feel that we have a right to rejoice in these martyrs of truth and love, yea, in the very pains and sufferings which they endured? that only as the nerves of our own moral being are weak and unstrung, only as we have become incapable not merely of doing, but even of appreciating, what is noble and great, do we grudge them those pains, do we wish for them one of these to have been less; seeing that these were the conditions of their greatness, that without which it could never have been shown, without which it might never have existed?

Even the heathen moralist could say of God in his dealings with good men, "*fortiter* amat." There is no weakness in his love; it is love according to which He does not spare his own, but thrusts them forth to labor and difficulty and pains, in which alone they can be perfected; even as the same heathen could affirm that God had joy in nobly suffering men; not, of course, for the sufferings' sake, but for the virtues which were manifested therein. And should not the God and Father of our Lord Jesus Christ have pleasure in the faith, the love, the obedience of his Son? Yea, it was a joy such as only the mind and heart of God could contain, that in his Son this perfect pattern of self-forgetting, self-offering love was displayed. We do not shrink from accepting in the simplest sense the assertion of the Apostle, that Christ, giving Himself for us on the Cross, became therein and thereby "a sacrifice of a sweet-smelling savor" unto God; that He was well pleased therewith, and said at length what He would never else have said, "I have found a ransom."

Christ satisfied herein, not the divine anger, but the divine craving and yearning after a perfect holiness, righteousness, and obedience in man, God's chosen creature, the first fruits of his creatures; which craving no man had satisfied, but all had disappointed, before. There had been a flaw in every other man's escutcheon · every other, instead of repairing the breach which Adam had made, had himself left that breach wider than he found it. But here at length was one, a son of man, yet fairer than all the children of men, one on whom the Father's love could rest with a perfect complacency, in regard of whom He could declare, "This is my beloved Son, in whom I am well pleased," in whom He had pleasure without stint and without drawback. And that life of his, the long self-offering of that life of love, was crowned, consummated, and perfected by the sacrifice of his death, wherein He satisfied to the uttermost every demand which God could make on Him, and satisfied for all the demands which God had made upon all the other children of men, and which they had not satisfied for themselves.

But if the question is here asked, How could one man satisfy for many? how by one man's obedience could many be made righteous? the answer is not far to seek. The trandscendent worth of that obedience which Christ rendered, of that oblation which He offered, the power which it possessed of countervailing and more than counterbalancing a world's sin, lay in this, that He who offered these, while He bore a human nature, and wrought human acts, was a Divine person; not indeed God alone, for as such He would never have been in the condition to offer or to die; nor man alone, for then the worth of his offering could never have reached so far; but that He was God and man in one person indissolubly united, and in this person performing all those acts, man that He might obey and suffer and die, God that He might add to every act of his obedience, his suffering, his death, an immeasurable worth, steeping in the glory of his divine personality all of human that He wrought. Christ was able so summarily to pay our debt, because He had another and a higher coin in which to pay it than that in which it was contracted. It was contracted in the currency of earth; He paid it in the currency of heaven. Nor was it, as some among the schoolmen of the middle ages taught, that God arbitrarily ascribed and imputed to Christ's obedience unto death a value which made it equal to the needs and sins of the world, such a value as it would not have had but for this imputation. We affirm rather with the deeper theologians of those and of all times, who crave to deal with realities, not with ascriptions and imputations, that his offering had in itself this intrinsic value, that there was no ascription to it, as of God's mere pleasure, of a value which it did not in itself possess; for then the same might have been imputed to the work of an angel or of a saint; the whole exclusive fitness of the Son of God undertaking the work would then pass away; and another might have made up the breach as well as He. We affirm rather that what the Son of God claimed in behalf of that race whereof He had become the representative and the Head, He claimed as of right, although, indeed, that right was one which the Father as joyfully conceded as the Son demanded. Without a satisfaction such as this, the eternal interests of that righteousness whereof God is the upholder in his own moral universe would not have permitted Him to be, as He now is, the passer-by of transgression, the justifier and accepter of the ungodly.

Such, my brethren, is the church's faith in respect of the atonement. That atonement is not, as some would persuade us, a one-sided act; it looks not one way only, but two; having a face with which it looks toward God, as well as one with which it looks toward man. It is no mere reconciling of man to God, as though its object were to remove the distrust, to kill the enmity in man's heart, to persuade him to throw down his arms, and yield himself the vanquished of eternal love. It is most truly this, but it is much more than this. It is a reconciling not merely of man to God, but of God to man; whose love could not have gone forth upon the children of men in its highest forms, in those of forgiveness, acceptance, renewal, if this had not found place. Think not, then, my brethren, of Christ the peace*maker* as though He came only to *announce* peace, to say to the doubting and distrustful children of men, Why will ye remain at such a miserable and guilty distance from your Heavonly Father, when his arms are stretched out to receive you, when He is only waiting to enfold you within them? No doubt Christ did come bringing this message, did proclaim that those arms were open, and that Heavenly Father waiting to be gracious ; but He only brought this message inasmuch as He *made* the peace which He announced. "Having *made* peace by the blood of his Cross," "He entered into the Holiest of all, having obtained eternal redemption for us." In Him and through Him, through the sacrifice of his death, the disturbed, and in part suspended, relations between God and his sinful creatures were reconstituted anew ; his blood being shed to cleanse men from their sins, and not to teach them that those sins needed no cleansing, and could be forgiven without one.

And will any faith which is short of this faith satisfy the deepest needs and cravings of your souls? You may struggle against it with your understandings ; though, I think, very needlessly ; for it seems to me to approve itself to the reason and the conscience, quite as much as to demand acceptance of our faith ; but you will crave it with your inmost spirits. There are times when, perhaps, nothing short of this will save you from the darkness of a hopeless despair. Let me imagine, for example, one, who with many capacities for a nobler and purer life, and many calls thereunto, has yet suffered himself to be entangled in youthful lusts, has stained himself with these ; and then after awhile awakens, or rather is awakened by the good Spirit of God, to ask himself, What have I done? How fares it with him at the retrospect then, when he, not wholly

8

laid waste in spirit, is made to possess (oh, fearful possession!) the sins of his youth?   Like a stricken deer, though none but himself may be conscious of his wound, he wanders away from his fellows ; or if with them, he is alone among them, for he is brooding still and ever on the awful mystery of evil, which he now too nearly knows.   And now too all purity, the fearful innocence of children, the holy love of sister and of mother, and the love which he had once dreamed of as better even than these, with all which is supremely fair in nature or in art, comes to him with a shock of pain, is fraught with an infinite sadness ; for it wakens up in him by contrast a livelier sense of what he is, and what, as it seems, he must for ever be ; it reminds him of a Paradise for ever lost, the angel of God's anger guarding with a fiery sword its entrance against him. He tries by a thousand devices to still, or at least to deaden, the undying pain of his spirit.   What is this word sin, that it should torment him so ?   He will tear away the conscience of it, this poisonous shirt of Nessus, eating into his soul, which in a heedless moment he has put on.   But no ; he can tear away his own flesh, but he cannot tear away that.   Go where he may, he still carries with him the barbed shaft which has pierced him ; "hæret lateri letalis arundo."   The arrow which drinks up his spirit, there is no sovereign dittany which will cause it to drop from his side— none, that is, which grows on earth ; but there is, which grows in heaven, and in the church of Christ, the heavenly enclosure here.

And you too—if such a one as I have pictured should

be among us to-day—you too may find your peace, you will find it, when you learn to look by faith on Him, "the Lamb of God, that taketh away the sin of the world." 'You will carry, it may be, the scars of those wounds which you have inflicted upon yourself to your grave; but the wounds themselves, He can heal them, and heal them altogether. He can give you back the years which the cankerworm has eaten, the peace which your sin had chased away, and, as it seemed to you, for ever. He can do so, and will. "Purge me with hyssop, and I shall be clean; wash me, and I shall be whiter than snow;" this will be then your prayer, and this your prayer will be fulfilled. The blood of sprinkling will purge, and you will feel yourself clean. Your sin will no longer be yourself; you will be able to look at it as separated from you, as laid upon another, upon One so strong that He did but for a moment stagger under the weight of a world's sin, and then so bore, that bearing He has borne it away for ever.

SERMON XVI.

THE KEYS OF DEATH AND OF HELL.

And He laid his right hand upon me, saying unto me, Fear not; I am
the first and the last: I am He that liveth, and was dead; and behold, I am alive for evermore, Amen: and have the keys of hell and
of death.—REV. i. 17, 18.

Easter Day.

GLORIOUS things are spoken of the *City* of God;
but of the *Son* of God, as might justly be expected,
things are spoken which are far more glorious still;
nor does He, the King of Glory, shrink from speaking
these glorious things of Himself. And yet I know not
whether, amid all the magnificent titles which He
bears, there is any title, any blazon, any style more
magnificent than this of my text, "I am He that liveth,
and was dead; and, behold, I am alive for evermore,
Amen; and have the keys of death and of hell" (for
that, and not "of hell and of death," is the true order
of the words, as in the best copies of the Greek). But
whether there be, or be not, loftier dignities even than
this, I am sure that there are none which would better
become, few that would become so well, the joyful
solemnities of this Easter morn. For here we have
the glory of Christ, not as He is God, and as such is
the Life, the Fountain of Life, for all created things:

(172)

by whom and in whom they live and move and have their being ; but Christ as He is the *Resurrection* and the Life, as He is Life in conflict with death, and overcoming it, as He is Life, swallowing up death in victory,—Christ, therefore, as He is Man (for only man could die) ; and yet as Man, as the son of Man, triumphing over death and hell and all the powers of the grave ; having burst their bonds asunder, because it was impossible for Him to be holden by them ; and now having risen to the power of an endless life, death having no more dominion over Him. "I am He that liveth"—this much He might have said as God ; but this was not all which we, the dying children of men, who dwell in houses of clay which the moth crushes, who shall presently lie down in our graves, and make the worm our bedfellow there, require. The tidings are far more glorious, infinitely more blessed, than this ; for they are these, and tell of death overcome, of the grave giving back its prey : "I am He that liveth, and *was* dead ; and, behold, I am *alive* for evermore."

And yet it is not this portion of my text which I propose mainly to dwell on to-day ; but rather on the words which immediately follow, "and have the keys of death and of hell." But here, before proceeding farther, and as something necessary for the understanding of this proclamation, let me remind you that our English word 'hell' is used in two very different senses in the authorized Version of the New Testament, and is the rendering of two very different words, now of one, and now of the other. Sometimes it stands for the place of torment, Gehenna, which word ' Gehenna' we have in a measure adopted into our own tongue; sometimes ' hell' is the translation of another word, namely, ' Hades,' which has also found a certain measure of acceptance with us; and ' hell' then means the whole invisible world, whither the spirits of all men, after they are delivered from the burden of flesh, of good men and bad alike, are gathered, waiting there the judgment of the great day; the good waiting their perfect consummation and bliss, and the bad that dreadful hour when, body and soul being reunited once more, they shall receive in their bodies and in their souls the due reward of their deeds. Now, in the passage before us, it is this last, this Hades, the world of the unseen, the world beyond the grave, which Christ claims for his own, *over* which He has obtained dominion, *of* which He holds the key; that key being the sign and token of his dominion; so that, holding that key, He can open, and no man can shut; He can shut, and no man can open.

A far more august dominion this, than if He had claimed to have the key of ' hell' in our common and narrower acceptation of the word, that is, of Gehenna, the pit; to be the jailer of that dark prison-house and miserable abode of the lost. ' Hell,' in the last sense of the word, is only a little obscure corner of the immeasurable dominion which is his. Not Gehenna merely, but Hades, the unknown, mysterious, invisible world, lying beyond our ken, almost beyond our guess, a world so near us, and yet so unimaginable by us, it is in all its extent a province of his empire. Not merely as He is God,—for this of course, and this from everlasting,—but through the grave and gate of death He as a man, and as our forerunner, entered into this Hades,—"went down," as we say in the Apostles' Creed, "into hell;" preached there, as St. Peter declares, to the spirits in prison. Seeming to be Himself a prisoner there, He was yet the breaker of the prison, first for Himself, and then for a multitude besides. Smiting the bars of iron asunder, He returned to the light of day; the wearer of that triple crown which another has blasphemously assumed; the wearer of it, because He was the winner of it, and because He was henceforward the Lord of heaven and of earth and of hell; so that at his name, at the name of Jesus, that is, the *human* name of the Lord, every knee should bow, of things in heaven, and things on earth, and things under the earth.

Such, my brethren, is the style, such are the dignities of the Prince of Life, who, having Himself tasted death, and gone down into hell, and having overcome death, and burst the gates of hell, henceforward wears at his girdle the keys of both, in token of his supreme authority over both.

Let us pause here, and ask, What this is to us? how it concerns us? what Easter lessons we, considering these words, may take with us home this day?

And first, Christ has the key of death. Our times are in his hands. *He* measures out to us the handbreadth of our life, longer or shorter as it may be. We do not die at random. The thread of our days is not cut short by the shears of a malignant fate, is not snapped as by chance, or by the blind walk of mortal accident. There is no chance, no haphazard here; but we live so long as Christ wills, and we die exactly when Christ wills. Life and death are his; and if we are his, then what is his is also ours, and life and death are ours also. Oh, comfortable thought for those that are Christ's! It is appointed unto them, as unto all, once to die; but they die at the right time. They are taken from the evil to come; or when they are at their best; or when God has no more work for them here to do; or when they may glorify Him more by their deaths than by their lives. How often God's saints and servants seem to us to die at the wrong moment; too early, when they were greatly needed, for not half, not a tithe of their work was done; or too late, when they seem to have overlived themselves, and nothing but the dull, dead ashes of what once they were to survive; or in some other way to have missed the fittest opportunity. So to us, in our short-sighted vision, it may appear; but it never is really so. As grace had the ordering of all the rest of their lives, so of this its most serious concluding act. Christ has the key of death, He, that is, who is at once the highest Wisdom, the highest Power, and the highest Love; He will not then turn that key till the fittest moment has come.

But if this is a comfortable thought for those who love and serve Christ, it is a thought of terror and dismay for the careless and the disobedient. Their times also are in his hands. To the proudest, boldest sinner He can say, and does say, Thus far shalt thou go, and no further; and here shall thy proud waves be stayed.

He sets them their bounds which they cannot pass. Where is he, perhaps he is among us this morning, the secure sinner, who is counting his life his own; who is laying out far-stretching plans for the future; who is saying to his soul, "Soul, thou hast much goods laid up for many years; eat, drink, and be merry;" who is counting that as he *has* lived in neglect or defiance of God's laws, so he may live in neglect and defiance of them still, and that no evil will overtake him? Shall it be so indeed? God's judgment may be far above out of his sight, but Christ, whom he is defying, has the key of death. One turn of that key, and how will it be with him? What if the decree should go forth against him, "This night shall thy soul be required of thee"? He may have borne it hitherto with a high hand against God, but will he do so any more? What will resistance profit him, when God changes his countenance and sends him away? Lay this, then, to heart, I beseech you, that Christ is the Lord of the spirits of all flesh, that He kills and makes alive, that He has the key of death, and that those who love Him, and those who hate Him, shall alike find this to be true.

But He has another key, the key of hell, or of Hades. He orders, that is, not merely the time of our departure out of this world, but the whole manner of our existence in another; in that world into which at death we pass, and in which we remain until the judgment of the great day. This too is a most comfortable thought, that He will be with his people there. For that state of existence into which we are ushered when we leave this warm tenement of clay and all this familiar world, that land without form and void, what a dim mysterious terror broods over it for us. Millions and millions of the children of men have travelled to it, and yet for us it is the same undiscovered country which it was before one child of Adam had girded himself up for that, his longest journey and his last; for of all these millions who have gone to it none have returned; or if one or two have come back, a Lazarus, or a little maiden, after briefest sojourn on the frontiers and outer confines of that land, their finger has been upon their lips; those lips have been sealed; and, even if they knew, they have not told us anything of the secrets which lie beyond the grave. That invisible world which is so near us, is still divided from us by a curtain which none has lifted; and we are left dimly and darkly guessing at all which is beyond. And yet, though we know no more of that mysterious kingdom than Adam knew when as yet his firstborn had not died, we have strong comfort in this, that One there is who *does* know, who has gone down into that strange, and for us unimaginable world, only peopled with the forms of our fear; who has returned from it, and who says to them who must descend thither as He descended, *Fear not;* I have the keys of that invisible world; I have been Myself before you through it; I will be with you in it; my rod and my staff shall comfort you there.

And then He goes on to say, I open, and no man can shut; I shut, and no man can open;* these also

<hr>

* Rev. iii. 7.

words of joy for believing souls, though words of terror and despair for the impenitent and unbelieving. Thus He opened Paradise to the penitent thief. For Paradise, which is not heaven, but rather the blissful waiting-place of happy souls, as yet not having received their perfect consummation and bliss, this, a part of Hades, is included in it. It was to this that Christ's own soul descended, while his body lay in the grave. He knew that He should have the key of it, that He could open it and none could shut, when, in reply to that word of faith, "Lord, remember me when Thou comest in thy kingdom," He made that confident answer, "This day shalt thou be with me in Paradise." And as He opened it to that poor penitent malefactor, so to Zacchæus the publican, when He declared, "This day is salvation come to this house;" and so to that woman who had been a sinner, when He said unto her, "Thy faith hath saved thee; go in peace." There were indeed many that would gladly have shut the door against these; proud, self-righteous Pharisees, who marvelled and who murmured that Christ was gone to lodge with sinners, or that He suffered such to touch Him, and who would have fain reversed the sentence of his grace. But when He opens, none can shut. His is the power of the keys. Men may mistake; they may make sad the soul which He has not made sad; they may retain the sins which He has remitted; but then his sentence shall stand, and not theirs. Or, worse than mistaking, they may grudge the grace extended to others; but while, thus grudging, they may shut the kingdom against themselves, they cannot shut

it against the objects of his grace. For the keys of
the invisible world, of Paradise, which is the outer
chamber and vestibule of heaven, and of heaven itself,
are in his hands. If He be on thy side, O thou penitent soul, fear not, though all the world be against
thee. If He absolves, who shall condemn thee. Shall
the world? its mouth shall be stopped. Or Satan?
that accuser of the brethren is cast out. Or thine own
conscience? He has spoken peace to it, and thou
wilt forgive thyself when thou knowest thou art forgiven of Him. Or the things written in the book
against thee? the red line of his blood has been drawn
across that page of the book in which thy sins had
been recorded, and has cancelled the writing there;
and instead of the bitter things of that book, thy name
shall be found written in another, even in the Lamb's
book of life. When He opens to thee, none can
shut.

But it is also true, that when He shuts none can
open. When He shuts heaven, none can force their
way *into* it; when He shuts hell, none can force their
way *out* of it. Wilt thou take heaven by violence?
There is a violence by which it *is* taken, the violence
of prayers and tears; but all other violence is in vain.
Wilt thou take it in thine own way, and not in God's;
seeking to establish thine own righteousness, and not
accepting the righteousness of Christ, thinking to force
thy way into the kingdom by some self-willed efforts,
self-chosen services of thine own, to enter the sheephold
not by the door, but climbing up, a thief and a robber,
by some other way? In vain. No man cometh to the

Father but by the Son. What He shuts against thee none can open. And, ah! it is also true, and I dare not leave it unsaid, if thou shouldst provoke Him to the uttermost, and He should once shut upon thee the gates of the dark prison-house, thou wilt be bound there by everlasting chains; for the gates, be they of heaven or of hell, which He shuts no other can ever open.

SERMON XVII.

SCRIPTURE ITS OWN BEST INTERPRETER.

Search the Scriptures.—JOHN v. 39.

"SEARCH the Scriptures," this is the commandment of Christ our Lord. "Do not search the Scriptures; you know not what mischiefs will befall you if you do," this is the commandment of that church which exalts herself as the only faithful guardian of Christ's words and authoritative interpreter of his will. For indeed the church of Rome, as is sufficiently familiar to us all, has been ever wont to magnify the difficulties and obscurities which are to be found in the Scriptures, to exaggerate these to the uttermost. She has spoken of the Word of God as though it was a labyrinth in which men, venturing without her clue, would be sure to lose themselves; a two-edged sword, which they who dared to wield for themselves would not fail to wield to their own hurt and harm; a dead skeleton, until she had breathed into it the breath of life. And many other things she has spoken concerning Scripture, or suffered her children to speak unrebuked, dishonorable to its authority, its sufficiency, its perfection.

Nor is the motive which has induced her to utter such words of disparagement hard to discover. The intention, indeed, is obvious,—to deter the faithful from the independent study of the Word of God; a study which would be little likely to prove favorable to her pretensions; and further, to drive men in despair of any secure guidance to be found elsewhere, into the arms of an infallible church.

But we, my brethren, who would fain believe that the Scripture is not the most unsafe, but the safest, study in the world, we gladly fall back on this word of Christ; and resting upon it and other like words, as, for instance, on St. Paul's declaration that all Scriptures " were written for our learning," we are sure that the Bible cannot be any such ambiguous, dark, and dangerous a book; but one in the main plain and clear; a manual of instruction for heaven, which they who consult, though they be wayfaring men, unlearned and unlettered, shall not err therein. Asserting this, we do not mean in the least to deny that in Holy Scripture are deep things and hard things, places beyond our depth, or even our sounding, mysteries which are and will remain unfathomed to the end; but only that the things needful for life and godliness are perspicuous and clear, the great truths by which men live are plain; that the difficulties which men sometimes find in regard of these, and which have hindered some from coming to a clear consent with the great body of faithful men in respect of these, are oftener moral than intellectual, born rather in the region of the heart than in that of the understanding.

And as from these declarations of Christ and his Apostles we assert what our Reformers were wont to call the perspicuity of Scripture, so also, in contradiction to the Roman teaching, we hold that it, being the Word of God, can receive no law of interpretation from aught above it, being itself above all. We regard it, not as a treasure of which another has the key, but itself as treasure, and key to the treasure, both in one. Scripture is its own best and most legitimate interpreter. You observe, I do not say, and the church of England has never said, that the interpretation of Scripture is to be sought *only* from itself; for this, which some have taught, is the pushing of a truth into an error; and so the whole past experience of the church, and the whole weight of the creeds, and the accumulated wisdom of all the holy and good men who have occupied themselves with its study, would be slighted and disallowed. Receiving a law only from itself, it gladly receives secondary helps for its understanding from every quarter which can yield them; and they are proud and little likely to come to the knowledge of the truth, nay, sure to miss it, who in so serious and solemn a matter, and in a vain conceit of their own powers, despise these helps. At the same time, this does not alter the fact that in every case the ultimate tribunal to which appeal must be made is the Scripture itself, and not any authority outside of the Scripture. It is its own best and most legitimate interpreter.

But is not this absurd? the objectors urge. Must there not be somewhere a living interpreter to resolve its doubts, to lead into its truth (which indeed there must, though not that one whom they intend)? How can men left to themselves ever come to any certainty about its meaning, abounding as it does, even according to your own admission, with places obscure, perplexed, and difficult, with many things most hard to be understood? And then they go on to demand, Is not every past heresy, professing as it has done to build upon Scripture, every past misinterpretation of the Word into which men have fallen, a witness and a warning of what must inevitably follow when men are turned loose upon the Scripture, to wander at random there?

To the first objection a reply has already implicitly been made. While we freely admit the partial obscurity of Scripture, we do not the less constantly affirm that it employs such plainness of speech in regard of all necessary truth, that a simple man seeking and using such helps as he would be guilty of pride and presumption if he did not seek and use, would assuredly gather it therefrom.

And if we are further asked, In what way have those who admitted no authority superior to the Word itself —our Reformers, for instance—dealt, or in what way did the early Fathers,—who only did not refute because they had never so much as heard of the pretensions of Rome,—deal with those avowedly more difficult and obscurer portions of the Word, for the purpose of reaching their meaning? our answer is this. Having obtained a secure starting-place in those passages which are plain and clear and lifted above all doubts, and walking in the light of these, they found them to lend of their own clearness to many others, which would without them have remained more or less obscure ; just as one diamond, cut and polished, serves in turn to cut and polish others. Or, to use another image, from these plainest passages, as from an impregnable citadel, the interpreter would go forth to the subdual of those which, without presenting exactly the same perfect plainness, yet did not offer any serious resistance ; which having overcome, he would enlist them too in his own ranks, range them in their place and order there, and then advance as with larger numbers, an army swollen by these successes, to the subdual of those which presented a still stronger front of resistance ; thus ever enlarging the circle of his knowledge, like a conqueror who uses the nations which he has conquered that by their help he may in turn conquer others.* For him duly equipped for his work, so searching the Scripture, and ever using it as a key to unlock its own treasures, there will remain in the end only those few passages unexplained, which probably always will so remain, will survive, like untaken fortresses, in perpetual witness that this Word of God is higher, deeper, larger, than every intellect of man.

In other words, Scripture is to be interpreted according to the analogy of faith. But what, it may be asked, do we exactly mean by this phrase, drawn no doubt originally from Romans xii. 6, where St. Paul lays down the rule, that if a man prophesy, expound, that is, the Word, he shall do it "according to the *analogy*," or, as we have it, "according to the *propor-*

---

* Augustine (*De Doct. Christ.* ii. 14): Ad obscuras locutiones illustrandas de manifestioribus sumantur exempla, et quædam certarum sententiarum testimonia dubitationem incertis auferant.

tion of faith"?   Let his prophesying or preaching be in conformity with the received rule of faith, in agreement with the things otherwise and already received by faithful men.   Every part of Scripture, St. Paul would say, must be so explained as to place it in harmony and agreement with the great body of truth drawn from the other parts; faith meaning here, not an inward quality and activity which God works by his Spirit in the hearts of men, but *the* faith, the sum total of the truths once delivered to us, which, as delivered by God, are the rightful object of our faith.

I will illustrate what is meant by the analogy, or proportion, of faith, and the safety of interpreting Scripture in conformity to it, by one or two examples.

Our Lord has in one place said, speaking of the day of his own return to judgment : " Of that day and hour knoweth no man ; no, not the angels which are in heaven, *neither the Son*, but the Father."*   These words, " neither the Son, but the Father," if taken alone and without the corrective of other passages, might appear to favor the doctrine of those who hold that the Son is not God in any such sense as the Father, as not possessing the same divine attribute of omniscience with the Father ; and this text was, as we know, the main stay of these heretics of old, their stronghold, as they deemed it.   But seeing there are other Scriptures far more numerous, far more explicit, not mere consequences and deductions, as is the Arian conclusion from his text, but distinct declarations of the Son's

---

* Mark xiii. 32.

equality in all things with the Father, it is plain that this one Scripture must be subordinated to, and must receive its law from, those many, and not, on the contrary, those many from this one; that distinct assertions must stand their ground against more or less remote deductions, however it may seem to some that these last necessarily follow from this or other Scriptures which they plead.

Take another illustration. The precept of St. Paul is familiar to us all: "If thine enemy hunger, feed him; if he thirst, give him drink; for in so doing thou shalt heap coals of fire on his head."[*] It is familiar also no doubt to some among us, how these last words, "thou shalt heap coals of fire on his head," have been explained; that is, Thou shalt, through his continued obduracy and obstinate rejection of thy proffered love, draw down at last heaviest judgment, even as coals of fire to scorch and consume him, on his head. But the analogy of faith at once forbids any such explanation as this. All will admit that the pervading, the constant teaching of the New Testament is, Love thine enemy, do him all the good which thou canst. But this precept of St. Paul, interpreted as above, would not be, Love him; it would be, Under the semblance of love seek to do him all the hurt which thou canst. Paul would, in fact, be teaching us, not how best to love, and loving to win back, an estranged brother, but how to hate him more artificially and effectually than the common haters of this world. Seeing, then,

---

[*] Rom. xii. 20.

that such an explanation would set this passage in opposition with that which is on all sides acknowledged
to be the teaching of the Gospel of Christ, it cannot
be the right one.   Of one thing we are sure, that
whatever St. Paul may have meant, he did not mean
this.   The precept *must* be a counsel of love, and not
a counsel of hate.   With this foregone conclusion we
come to the consideration of it, and no explanation
can demand our assent which issues in any other result.

We are fully authorized in thus refusing our assent.
Even in the interpretation of human writings, we presume unity, and do not willingly believe in respect of
any great writer or thinker that statements of his are
irreconcilable one with another.   We are hardly persuaded to accept such an explanation of any one passage as would set it in contradiction with what he has
constantly affirmed elsewhere.   And yet it is always
possible that there may be here not merely apparent,
but real, contradiction.   The intellect of man is limited; the truths which are above its horizon at one
time may be below it at another; not to speak of innumerable infirmities which cleave to it.   We do not,
therefore, absolutely demand of an expositor so to
interpret his author that every part of his writings
shall be in perfect agreement with every other.

But this self-contradiction, which is possible for man,
is impossible for that Holy Spirit who is the author of
this Book.   All things there being true, are not merely
true, but are true together ; and the interpretation, if
one may so speak, must be *panharmonic*, that only

being the meaning of any one part of Scripture which consents with the meaning of all. In the recognition of this rule, and in the observance of it, there is that which will, under God, evermore save us from those perils and mischiefs with which Rome threatens us, if we presume to go forth seeking the meaning of Scripture otherwise than under her infallible guidance.

And when she points to the many who have wrested God's Word to their harm, have missed its true meaning, and built on their own erroneous interpretation of it huge systems of error, to their own loss and that of many more, admitting this, what argument is there here, we ask, for withholding the Scriptures from all? Men have rashly committed themselves to the seas and been drowned. Shall none therefore go forth in ships? Men have wounded themselves with their own weapons. Shall a whole nation therefore be disarmed, and lie naked and defenceless in the presence of its foes? We do not deny that there are dangers here, as everywhere else. There is a trial linked with all other of God's gifts; why should there not be a trial linked with this, one of the very choicest and the best? Men may wrest Scripture to their harm, abusing even this excellent gift of God; while yet, be it remembered ever, the root of the mischief will have lain for them, not in the weakness of the intellectual, but in some perversity of the moral, nature. God has set so close and mysterious a connection between the conclusions of the intellect and the desires of the heart, the darkened heart is so sure to issue in the darkened understanding, men are so prepared to believe what they wish to believe, that it is nothing strange if oftentimes they err concerning Scripture, and read other things in it than those which the Spirit of God has written. Nor, continuing morally what they are, would they have been a whit nearer to the kingdom of heaven, if, instead of being searchers for themselves, they had been the passive recipients from others of the most correct body of doctrine ready made to their hands. Not in this would their help have lain; but in the purifying of the heart, and so of the understanding, through the unfeigned love of the truth.

" Search the Scriptures,"—this then is a precept of Christ's which we need not fear to obey; from obedience to which we need not be deterred by any confident assurances of men that the fruits which hang upon the branches of this tree of life are too high for us to reach; or that for us, rashly stretching out our hand and gathering them, they shall not be fruit of a tree of life at all. Grant that of this fruit some may hang, as no doubt it does, on the topmost branches where we cannot attain to it; still there is precious fruit in abundance on the lower branches, hanging within the reach of all, which all may gather who will. As little need we be scared by the threat, that, rashly plucking, we may be plucking not life for ourselves, but death. We know the meaning of these threatenings; we know in what interest they are spoken; and knowing this, we know that there is nothing in them which need make us afraid. Be assured, that for one who has perished through reading the Scriptures amiss, nourishing from them a proud perverse humor of his own, a thousand, ten thousand have perished through not reading them at all.   And there, in that not reading them at all, or at any rate not searching them at all, your far more real danger lies.   The stone has been rolled away that stopped these walls of salvation so long ; but yet do not, I would beseech you, forget that your carelessness, your indifference, your sin, may as effectually, and far more guiltily, close them for you than ever a tyrannous hierarchy closed them for your fathers.   We boast of an open Bible ; but what were so sad, what would involve so great a guilt, as a Bible which is at the same time open and unread ?

SERMON XVIII.

ELIJAH'S TRANSLATION AND CHRIST'S ASCENSION.

And it came to pass, as they still went on, and talked, that, behold,
there appeared a chariot of fire, and horses of fire, and parted them
both asunder; and Elijah went up by a whirlwind into heaven.—
2 KINGS ii. 11.

Ascension Day.

THERE is nothing altogether abrupt, unprepared,
wholly unlike every thing which went before it, in
the New Testament. There are almost none of the
leading events of our Lord's life that have not their
nearer or remoter analogies and parallels in the lives
of some one or other of the Old Testament saints;
God in this way testifying that He is the author of
both Covenants; one purpose, one scheme, one intention running through them both, knitting them together, so that it is impossible to detach them from one
another, to ascribe divine authority to the one, and at
the same time to withhold it from the other. To give
an instance of what I mean: there is an anticipation,
a feeble one indeed, but still an anticipation, of the
Transfiguration of Christ in the skin of Moses' face
shining, as he also came down from the mountain
where he had been talking with God.* The glory,

* Exod. xxxiv. 29.

indeed, of Moses' transfiguration, if we may call it by so august a name, was infinitely less than the glory of Christ's; but this only agreed with the relative position of the two—Moses a servant in the house of another, Christ a Son in his own.

Not otherwise the Ascension of the Lord, which we celebrate to-day, was prefigured, foreshown, and, we may say, anticipated in part, by the translation of Elijah; and the church has marked her sense of the inner connexion in which the two events stand to one another by appointing the chapter from which my text is drawn, the chapter which records the fact and the manner of Elijah's taking up into heaven as one of the lessons to be read in the services appointed for to-day. We may expect to find, in comparing the two narratives, points of likeness, and points of difference: points of likeness, for the kingdom of God is one, one through all ages; its leading events, therefore, will repeat themselves again and again: points of difference, because there is growth in it, advance, development; the bud passes into the flower, the shadow into the substance, the type into the antitype, and God, who spake long and often by his servants, speaks at last by his Son. Nor will such an expectation as this be disappointed. There is already much of Christ's Ascension in Elijah's translation; but at the same time there are features in the later and more glorious event which exist not at all, or only in their weak beginnings, in the earlier: there are points of unlikeness, even of absolute contrast between the one and the other. Let us a little consider that earlier event to-day, reading it, as we go along, in the light thrown upon it by the later.

Elijah's work is now done; his long controversy with Israel, with an apostate king and a rebellious people, is drawing to a close; he shall no longer prophesy as in sackcloth, denouncing heavy things to his people,—shutting up heaven with a word, withholding for long years the rain and the dew from the earth,—slaying the wicked prophets of Baal; a man of peace, yet by a miserable necessity bringing a sword. All this has ended now. It has been revealed to him that his warfare is accomplished; his rest and reward are near. He shall be withdrawn in a wonderful way from the earth. He knows not, indeed, that this which has been revealed to him has been revealed also to his faithful servant and minister, Elisha; he makes, therefore, more efforts than one to leave him behind, seeking, as was so natural, that no eye of man should witness the wonderful and mysterious change whereof he should be the subject. But Elisha cleaves to him with a clinging affection : "As the Lord liveth, and as thy soul liveth, I will not leave thee." He counts, and rightly, that there will be some boon and blessing for him, some legacy of love, if only he be with his master to the last, and behold him in the very moment of his departure. He will not take a dismissal, and the pertinacity of his faith at length meets with its reward. Elijah no longer seeks to dismiss him; on the contrary, suggests to him that he should put himself in the way of a blessing, "Ask what I shall do for thee before I be taken far away from thee;" whereupon the longing

desire and expectation of Elisha's soul clothe themselves in this petition : "I pray thee let a double portion of thy spirit be upon me."

These words, I would observe by the way, have been
often misunderstood, as though Elisha had claimed
twice as much of the spirit as that portion which Elijah
had for his own. Now none could impart more than
he actually possessed—as much perhaps as he possessed, or a part of what he possessed, but certainly
not more. Neither does Elisha ask more. All that
he asks is, to be recognized as Elijah's eldest son,
that to him, among the spiritual sons of the prophet,
the rights of primogeniture might pertain. It was a
part of these rights, of the privileges of an eldest son,
that the father might bequeath, or indeed was bound
to bequeath, to him a double portion of his inheritance,
twice as much as he bequeathed to any other ;* and it
is this, not a portion twice as much as Elijah himself
actually had, that Elisha sought. The whole course
of the after history would, indeed, sufficiently refute
this latter interpretation ; for, even granting that the
miracles of Elisha are more in number than those of
Elijah, and appeal is sometimes made to this fact, yet
none who reads this history with any true insight can
deny that in Elijah we have the loftier figure, the more
heroic nature, the more predominant spirit ; that Elisha, the scholar, might indeed carry on the work which
Elijah, the master, had auspicated and begun, might
complete, but could scarcely have commenced, that

* Deut. xxi. 17.

great, and in many respects most successful, protest against idolatry which his mightier precursor was first raised up to bear.

But in all this story a higher meaning is ever present with us as we read. We read of Elijah, but we feel that a greater than Elijah is here. Our thoughts carry us on to One who, like the prophet of the elder dispensation, had finished the work upon earth which his Father had given him to do; who had borne the burden and the heat of a yet fiercer day than the prophet had ever borne, endured with a diviner patience, with not even one passing movement of impatience, a worse contradiction of sinners, had drunk the cup of a bitterer agony, had been baptized with the baptism of a more searching pain; and who, now about to leave the earth, announced to his faithful disciples that legacy of love, that promise of the Father, that double portion of the Spirit, which He would bequeath to them, and which should compensate them for his bodily absence in those coming times when they should behold no more Him whom the heavens had received out of their sight.

But to proceed: the actual translation of Elijah is recorded in those words which I have chosen for my text: "And it came to pass, as they still went on, and talked, that, behold, there appeared a chariot of fire, and horses of fire, and parted them both asunder; and Elijah went up by a whirlwind into heaven." Compare with this the Ascension of our blessed Lord: "And it came to pass, while He blessed them, He was parted from them, and carried up into heaven." The placing of one account side by side with the other is very instructive, and suggests many points of comparison. Elijah is translated, a chariot of fire and horses of fire are commissioned to snatch him away from the earth, and carry him to heaven; but our Lord is borne upward by his innate power; He is not translated, He ascends. He came *from* heaven, and He returns *to* heaven, as to his natural home. The wonder is, not that He should now at length *go* to heaven, but that He should so long have tarried upon earth. Calmly, majestically, He ascends, carrying with Him that body which He had redeemed from the grave. No fire-chariot is needed for Him; and why? there is nothing of earthly dross requiring to be burnt out of Him, no wondrous transformation, no last baptism of cleansing fire before He can endure to pass into the presence of his Father; but such as He was upon earth, exactly such He passes into the heavens. No shock, no whirlwind, no violent rapture in his case; for in his Ascension there is no breach of the laws of his natural life, but all is in exactest conformity with them. Surely in all this matter the comparison between the servant and the Son brings out to us the greatness indeed of both; but at the same time the transcendent superiorities of the Son, who in all things hath the preëminence.

In what follows after Elijah has been taken up, we may have a dim foreshadowing of the history of the church, above all the apostolic church after the Ascension of its Lord. Elisha, we are told, the faithful disciple, "took the mantle of Elijah which fell from him, and smote the waters, and said, Where is the Lord God of Elijah? and when he also had smitten the waters, they parted hither and thither, and Elisha went over." The significance of this lies in the fact that it is exactly the same miracle* which Elijah himself had a little while before performed. Are we not here reminded of Him who, being Himself anointed with the oil of gladness above his fellows, did yet, when He left the earth, not so leave it but that He left behind Him gifts and graces and powers with his church, endowing it with these from on high; and so effectually endowing it, that the works which He did, it was able to do the same, fulfilling to the very letter that promise which He had made :. " He that believeth on Me, the works that I do, he shall do also, because I go unto my Father?" These powers, these gifts. these supernatural endowments were, so to speak, the mantle which fell from our ascending Lord, the mantle which the church took up, with which it has arrayed itself: in right of possessing which it claims to be the inheritor of its Lord's commission ; in the power which that imparts, seeks ever to carry on and to complete its Lord's work, to repeat and multiply his works of grace and mercy and power in the world.

And if we, brethren, have seen, like Elisha, our Master taken from our head, if a cloud has received Him out of our sight, what shall be our conduct, what remains for us to do ? Both narratives are abundantly instructive. Elisha wasted not his time in idle lamen-

* See ver. 8.

tations; there was but that one cry, "My father, my father, the chariot of Israel, and the horsemen thereof!" and then he girt himself to his own work, though a work to be performed in his Master's strength. And the Apostles, they stood not for long idly gazing up into heaven, watching the track of their departing Lord and the path of light that He had left; but returning to Jerusalem, "continued with one accord in prayer and supplication," waiting for the promise of the Father; which no sooner had they received than they became witnesses to Christ "in Jerusalem, and in all Judæa, and in Samaria, and unto the uttermost part of the earth." They felt, and they felt rightly, that they were not weaker through his departure, but stronger. Those words of his, "It is expedient for you that I go away," had been a hard saying to them at the first; but it was not long before they understood them, before they tasted of the sweet which lay concealed in their seeming bitter, before they understood that a Lord in heaven, sitting at the right hand of God, receiving there gifts *for* men, and shedding abroad those gifts *upon* men, this was better than a Saviour upon earth, limited by conditions of time and space, with a Holy Ghost not yet given, because the Son of God was not yet glorified. They understood this; and let us, my brethren, ask of God that we may understand the same,—what this, our Lord's Ascension and sitting at the right hand of God, is for us and for all believers; why Ascension-day, if it does not quite attain to the dignity and honor of the first three among the Christian festivals, Christmas-day, and Easter-day, and Whit-Sunday, is yet only a little inferior to *them ;* while it transcends in the dignity and importance of the event which it commemorates every other day in our Christian calendar.

Very briefly, then, Christ's Ascension is, in the first place, the complement of his Resurrection. It was not enough that He should rise from the dead and walk this earth again. He must show that not earth, but heaven, is his home, and the centre to which He is irresistibly drawn. He must take his place as the Universal Bishop, the Bishop of all souls ; no longer the Shepherd of one little flock in Judæa, but the Great Shepherd of the sheep gathered in from many flocks into a wider fold. Christ's Ascension enables you to regard Him as the King of Glory, Head over all things in the church, and as such having received gifts for men. True, there were gifts and blessings before, but not in such largeness ; they were restrained, the full fountains of grace were not yet unsealed. A few drops of blessing had sprinkled a single family, a single nation ; but now in full fountains it overflowed the world. The dew was hitherto upon Gideon's fleece only, and it was dry upon all the earth besides ; but now there was to be dew on all the ground.*

There is another aspect under which Christ's Ascension may be regarded ; that which it is the object of the Epistle to the Hebrews more than of any other Scripture to bring before us. We have now not a King only sitting on the throne of power, but a High

* Judges vi. 37–40.

9*

Priest as well, who has passed within the veil, there to appear before God for us, to carry forward in heaven the work which He auspicated on earth ; who died for us once, but who lives for us for evermore. He made one offering for sin ; but He pleads the virtue of that offering continually. There is always a way for us to the Father ; for He who first opened that way keeps it open for us still ; else our sins would presently obstruct it anew, and all boldness and freedom of access to the Father would in a little while be as effectually lost again as though it had never been won ; but now, if any man sin, we have an Advocate, Jesus Christ the Righteous. And such we have, and have only, because He has made good his own words, " I ascend to my Father and your Father, to my God and your God."

One word more. It is plainly the intention of our church to suggest,—she does it by her Collect for to-day,—that we should find in the contemplation of our ascended Lord a motive to heavenly-mindedness ; for where our treasure is, there our heart should be also. Christ is our treasure—we profess at least that He is so ; and He is in heaven. Let our hearts be there also ; let us, according to that word of the Apostle, " seek those things which are above, where Christ sitteth on the right hand of God." And how does He sit there? for in the answer to this question is an additional motive to holiness. In his human body ; in that humanity which He, the Eternal Word, has married to Himself forever. It is not now, as before the Incarnation, the Son of God only that is in the bosom of the Father,* but the Son of man also that sitteth at the right hand of the Majesty on high. Taking this flesh of ours, this nature which we bear, from his Virgin Mother, and purifying it in the act of taking, He kept it pure, kept it unspotted, made it the organ and instrument of that divine life which He lived upon earth, and in the end offered Himself in it, the Son of Mary, Jesus of Nazareth, as a sacrifice of a sweet-smelling savor; and this done, and death overcome, presented Himself in it, with the prints of the nails in his hands, of the spear in his side, for the worship of angels, for an equal place with his Father on the throne of heaven. Treat, then, with reverence and respect your mortal bodies; possess them in sanctification and honor. They are akin to his body. You have nourished them,—I trust you will again nourish them to-day,—with his blessed body and blood, which is the very salve of immortality. They may be made the organs of a divine life in you, as that body which He assumed was the organ of a divine life in Him; and then where He is, you will be there also.

* John i. 18.

SERMON XIX.

CHRIST RECEIVING GIFTS FOR MEN.

Thou hast ascended on high, Thou hast led captivity captive: Thou hast received gifts for men; yea, for the rebellious also, that the Lord God might dwell among them.—PSALM lxviii. 18.

Whit-Sunday.

THESE words, drawn from a Psalm of David, form part of a magnificent hymn of triumph which he composed when, after some great victories gained over the enemies of God and of Israel, he and his people, returning from the war, brought back with gladness and solemnities of triumph the Ark of God, which had gone forth with their armies, to its resting-place in Jerusalem once more. But the words which the Holy Spirit dictated and suggested to David were so over-ruled, so ordered by that same Spirit, that they might fitly be applied, many of them, to a far mightier tri-umph than this—the victory of the Son of God over all *his* enemies; the going up, not of the Ark of God into its former resting-place at Jerusalem, but the go-ing up of the Son of God to his own place in heaven; the distribution of gifts, not such as David or some earthly monarch might distribute on some high day of rejoicing, gold and silver, sheep and oxen, for the nourishing of an earthly gladness, but such higher gifts as *He* gives from whom comes every good and every perfect gift.

St. Paul saw that this meaning lay in the words, that such application of them would be in accordance with the mind of the Spirit; and therefore, treating in the Epistle to the Ephesians of the Ascension of Christ, and the outpouring of the gifts of the Spirit which followed that Ascension, he cites, as you may remember, at least in part, the memorable words of my text; and, so to speak, claims them for Christ, and sets his seal to their fitness for the services of this day. His words are, "But unto every one of us is given grace, according to the measure of the gift of Christ. Wherefore He saith, when He ascended up on high, He led captivity captive, and gave gifts unto men. Now that He ascended, what is it but that He also descended first into the lower parts of the earth?" These last words being the Apostle's own, he indicates in them that Christ's ascent into heaven was a consequence of his descent upon earth, yea, and under the earth. He went down, and therefore it was that He went up; He humbled Himself, and therefore it was that God exalted Him; He chose for Himself the cross of shame upon earth, and therefore it was that God gave Him the throne of glory in heaven; He ascended, but He had first descended.

The words are well worth our dwelling on. It is not for nothing that St. Paul lays such an emphasis upon them; for indeed he is giving us here the secret of all true glory—that it rests and is based on humility.

Lucifer, the son of the morning, the prince of the apostate angels, he too had said, "I will ascend into heaven; I will exalt my throne above the stars of God."* But what came of his ascension, based as it was not on humility, but on pride? He who sought to be the highest, became the lowest. He fell, as only an angel could fall, from the height of heaven to the depth of hell. But Christ, *He* also ascended; only He had first descended, had taken the form of a servant, had been willing to be accounted the lowest and the last, and thus attained of right to be highest and the first. As his descent, so also his ascent. "Thou hast ascended on high." When the Apostles, as they stood upon Mount Olivet, followed with straining eyes the track of their departing Lord, with these they could follow Him but a little way; presently a cloud received Him out of their sight. But by faith they could follow, and we can follow, far. We know whither He was bound, that he was going far above all heavens, to *his* Father and to *our* Father, to the right hand of the throne of God, there to sit, the Man Christ Jesus, wielding the sceptre of the universe, the supreme Lord of earth and of heaven and of hell; "angels and authorities and powers being made subject unto Him." Truly it was *on high* that He ascended.

But this was not all. "Thou hast led captivity captive." Perhaps we shall best understand these words by imagining to ourselves some earthly monarch who has triumphed gloriously over his foes, who has

---

* Isaiah xiv. 13.

delivered a multitude of his own people whom those foes were oppressing, whom they had brought into bitter bondage; and is now returning to his capital city, bringing home the fruits and trophies of victory, and among the most signal, and to him far the most precious of these, his own people whom he has delivered. They were captives once; but he has redeemed them out of the hands of their enemies, and is thus leading their captivity captive. If they are captives still, it is his captives they are; and that captivity they are well content to undergo, for it is only liberty under another name. Take, for instance, Lot. You may remember how he with all his household fell into the hands of the confederate kings, and how Abraham, hearing of the misfortune which had befallen his nephew, armed himself and his servants, pursued and smote the spoilers, and rescued Lot out of their hands, and in this way led his captivity captive,—gave him in fact his liberty again, only binding him by ties of a dearer obligation to himself. Or contemplate David, when, returning to Ziklag, he found that the Amalekites had burned the city in his absence, and carried away the wives and children of himself and of his people; contemplate him pursuing, overtaking, destroying those, rescuing these dearly-beloved out of their grasp, and you will have in this and that other exploit some faint earthly image of that work of rescue and recovery which Christ our Lord, Son of Abraham and Son of David, wrought for us, led away as we were into slavery, the thralls and captives of Satan and of sin. He also pursued and overtook, smote the spoiler, brought back again the spoiled; saw in them whose bonds He had broken, whose captivity He led captive, the best fruits of the travail of his soul, the choicest trophies of his war. And, indeed, were they not? What signs and tokens of his power like these—when sinners become saints, when servants of dead idols are changed into servants of the living God, when Sauls are transformed into Pauls, slaves of sin into freemen of Christ? It was for this, brethren, that Christ lived, and died, and rose again, and ascended into heaven, namely, that we might be thus transformed, that we might be thus made free, that the chains of evil customs and sinful habits might fall off from our souls; that He might thus lead our captivity captive, and bring us into the liberty of the glory of the children of God.

But how should this be? How should this be brought about? The mere pattern and example of his holy life was not sufficient. We might have seen and admired that afar off; we might have derived a certain limited amount of good from the contemplation of it; but more than this, much more than this, we needed. He must not be merely the pattern of a new and higher life; He must be the *power* of that life; they who are his must be endued by Him with power from on high. And it is even so. The work of men's deliverance, which He began while He was on earth, He carries on and completes from heaven. He "received gifts for men," the manifold gifts of the Holy Ghost. He had been Himself, the Man Christ Jesus, anointed with these, with the Holy Ghost and with power, during the time that He tabernacled on earth. The Father gave not the Spirit by measure to the Son, but anointed Him with the oil of gladness above his fellows. All gifts and graces without stint and without measure, the sevenfold gifts of the Holy Ghost, were his. The Priest, the Prophet, the King of the New Covenant, He was able, "because of the anointing," to fulfil duly upon earth the offices which pertained to each ; while, being in heaven, He is no longer there the Receiver, but the Giver,—the Giver of all good gifts to the children of men ; whom He has not forsaken, whom He has not forgotten, (how should He, when He bears their nature still, is bone of their bone, and flesh of their flesh ?) and, above all, of that gift in which every other gift is shut up and included,—the gift of the Holy Ghost, which is the crowning gift of all. How transcendent a gift this is, we can best understand when we remember that Christ, who would not and could not deceive, proffered it to his mourning disciples as a substitute for Himself, as a sufficient compensation for his own absence? He was Himself one Comforter, and the Holy Ghost, whom the Father would send in his name, should be another ; yea, in some sort it was expedient that He should go away, for the presence of that other Comforter with them should *more* than make up for his own absence from them.

Such were the gifts, or such rather was the gift, which He, being glorified, received *for* men and imparted *to* men ; yes, and imparts evermore ; for when we contemplate, as to-day we are doing, these pentecostal gifts, we must not think of them as given once for all, as though on one signal occasion heaven was opened and the Spirit descended, and then, this done, that heaven was again shut, and the streams of blessing withholden again. Not so; He who gave once, gives always. The pure river of water of life, clear as crystal, proceeds evermore out of the throne of God and of the Lamb.* These are gifts *for men:* and as long as there are men needing these gifts, they will not cease. And that will be always, even to the end of the world. In a world of sorrow such as ours, when will the office of a Comforter cease? In a world of sin such as ours, when will the office of a Sanctifier be out of date?

Surely a blessed thought, my brethren, that these gifts of Pentecost, whose first imparting we celebrate to-day, belong as truly to us as they did to the apostles, on whom, as upon this day, they lighted visibly and audibly to all. He who is the Author of those gifts descends not now upon us with a mighty rushing wind, and with tongues of fire. These outward tokens, addressing themselves to eye and ear, are wanting at the present; but He is with us still. The church would not exist for an hour without Him, without his presence and his power. He is with us still, enlivening, purifying, enlightening, healing, strengthening, comforting, convincing of sin, taking of the things of Christ and showing them to the contrite sinner, converting the soul, moving on the face of the waters of baptism, and making them to be waters of regeneration, causing common bread and common wine to be

---

* Rev. xxii. 1.

to the faithful receiver the body of Christ and the blood of Christ, and from the rich treasure-house of his manifold gifts dividing to every one severally as He will.

But perhaps there may be some one here present who is saying in his heart, Christ, the ascended Lord, may have gifts for men, manifold gifts of grace and of the Holy Spirit for manifold sorts of men; but He can have none for me; I have so grieved that Holy Spirit, I have so resisted his godly motions in times past, I have done such despite to the Spirit of grace, that He will never more plead with me, knock at the door of my heart, or seek to make his habitation there; I am a dry tree, which at no scent of water can ever again blossom or bud. But hear me, or rather hear God, how He has prevented thine unbelief, and will give no room for thy despair: "Thou hast received gifts for men; yea, for the rebellious also, that the Lord God might dwell among them." And these are not mere words. They were shown to be very truth; God set his seal to them on that great day of Pentecost, when they received for the first time their perfect fulfilment. Who were those three thousand who on that birthday of souls heard the Word gladly, and were added to the church of the living God? They were for the most part no other than the men who had been rebellious to that very day; who had, as St. Peter plainly told them, taken the Lord of Life, and with wicked hands crucified and slain. And these very rebels, with all that blood upon them so newly shed, even the blood of God, they were now made willing in the day of his power. They were pricked to the heart; convinced of sin, convinced of righteousness, convinced of judgment to come ; and cried out of the depth of penitent hearts to Peter and the rest, "Men and brethren, what shall we do?" And what if you have been rebellious, and what if you have been enemies, enemies by wicked works? It was while we were yet enemies that Christ died for us ; it is while we are yet enemies that He comes to us in the power of his Spirit, knocks at our closed hearts, that He may find entrance there, and that so the Lord God may dwell among us.

. Oh, then, say not thou, These gifts are not for me. They *are* for thee ; they are for men, and for the rebellious among men,—for them of whom it might have been said unto this very day, " Ye do always resist the Holy Ghost." But this day, O friends, is a day of power ; it is a day of grace ; it is a day of gifts. Heaven is open. He with whom we have to do is He " that hath the seven spirits of God,"* who can take you out of the mire, and set you among princes. Ye have lain among the pots, and yet your wings may be as the wings of a dove that is covered with silver wings, and her feathers like gold.† Do not limit his power ; do not shorten his hand ; do not think hard things of his love. Ask Him to work his work in you, and He will work it: He will make your old heart new, and your dead heart alive ; and your heart, which, it may be, was as a cage of unclean birds, as a

---

* Rev. iii. 1.   † Ps. lxviii. 13.

robber's den, where every thought and every imagination was as a robber of God and his glory, He will make even that a temple of the Holy Ghost, a habitation of God through the Spirit. He *can* do this, and, if only you will allow Him, He *will*.

SERMON XX.

THE HOLY TRINITY IN RELATION TO OUR PRAYERS.

And they rest not day and night, saying, Holy, holy, holy, Lord God
Almighty, which was, and is, and is to come.—Rev. iv. 8.

Trinity Sunday.*

ALREADY, since the commencement of our Christian year, which I need not remind you begins with Advent Sunday, we have kept three great festivals, not to speak of many lesser ones, interspersed among, or grouped around these which are the three first and greatest of all. We have celebrated Christmas-day, which may be fitly called the festival of the Father; for upon that day the Father sent the Son to be the Saviour of the world. We have celebrated our Easter feast, which may be fitly styled the festival of the Son; for upon that day He was declared the Son of God with power by the resurrection from the dead. We are fresh from the celebration of Whitsunday, which is most truly the festival of the Holy Ghost, the Spirit of the Father and of the Son, who was upon that day shed abroad from heaven on the hearts of the waiting disciples. And now at length, having thus

* Preached at one of the Special Evening Services in the nave of the Abbey.

(214)

declared the glory severally of the Father, and of the Son, and of the Holy Ghost, we keep, as the crown and consummation of all, the feast of the Holy and Blessed Trinity, weaving these three glories into one glory, proclaiming these three Persons to be but one God, who is blessed for evermore ; we join our songs with the songs of the four living creatures before the throne, of the four-and-twenty elders, of Cherubim and Seraphim who continually do cry, " Holy, Holy, Holy," —three Holies, and yet but one Holy,—even the " Lord God Almighty, which was, and is, and is to come."

Perhaps there may be some here, one and another, who, as they listen to these words, are saying in their hearts, I cannot understand this of the three Persons, who yet are but one God.   Doubtless you cannot ; we were not meant to understand it ; we were not formed to contain God's truth, but to be contained by it, as by something larger, mightier than ourselves. This, which we speak of, is a mystery ; and Revelation, which means unveiling, an unveiling of God, of his character, of his being, must have mysteries, yea, many and deep ones.   You may perhaps have heard a line from a famous English poet, which, if not quoted very often now, was a few years ago a great favorite with some.   It is this—

> " Religion ends, where mystery begins."

Now, my dear friends, I take on me to affirm that there never was a falser, and, despite a certain clever sound which it has, there seldom was a shallower, word spoken than this.   Plain things there are in religion ;

all necessary things are plain ; but there are also deep things—yea, the deep things of God, hard to understand, or which pass our understanding altogether. We might as well expect to take up the great sea in the hollow of our hand, as to embrace God—the whole mystery of his being—in our minds ; the finite to embrace the Infinite ! the creature to comprehend the Creator ! the child of time Him that is from everlasting to everlasting, who was, and is, and shall forever be ! Why, that would not be God at all, but only some dream and fancy of our own minds, whom we could understand, whom we could fathom in all his mysteries. Man knoweth the things of man ; but only God knoweth the things of God. *We see but the skirts of his glory.* Some things we understand about Him. Other things we are told, and bidden humbly and devoutly to receive and believe, and to live by them. For they may be life to the soul, and strength to the spirit, even while the mind, the intellectual faculty, is quite unable to master them, or to bring them within its own forms and conditions. It is thus with the mystery of the Trinity, of the Father, the Son, and the Spirit, three Persons and one God. Angels live by it, as men must live by it ; and yet I suppose that it transcends the minds of angels, as much as it transcends the minds of men. They do not seek to fathom it. It is enough for them to stand before the throne, to veil their faces there, to cry one unto another, " Holy, Holy, Holy, is the Lord God of Hosts ; the whole earth is full of his glory,"—to praise, to worship, to adore.

O brethren, what a glimpse of heaven, and of the

whole company of heaven, is vouchsafed us in this 4th chapter of Revelation, from which my text is drawn—praise, worship, and adoration all their business and all their delight! Once they *prayed*, but prayer is now transfigured into praise.· What need of prayer? They have nothing to ask. Their warfare is accomplished ; there is no one now who can take their crown ; sin and Satan are forever bruised beneath their feet ; they see God's face ; his name is written in their foreheads ; they are as pillars in the temple of God that shall go out no more. He has put a new song in their mouths, so glad, so glorious, so divine, that even the faint echoes of that song which reach us here make sweeter music in our ears than all the mirth and melodies of earth !

We cannot at this present learn that song of theirs. We *may* learn it hereafter. It *may* be hereafter fitted to our lips, as it is to theirs, but not now. We still bear about with us the burden of the flesh. We are still compassed with infirmities. We may be striving —I trust many of us are striving—to lead godly lives ; such lives as of God's great mercy shall lead us up at last to the steps of the throne, and the presence of Him that sitteth upon it ; but, oh, what recurring temptations are our portion here, what struggles against our grosser animal nature!—what harsh discords around us, what harsh discords within us!—with how many things to sadden, and how many things to depress! How shall we sing the Lord's song in a strange land? Praise God we may and ought, for praise is comely, and He giveth songs in the night ; and voices out of the great deep may yet be voices of thanksgiving; and men have praised Him as Jonah did out of the whale's belly; and as Paul and Silas did out of the inner dungeon; and as the Three Children did out of the burning fiery furnace. But the clear hymns of joy, of joy untroubled with any sorrow, the harmonies in which no discords mingle, those are not of earth, but of heaven. They are fitted to the lips, not of those who are exiles still in a far foreign land, seeking a country, but of those who have sought and found; who, once beaten and buffeted by the waves of the troublesome world, are now at length in the haven of everlasting rest, where they would be.

Friends and brethren, would you learn that new song? Do you desire that the issue of your lives may be, that they shall lead you at length to the Golden City, the New Jerusalem, the presence of God, a place before his throne? Do you desire to leave behind you all which has here debased and degraded you, which is debasing and degrading still—your sins and all the guilty memories which they have bequeathed? Do you desire to emerge out of this darkness into that heavenly light, to praise God for evermore? I know you desire this. Quite apart from the mere wish to escape from punishment and pain, there are yearnings and longings in the heart of every one of you, which nothing has been able quite to crush or to subdue—yearnings and longings which can only find their satisfaction in God, and which you feel can only find their satisfaction in Him. And yet how shall that be the issue and the end, if the paths which you are treading now are too many of them such as will lead you *from* God, and not *to* Him? How shall you praise Him there, if you do not pray to Him here? Suffer me, then, under the suggestions of my text, moved also by the fact that this is Trinity Sunday on which we are here gathered together, to speak to you a little of prayer, in connection with the three Persons of the ever-blessed Trinity; and may *we* so learn to pray to God now, that we may praise Him for evermore!

You may remember some words of St. Paul, where, speaking of Christ the Lord, he says, "Through Him we all have access by one Spirit to the Father.* In this little verse we have mention of all the three Persons. There is the Father *to* whom we have access, or approach in prayer; there is the Son, *through* whom we have this access; and, lastly, there is the Spirit, *in* whom this access, this open way to God and to the throne of grace, is ours.

And, first, it is access *to* the Father; He is the ultimate object of our prayers. I do not say that we may not most fitly pray to Christ. He too is God. Our church, in more than one of her Collects, expressly addresses herself to Him, makes her supplication to Him. Still these are the exceptions, and not the rule. They are more often brief ejaculations of the soul that go forth to Him, as those in the Litany: "O Lamb of God, that takest away the sins of the world, grant us thy peace;" or as this, "O Son of David, have mercy upon us." It is these, rather than more set deliberate prayers, which are addressed to the second Person of the

* Ephes. ii. 18.

Trinity. We have *access to the Father*, and our prayers must not stop short till they mount up to Him. The prayer of all prayers, that with which the Son of God taught us to pray, begins with " Our Father." O words of comfort and strength unutterable for the children of men! Conceive to yourselves what it would be, how it would fare with us, if God only presented Himself to us as a God of nature, a God of power, a Maker of heaven and earth, with a certain vague general benevolence and good-will toward us, in common with the other creatures of his hand. Think what this would be, in our trials, our temptations, our remorse of conscience, our agonies, this God of *nature*, as compared with what *is*, a God of *men*, a Father in heaven, who opens wide a Father's arms to his wandering and suffering children here, and will embrace with a Father's love, and draw them close to a Father's heart. Here is the magic of that word of the Gospel which we declare, here is its secret, attractive power — that it wakens up in the hearts of the poor prodigals of earth such thoughts as these, " I will arise, and go *to my Father*." To my Father! what words are these, of what strong consolation! How many that have wandered far, whom their sins have overtaken and found out, bankrupt in hope, bankrupt in health, bankrupt in character, bankrupt in everything, steeped, it may be, in infamy and scorn, whom the world had ruined and then cast off, desolate, forsaken, pierced through with many sorrows, in hospitals, in prisons, in far places of their exile, how many of these have found the consolation that is in these words, and *have* arisen and gone to their God, because their God was their Father as well.

And what though we may not have eaten all the bitter fruits of our doings, as they have done of theirs, though we may have never sounded the depths of their desolation and despair, yet do we not need every one of us evermore to take on our lips these same words? for we too have all departed—some, indeed, more widely than others—but all have departed from our God, all have need to exclaim, " Father, I have sinned before heaven and against Thee." And prayer, it is such a confession as this; followed up, indeed, by a making known of *all* our wants to God—but still to God as a Father, as *the* Father, from whom every other father, every father upon earth, has drawn whatever little of love, care, pity, tenderness, compassion he may have for his children*—this love of the earthly parents, of fathers and mothers here, being to us a faint shadow and a dim teaching of what is the love that beats in the heart of Him who is the Almighty Father in heaven.

But if prayer is thus *to* the Father, it is, as St. Paul declares, *through* the Son. He is the daysman that must lay his hand upon us both,—upon God and man, upon God in heaven and man upon earth, upon God holy and man unholy,—and must bring them together, face to face, so that man may see God's face, and not perish in the seeing; may enter into God's presence, and not be consumed by the intolerable brightness of that presence; may speak with his unclean lips to

* Eph. iii. 15.

God, and yet, unclean as those lips are, may speak not in vain, but words which shall prevail. When we affirm, or rather when Scripture affirms, that all approaches to God the Father, all approaches in prayer or otherwise, are through God the Son, that no man can come to the Father but by Him, while by Him all may come near, it affirms herein the absolute holiness of God, the deep sinfulness and defilement of man, which renders him quite incapable by himself of holding communion, of entering into fellowship, with God; which has put a broad gulf between these two ; but it asserts likewise that this gulf, which no other could bridge over, has yet been bridged over by Christ; that He by his life, being at once God and man, the two natures in one person united, by his death, making a sacrifice for the sins of all mankind, has brought near those who were before far asunder ; that there is now freedom of access, an open way to the Father, through the Son.

O brethren, think not in your prayers to draw nigh to God making mention of any other name, except that Name which is above every name, the Name of Jesus, or making mention of any other righteousness but his—least of all, making mention of your own. Remember Cain and Abel, and their several offerings, and how "the Lord had respect to Abel and his offering ; but to Cain and his offering He had not respect." And why not? what was the difference? The offering of Cain was of the mere natural fruits of the earth; the offering of Abel was of the firstlings of his flock. There was therefore blood, a prophecy of the blood of Christ, in Abel's offering; there was none in Cain's; and without that precious blood-shedding there is no remission of sin; without faith in that blood-shedding no approach to the Father. Therefore was it, because Abel pleaded the blood of Christ in those firstlings of his flock, because Cain thought he could be accepted without that blood, that the Lord had respect to the offering of one, but had not respect to the offering of the other. Oh, beware of profane prayers; and all prayers are profane which leave out, which do not rest on, the Atonement. When you enter into the presence of the great King, would you find favor with Him, and have his golden sceptre stretched out to you in grace; would you, a suppliant Esther, trembling between life and death, hear words like these from his lips, "What wilt thou? and what is thy request?" see, then, that you enter ever into that presence making mention of the name and of the righteousness of Christ, with his blood newly sprinkled by faith upon your soul. Say to God, I dare not draw nigh to Thee, holy as Thou art, unclean, leprous, sin-spotted as I am, except through Christ; my prayers, they could never come up to Thee, except they were offered in the golden censer of my great High-priest, and mingled with the incense of his perfect obedience and his prevailing intercession. This is to draw near to the Father through the Son, and this is the only way by which we can draw near to Him.

But, thirdly and lastly, it is *in* the Spirit that this access is ours. What may this mean? Prayer, my brethren, is a work of grace, and not of nature. We pray because God, God the Holy Ghost puts it into our hearts to pray, helps our infirmities, suggests to us what things we ought to pray for, and how. Look at a ship without a wind, becalmed in the middle sea, its sails flapping idly hither and thither; what a difference from the same ship, when the wind has filled its sails, and it is making joyful progress to the haven whither it is bound! The breath of God, that is the wind which must fill the sails of our souls. We must pray in the Spirit, in the Holy Ghost, if we would pray at all. Lay this, I beseech you, to heart. Do not address yourselves to prayer as to a work to be accomplished in your own natural strength. It is a work of God, of God the Holy Ghost, a work of his in you and by you, and in which you must be fellow-workers with Him,—but his work notwithstanding. How many forget this; and what is the consequence? They make a few ineffectual attempts at prayer, and then they complain that they cannot pray, that they cannot lift themselves from the earth, that, despite all their efforts, their souls cleave to the ground. Of course they do, unless the breath of God lifts them up from the earth. My dear hearers, is not this the secret of your dead, fruitless, heartless prayers? does not this explain the fact that so many of you, who are listening with tolerable attention to these words of mine to you, yet made little or no attempt to join in the prayers which went before the sermon, which should have been words of yours to God; of the fact, perhaps sadder still, that so many of you are living without private prayer, without anything which deserves the name of secret fellowship and communion with God? I know all your outward difficulties in this matter of prayer, or at least I am able to guess at them : difficulties from the crowded habitations of some, where it is almost impossible to be alone ; difficulties from the tyrannous demands of your daily toil, leaving you, as it seems, little or no leisure to attend to anything beside. And yet, put these with all other outward difficulties together, and they are not sufficient to explain the fearful extent to which the habit of private prayer has perished among our people. The evil lies deeper yet ; the root of it is this, that we have ceased to believe that we are in a kingdom of heaven, that we have been baptized into all the gifts of the Spirit ; that He, the Spirit, in this his kingdom, is blowing indeed where He lists, where He pleases, but that nothing pleases Him a thousandth part so well as to breathe upon our souls, to quicken them with life and power, with the spirit of supplication and the spirit of prayer.

Prove if it be not so. Brethren beloved in the Lord, with such helps, with such divine assistances, why will you continue, so many of you, without prayer, and therefore practically without God in the world? Say not that you have no time. You have time for sleep, time for meals, time for the newspaper, time for the club, time for trivial talk, time for everything but for God. Say not that you are no scholars, that you do not know how to pray. God will teach us, God the Holy Ghost ; and who teaches like Him? Cast yourselves on his teaching, upon his guidance, and He will lead you up, through the mediation of the Son, to

10*

the throne and presence of the Father. Yes, and weak as you are now, weak as in yourselves you shall ever be, you shall yet go on from strength to strength, till you too appear before the Lord in that heavenly City which needeth no light of the sun, for the Lord God is the light thereof, where " Holy! Holy! Holy!" is the song of praise through eternity of elect angels and redeemed men.

SERMON XXI.

ONE BODY AND ONE SPIRIT.

There is one body and one Spirit.—EPHES. iv. 4.

NO one, I think, can have failed to observe how often the church of Christ is by St. Paul compared to a human body. Thus, in the Epistle to the Romans, " For as we have many members in one body, and all members have not the same office, so we, being many, are one body in Christ, and every one members one of another." * And again, in his first Epistle to the Corinthians, " For as the body is one, and hath many members, and all the members of that one body, being many, are one body, so also is Christ," † or the church of Christ, as here is rightly understood ; and then he proceeds there, as you may remember, to draw out this comparison at length. Other like passages occur in the Colossians‡ and elsewhere. What, it may be asked, is the meaning of this comparison ? Why are the company of faithful men that are gathered under Christ, and united to Him, and in Him to one another, likened to a human body ? why called, as they so often are, the mystical body of Christ ? There must be some highest fitness in this comparison, some deep

* xii. 4, 5.　　　† xii. 12.　　　‡ ii. 19.

inner correspondence between these two, else the Holy Ghost would not have so often chosen to set forth the mysteries of the one by the aid of the other.

The Scriptures quoted seem to me to give an answer sufficient to this question. In the human body there is the greatest possible *unity*, and the greatest possible *variety*. One body, *there* is the unity ; many members, and each with its own office, diverse from every other, *there* is the variety. And it is exactly the same with Christ's church. That too is at the same time one and manifold—one, having the highest unity, in that it owns allegiance to one Lord, is inspired by one Spirit, has one faith, one baptism, one God and Father of all ; but manifold, in that the members which compose it have various gifts, some of this kind, some of that, some more, some fewer—are wise and simple, learned and unlearned, strong and weak ; some have one function and office to fulfil, and some another.

Let us follow up both these points a little more in detail ; first, that of unity, then this of variety or multiplicity ; and conclude by a brief consideration of some of the duties flowing out from the one and from the other.

And first, of the unity or oneness of the church, as set forth by the unity or oneness of the body. "The body is one," says the apostle. Notwithstanding the several limbs or members of which it is composed, one life animates the whole. The parts mutually subserve one another. They instinctively feel that they belong to one another ; that they owe to one another mutual help and support. The hand does not labor for itself alone, but the food it earns nourishes the whole body. The arm is lifted up to turn away a blow not merely directed against itself, but threatening to harm any other limb. The eye does not see for itself alone, but gathers in notices from the outward world which turn to the profit of all. Each serves the other, and is served by the other in turn; while the head thinks and the heart beats for all. Then, too, there is a certain harmony existing between all the members; they constitute a symmetry among themselves, so that one could not be taken away without destroying the perfection of all the others, more or less marring the grace and beauty of the whole frame. If the body lives, it lives in every part; if it dies, death reigns throughout it all. It is no cunning piece of mechanism, of which the several parts, the wheels, the cogs, the hammers, being as they are dead things, might exist independently of one another, and of the dead whole which together they compose; but the body is a living organism, possessing that wonderful and mysterious principle of life, by which all the parts of it are knit and bound together, as no other law but this law of the spirit of life could ever have bound or knit them together.

And so, too, the church is one—one mystical body, as we call it—having one Author, which is God, and one Head, which is Christ, and one informing Spirit, which is the Holy Ghost; having one country toward which all its members are travelling, which is heaven; one code of instructions to guide them thither, which is the Word of God; one and the same band of enemies seeking to bar their passage, which are the world, the flesh, and the devil; having the same effectual assistances in the shape of sacraments and other means of grace to enable them to overcome these enemies, and of God's good favor to attain the land of their rest. One has need to remember, at a time like the present, all these points wherein the unity of the church consists; else, looking out at the distracted spectacle which a Christendom at this day presents, torn and rent in pieces, divided into so many, alas! oftentimes hostile, camps, we might be tempted to think that this unity was nowhere, that Christ's promises had failed.

The sins, indeed, of the church, being, as they are, so far more dreadful than the sins of the world, have hindered those promises taking full effect. His prayer to his Father for his people, " that they may be one, even as We are one," has not had that glorious fulfilment which it might have had; the unity of the church has withdrawn itself from observation; and yet for all this, and despite of all the miserable divisions of those who call themselves by the same holy name, but yet seem only anxious to disclaim brotherhood one with another, God's word stands true. " There *is* one body and one Spirit;" and wherever there is on this redeemed earth, under whatever forms, mixed, debased, overlaid with whatever superstitions, any true love to God, and for God's sake love to man, any true affiance upon Christ and his sacrifice, any true obedience to the Spirit and his leadings, *there*, in the man of whom this may be affirmed, there is a member of this mystical body whereof the Apostle speaks. He may have learned to pronounce his anathema upon us ; we may refuse to include him in our narrow scheme of Christian fellowship ; but happily neither he nor we have a voice conclusive, or, indeed, a voice potential at all, to determine who are members of this body, and who are not. It is a body far wider than his anathema, than our narrow-hearted exclusiveness, would leave it ; and he, who would fain shut out us, and we, who would willingly shut out him, may both belong to it alike, God's charity being so much mightier than our want of charity,—He blessing where we would curse, He including where we would only exclude. Despite of all our divisions, enmities, debates, all our readiness to bite and devour one another, all our denials by word and deed of the truth affirmed in my text, that truth remains, that truth stands unshaken : "There *is* one body and one Spirit."

When I speak thus, I would not in the least imply that it is a matter of indifference whether we belong to a purer branch of Christ's church, or to one less pure ; to one holding the whole of God's truth, or only parts of that truth, though saving parts still ; all I seek to affirm is, that God acknowledges now, and will acknowledge at the last day, not those who have *our* mark upon them, but those who have *his ;* and as many as have thus "the spot of his children," ranged though they often be now in battle-array against one another, constitute in his eyes who sees not as we see, the one body, gathered under the one Head, which is Christ.

But secondly, as in the human body there is unity, so there is also variety, diversity, multiplicity, or what-

ever else we may please to call it. "All members
have not the same office." You remember, no doubt,
how fully St. Paul draws this out for the checking of
the vanity of his Corinthian converts, who probably
wanted, every one of them, to be everything in himself,
a desire abundantly characteristic of the Greek love
of display in those miserable fallen days of Greece.
The body, he reminds them, is not one member, but
many; and then he shows the necessity of this : "If
the whole body were an eye, where were the hearing?
if the whole were hearing, where were the smelling?"
"The eye cannot say unto the hand, I have no need of
thee ; nor again, the head to the feet, I have no need
of you ;" and so on. And then he proceeds, as none
of us can have forgotten, to apply all this, to transfer
this, which is true of the natural body, to the spiritual
as well, to show how the same tempering of the parts
holds good in it also. There are also "diversities of
gifts," "differences of administration," some having one
gift, some another; some in a more honorable place, and
some in a humbler ; some furnished with ten talents,
and some with five, and some only with one ; all which,
as it was true in his days, so is it in ours. The church
is most truly a body in this sense also, that its different
members have different functions and offices to perform, all these being severally assigned to them of
God ; and then, and then only, it makes equable and
harmonious growth, increases with the increase of
God, when each, holding by the Head which is Christ,
yet abiding in his own place, seeks diligently to fulfil
the duties of that place, be it high or low, glorious or

inglorious, in the sight of men or out of the sight of men, easy or hard ; and is contented to be hand, or foot, or what else it may be ; counting it glory enough to be a member in Christ's body at all, and to have any office and ministry pertaining to the good of that body.

These things being so, let us occupy ourselves for such a time as remains to us, with considering some of the lessons which we may derive from the truths which have been just stated.

And first, we are members of a body. Let us never forget this. It is only too easy to do so, to nourish a selfish isolated religion, apart from our brethren, neither seeking to give good *to* them, nor hoping to get good *from* them. When offences abound, when others misunderstand us, when they do not sympathize with us as we expect, when they seem to us prejudiced, bigoted, narrow-minded, eager about secondary matters, what a temptation it is to say we will have nothing, or as little as possible, to do with them, to give up the attempt at working with them for a common end, and to resolve that we will cultivate a solitary piety for ourselves, apart with our God. Of course this would be much more pleasant, if we were set here to seek out what is pleasant for ourselves,—more pleasant, that is, to our selfish nature ;—many rubs and annoyances would in this way be avoided ; we fancy, too, that thus we should grow much faster in spiritual things than clogged as we are and hampered by others, by their slowness, their narrowness, the thousand obstacles which they seem to place in our way. All experience, however, proves the contrary. The spirit of selfish isolation in religious things is mischievous, and, if pushed very far, is fatal, to the life of God in the soul. The church is a body; it must grow together, and by that which every joint supplieth. To separate from our brethren is to separate from Christ; for He is with the body, being Himself the Head of the body, from whom all the life of every member of it flows. Life is not, indeed, in the body, and in fellowship with the body, *because* it is the body (that were to make the church life-*giving*, when in fact it is only life-circulating, life-distributing), but it is in it because it is in union with the Head, the one fountain of life for it, and for every member of it in particular; divided from whom they are as branches broken off from the true Vine, and which can only wither and die. This, then, is our first lesson, that we do not yield to the temptations, and at certain periods of our spiritual course they will not be slight temptations, which would lead us to separate ourselves, if not wholly, yet in part, from the body of Christ, and to set up a selfish independent life of our own.

Take another lesson, or, in fact, only the same, regarded from another point of view. If we are thus members one of another, many are the debts which, as such, we owe the one to the other. Thus we owe one another *truth*. You remember the words of St. Paul: "Speak every man truth with his neighbor;" and why? "for we are members one of another." *He* found the motive here, and so should *we*. In the natural body, the members do not play false one to another.

What the ear hears, it conveys faithfully to the mind; the eye does not see safety when there is danger,—a plain, for instance, when there is a precipice,—or seeing, refuse to give notice, or give false notice, of what it has seen to the other members. The natural body could not exist, it must presently perish, but for this which we may call the truthful dealing of the several parts among themselves. And we too, in Christ's spiritual body, we in like manner owe this truth to one another; that we do not flatter one of us the other in his sins;—nay, brethren, how good it would be if Christians would resolve not to *suffer* one another in their sins. Of course in this loving rebuke of which I speak, time, and place, and years, and condition, and many other points, would have to be considered; and there is a time to keep silence, as well as a time to speak: but yet, with all these abatements made, I am sure that if we did more feel that we were members one of another, and owed, therefore, the truth to one another, we should be acting a manlier, braver, more consistent part; by some seasonable word we might elevate the whole spiritual life of a brother, or perhaps arrest him in the sin which in the end shall be the total shipwreck of his soul.

But once more. If we are members of one body, we owe *love* one to another. In the natural body, if one member suffers, all the others suffer with it. The pain and discomfort of one limb is, in fact, the pain and discomfort of the whole body. So should it be in the spiritual body. Our Lord and Saviour Jesus Christ, the Head of that body, so realized his own fellowship with the other members, so felt that when they suffered He suffered, that when they were wounded He was wounded,—that, as you may remember, when He arrested Saul the persecutor in mid career, it was with these words, " Why persecutest thou *Me?*" He did not say, " Why hast thou stoned Stephen, and haled other of my servants to prison and to death ?" He did not say, " Why persecutest thou my members ?" But He, in heaven exalted forever far above all the spite and malice of evil men, could yet say, " Why persecutest thou *Me?*" not " my saints," but " Me." So was He afflicted in their affliction ; so did the blows aimed at them light upon Him. And Paul was in this, as in all else, a follower of Christ : " Who is weak, and I am not weak? who is offended, and I burn not?" Let *us* ask of God a tenderer, livelier, more earnest sense of the sorrows, needs, perplexities, distresses, fears, trials of our brethren ; a heart readier to feel, a hand readier, where this may be, to help ; that in this matter of sympathy or fellow-feeling we may not forget, to so great an extent as we often do, that we are members one of another.

But again, if the church, being thus one, has yet many members, and they all have different offices therein, which have been appointed them by Christ, we owe *honor* one to another. Let us learn to honor all men in their office, and because Christ has placed them there,—not those only whose offices are great and glorious in the eyes of the world—kings, and princes, and prelates, and nobles, men of wealth and men of genius, those from one cause or another the chief of the earth, but men of low estate, men of mean abilities, for their work's sake; remembering always that it is not the greatness of a man's position, nor yet the greatness of the talents which in that position he may use, which makes a man great in the eyes of God,—this is one of the world's lies,—but the zeal, the faithfulness, the diligence with which he actually fulfils the duties of that position, be it high or be it low. He that shuns and shirks the task of his life, shuffles it from him, does it deceitfully, or does not do it at all, is base, dishonorable, contemptible in the sight of God, though he wore a king's crown or an emperor's mantle; while the poorest digger and delver of the earth, the meanest and smallest among us, if faithful in his narrow line of things, is honorable in his sight, shall be crowned with glory and honor even before men, in that day when first shall be last, and last first. Be it ours, in part at least, to anticipate that coming day; to honor all men, since all were made in the image of God; but to honor above all, with the best honor and reverence which our hearts can render, and without respect of persons, those in Christ's church, be they high or low, in first place or in last, weak members or strong, learned or simple, who are seeking to approve themselves and their work in the sight of God the All-seeing; and may we esteem it the main business of our lives to be ourselves found in the number of these, and thus to obtain that "Well done," which shall be as freely given to the faithful dispenser of one talent as of ten or of a hundred.

SERMON XXII.

ON THE DEATH OF GENERAL HAVELOCK.*

A centurion of the band called tho Italian band, a devout man, and one that feared God.—Acts x. 1, 2.

SINCE we assembled for worship within these walls last Sunday, there has come a great, I may say a national, sorrow upon us; and tidings of a sad surprise have been heard with a pang of pain in every corner of this English land. Among many noble warriors, he whom we deemed, whom not improbably we rightly deemed, the noblest of all, has passed from us. England, Christian England, is at this moment mourning for that one among her Indian sons of whom she was proudest of all, and mourning the more because she had no opportunity of telling him how near to her heart he was, and how deeply engraven his heroic deeds, and he the author of them, would be upon her memory, how safely enshrined in her affections, for-ever.

It seems to me that the occasion will not be an un-fitting one to say something on the character, happily by no means an uncommon one now, of the Christian soldier; and the thought will be a calming and a soothing one, that he whom England is so mourning

* Preached January 10, 1858.

(238)

now eminently realized this character; and that in whatever light we may at this moment regard it, far sadder things may well come to pass than this of a Christian man dying in the fulfilment of his duty, having accomplished a mighty work, having won a nation's gratitude, leaving behind him an unspotted name, and exchanging a miserable scene of tumult and toil, of confusion and blood, exchanging this in a moment for the rest and Paradise of his God.

But before we can hope to say anything to the point on the character of the Christian soldier, something must needs be said first on that serious and terrible business in which he is engaged,—I mean upon war. We can only judge *him* aright, when we are sure that we judge aright the task which he has in this world set himself to do. Now there are two aspects in which war may be, in which practically it is, regarded. There is first theirs who regard it purely and simply as an outcoming of the spirit of Cain, of the first murderer, as nothing better than murder upon an enormous scale, as that which no amount of provocation, of loss or danger or dishonor to be averted, can justify; an uttermost denial of Christ and his Gospel of peace on the part of *all* who engage in it. They who in this way regard it would perhaps admit that one party engaged in a war may be *more* guilty than the other, but would not the less affirm that *both* must be deeply guilty; and of course, in their view, the crime which is necessarily involved in war extends to every one who takes any willing share in it. It is for every soldier an utterly unblessed and wicked trade, and never can be anything beside. Such is the judgment of the Quaker about war; such too the judgment of many others who, without adopting all his convictions, still consent with him in this: and they who maintain this position usually seek to strengthen their case by pictures, only too true, of the hideous horrors which war draws after it in its train — the wasted homestead, the desolated hearth, the burning village, the stormed city, the children left fatherless, and the wives widows; the field of battle, with its thousands made in God's image who lie maimed or mutilated, dead and dying there; and worse than all these, for they are *moral* evils, the recklessness of life, the savagery, the brutality which war generates, and in far wider circles than that of those immediately engaged in it.

But even those horrors (and I believe no words can paint them to the full, and all which we imagine about war falls short of the terrible reality) ought not to remove us from another and truer view of what war is, and of the light in which it should be regarded by us. We do not deny, on the contrary we too affirm, that war may be, and that it *often* is, this enormous wickedness, which those who would condemn altogether assert that it is *always;* we too affirm that every needless unrighteous war, undertaken out of greed, or pride, or ambition, or love of glory, or lust of dominion, is a crime huger, darker, deeper, entailing a more fearful guilt on its authors, be they princes or people,—and they are quite as often the last as the first,—than any other in the dread catalogue of human crimes, because it is a crime on a far more gigantic scale.

But this does not hinder us from affirming also that war may be a terrible necessity,—a duty which a nation must not shun or put back, as it would have the blessing of God upon it,—a most righteous thing, an act of faith in the Almighty Governor of the world, an appeal to Him and to his righteousness, when the appeal to any human tribunal is possible no longer. It is, I say, this act of faith; for it is a bringing the matter at issue into the court of heaven. It is a saying, Let God decide, the Lord of Hosts, the God of battles, the Giver of victory. Let Him weigh us and you in the balances, and let the balance, in which justice is wanting, kick the beam, even as we are confident it will do. Then, too, when wickedness has risen to so prodigious a height and strength that it defies and despises the restraints of human law, when the wand of justice is broken, and the voice of the judge is mute, then the sword must step in, —the sword, we do not fear to call it in such a case, of the Lord, even though it may be wielded by the hands of infirm sinful men, themselves, very likely, not all of them, nor any of them, not even the best among them, wholly free from the very guilt which they punish in others; but who yet, in punishing the far higher wickedness of others, are doing a work of God, a work of righteousness which it were woe to them if they, out of fear, or a shunning of the task and toil, or a lack of righteous indignation against evil, did deceitfully, or left undone altogether. What if the children of Israel, in the time of the Judges, had left unpunished the hideous outrage of the men of Gibeah, and of the Benjamites, who, making common part with them, in this way became

11

partakers of their sin?* If they had left these wicked
men unpunished, had shrunk from the task of punishing,—and you may remember they only did it at the
cost of some of their best blood,—would God, the righteous Lord, have left *them* unpunished? We may find,
I think, an answer to this question, if only we will call
to mind how it fared with the one city which would
take no part or share in executing that righteous
doom.† Or would He leave us unpunished if, under
any pretext, any plea, we had left unfulfilled in India
the terrible commission which He has given us of
avenging the innocent blood; which, being shed, defies
a land with a defilement which only the blood of the
guilty can cleanse away?

Then, too, when some make so much of the horrors
which war brings in its train, they do not err in dwelling upon these, and making much of them (none can
exaggerate them); they only err in dwelling *exclusively* upon these. War has its gains as well as its
losses. If it calls out in baser natures some of the
worst and most devilish passions of the human heart,
it kindles in others elevating and ennobling sentiments
of duty and self-sacrifice, which otherwise they would
not at all, or would have very feebly, known; lessons
are learned in this stern school which would never
have been learned in any other, but which no nation
can afford to forego. For, indeed, what would a nation
be, over which for century after century the great anguish and agony of a war, with all its elevating emo-

* Judges xx.   † Judges xxi. 8–10.

tions and purifying sorrows, had never passed ; in which wives had never given their husbands, nor mothers their sons, nor sisters their brothers, to the battle-field, to labors, to wounds, and it might be, to death ; happy if they might receive these beloved ones safe and sound again ; but not wholly unhappy if in duty's and in honor's path these had ended well, and paid even with their lives the debt which they owed to their native land ? How mean, how sordid, how selfish, would the whole spirit and temper of such a nation become, its heart unmanned, its moral nerves and sinews unstrung ! Oh, no ! the nations cannot do without the severe discipline of this terrible thing. For nations, as little as individuals, can do without tribulation ; and what is war but tribulation on an enormous scale, and visiting not, as at other times, this household, and then that, but visiting hundreds and thousands of households, bringing to them distress and anguish at the same instant. Fearful remedy as it must needs be esteemed, war *is* a remedy against worse evils—sloth, selfishness, love of ease, contempt of honor, worship of material things,—all which, but for it, would invade and occupy the heart of a people, and at length eat out that heart altogether.

And as the reactive influence which war exercises on a nation generally, that undertakes it in a righteous cause, is exalting, ennobling, purifying, so still more marked is its influence often upon those who are directly engaged in it. Some, of course, are hardened and brutalized by their familiarity with suffering, by the necessity which they often lie under of themselves inflicting it ; but many also there are, like " The Happy Warrior" of the poet,

> "Who doomed to go in company with pain
> And fear and bloodshed, miserable train,
> Turn their necessity to glorious gain ;"

and who are only made more tender and more gentle thereby.

It certainly is not a little remarkable, that of the four centurions, or officers of the Roman army, who are mentioned in the New Testament, every one comes before us in a favorable light, has more or less honorable mention made of him. ·To take the least notable case, that of Julius, the centurion who had Paul in charge as a prisoner during the long and perilous journey from Asia to Rome. He " courteously entreated Paul," was evidently attracted to him, had him in honor, or even in affection, would suffer, as far as in him lay, no harm to befall him.* But still more noteworthy, in his readiness to receive a profound religious impression, is that centurion who was charged to oversee the due carrying out of the sentence of crucifixion pronounced against our Lord. He had been no careless, no indifferent watcher of all that passed upon that cross, as is abundantly witnessed by that exclamation which, when the Lord had breathed out his spirit, he uttered, " Certainly ·this was a righteous man ;" or, as another Evangelist reports it, " Truly this was the Son of God."† He who at such a moment could make such

---

* Acts xxvi. 3, 43.   † Luke xxiii. 47 ; cf. Matt. xxvii. 54.

a confession was not very far from the kingdom of God. But more notable than either of these are two other centurions, who come prominently forward in the evangelical history. There is, first, that one in the Gospels, glorious in his humility, "I am not worthy that Thou shouldst enter under my roof,"—glorious in his faith, "say in a word, and my servant shall be healed ;" of whom Christ Himself bore this testimony, "I have not found so great faith, no, not in Israel."[*] And last of all, there is that other, "Cornelius, a centurion of the band called the Italian band, a devout man, and one that feared God with all his house, which gave much alms to the people, and prayed to God alway ;" to whom was vouchsafed the honor that he should be the firstfruits of the Gentile world.

Surely, with these examples before us, we shall scarcely affirm that the profession of a soldier is, and must be, unfavorable to the spiritual life. On the contrary, I am persuaded there are very many professions and callings in which there is far more imminent danger that the very work which a man has to do may choke and strangle the life of God in his soul ; while I think that the experience of every one of us will bear witness that among those whom we have known, educated to this profession of arms, we have found some of the gentlest, the most humane, the most considerate, the most careful to avoid inflicting unnecessary pain upon others, that we have ever been privileged to know ; not to say that among them are to be numbered

* Luke vii. 1–9.

many of the most earnest and zealous for the spread
of Christ's kingdom, many who would most rejoice if
that kingdom of peace might come, abolishing for ever
pride and rapine and lust and cruelty and covetousness
and ambition and wrong; and therefore abolishing
with these that dreadful business of their, which is
properly the putting down and repressing with a
strong hand these outcomings of human corruption,
before they have turned this earth into a hell.

It is such a man, and one, I believe, among many
such, who has just passed from us, from the field of his
fame, from the gratitude of his country, from the honors with which it hoped to attest this gratitude to
him and before the world. Many things have been
granted to us and to him; but some have been denied.
To us it has not been granted to welcome home, as we
fain would have welcomed, him who in darkest and
most perilous hour upheld so well the honor of England; who, inspiring others with the confidence which
he felt himself, took no account of odds, for he knew
that the battle is the Lord's, and that the Lord can
save by many or by few; who, rolling back the fierce
tide of war, and the first who did this, avenged where
he could not save, crowded into a few days victories
which would have illustrated a life, and then told of
deeds which will make the ears of Englishmen to tin-
gle and their hearts to burn to the end of time, as
though they had been common things, as though there
had been nothing unusual about them.

Some things also were denied to him. It was
not given him to see the final triumph of right and

truth, whereunto he had himself so mainly contribut-ed ; to repose upon laurels won ; to learn the place which he had for ever attained, as one of England's worthies, in the heart and affections of her people. This was not given him, nor yet to share (which he would have esteemed far more highly) in that mighty effort presently, as we trust, to be made, for the bringing of a new India out of the old, a Christian India out of that heathen India in which we have acquiesced too long.

But if something has been withheld, much has been granted both to us and to him. Much to us ; one more example set before us of work modestly, simply, nobly, grandly done ; of a man fit for high place who had embraced contentedly a low ; who would have been well satisfied, as everything declares, to have lived and died unknown to fame, simply doing his duty and looking for no earthly reward ; one more example of heroic daring, of the deeds which are wrought by faith, so that in these times also those that put their trust in the living God out of weakness are made strong, wax valiant in fight, turn to flight the armies of the aliens. Henceforward there is another star shining bright and unsullied in the firmament of England's fame, and beckoning onward all that gaze on it in the paths of truth and virtue and honor.

To him also much was granted. When fatigue and weariness and watching were at length breaking down the tabernacle of his earthly body, he at any rate knew that those to save whom he had dared so much were in safety at last. If he did not actually also know, he must have confidently guessed, the place which he had won in his nation's heart. And, far better than all this, he could take up, we humbly yet confidently believe, as few could do, the triumphant words of the Apostle, in contemplation of his approaching dissolution, and the goal, now so close, of his earthly career. He too could say, " I have fought a good fight ; " not the fight only with wicked men, but the fight of faith, in which he had overcome the world. He too could say, " I have finished my course ; " not that course, glorious as it was, which brought him through opposing hosts to the walls of Lucknow, to the city of strife, to the city of his death ; but that course which was bringing him to a better city, the city of peace, the city of life, the city of the living God, the new Jerusalem which is in heaven. He too could rejoice that there were laid up for him, not those fading wreaths, those corruptible crowns, with which we had fondly thought to encircle his brows, but that his should henceforth be that crown of righteousness which God, the judge of all, imparts to every one that has striven lawfully, and continued a faithful soldier and servant of Christ to his life's end.

Let us, my brethren, thank and praise God for all his gifts to us, and among his choicest and best for the great and good men whom He has raised up, whom his Spirit has quickened, and stirred to noble exploits, whom He has kept to the end, who have entered into his rest, and whose faith and patience we are invited to follow, that we may of the same mercy enter into the same heavenly rest.

SERMON XXIII.

GOD SEARCHING OUT OUR IDOLS.

*If we have forgotten the name of our God, or holden up our hands
to any strange god, shall not God search it out? for He knoweth the very secrets of the heart.—PSALM xliv. 21 (Prayer-Book
verson.)*

IT is good for us that we remember often that great
final judgment act, which shall at length, and once for
all, be accomplished ; when He who is the Judge of
all shall come with all his holy angels at the end of
the world, and shall assign to each that portion and
that place which shall be his thenceforth and for evermore.   And yet it is also good for us to remember that
He, the same Judge who shall judge the world in
righteousness *then*, is also judging it in righteousness
now; that He has not deferred all judgment to that
future, it may be far-distant day ; that He will not
then, for the first time, reward his faithful servants, or
repay his foes to their face.   It is good for us to remember that *now* his eyes are running to and fro on
the earth ; and He lifting up and casting down ; rec-
ompensing and punishing, promptly and swiftly, and,
so to speak, upon the spot ; leaving *much*, it is true, to
be redressed and adjusted and balanced, and finally

11*   (219)

set upon the square, on that great coming day ; but by no means deferring and postponing *all*. Even now his judgments are in all the world. It is for man, and not for God, that the word of the Apostle stands good, " Judge nothing before the time." There is no danger that God should judge before the time, who knows all, and sees all, and weighs all ; and it nearly concerns us that we do not, in the contemplation of a future judgment which He *will* execute, lose sight of a present which He *is* executing. It is this which I would invite you to contemplate to-day, and with this view have chosen for my text the words of the Psalmist, who plainly contemplates such a present judgment in these words of his : " If we have forgotten the name of our God, and holden up our hands to any strange god, shall not God search it out ? for He knoweth the very secrets of the heart."

The subject naturally and easily divides itself into three parts. There is, first, the sin,—forgetting God, and holding up the hands to some strange god. There is, secondly, the certainty of the discovery and punishment of the sin,—" Shall not God search it out ?" And, thirdly, the ground of this certainty, because He with whom we have to do is a discerner of the thoughts and intents of men,—" He knoweth the very secrets of the heart."

Let us consider these in their order. And first, the sin. The Psalmist contemplates this under two aspects,—as a turning *from* the true God, and then a turning *to* a strange or false god. They are not two sins, but one and the same sin, contemplated first on one side, and then upon the other. On its negative side, it is a forgetting the name of our God. Forgetfulness of God is continually set forth in Scripture as the chief feature and characteristic of ungodly men. God is not in all their thoughts. Those who defy Him, who set themselves in conscious opposition to Him, as in battle-array, or who speak great words against Him, who say out, like Pharaoh, "Who is the Lord, that we should obey him?"—such may be comparatively few; but those who forget him, who say, if not in as many words, yet inwardly in their hearts, "Depart from us, for we desire not the knowledge of thy ways," are many. Strange that in a world like this, so full of God, with everywhere the footprints of his power and his love to be seen, the rustling of the skirts of his robe to be heard; strange that in a world where God speaks to men in such a multitude of ways, ever changing his voice that He may be heard the better, calling to them by joy and by sorrow, by nature and by grace, by life and by death, by mercies and by judgments, by his works and by his Word, any should contrive to forget Him. It would seem to us stranger, more inexplicable still, if we had not the sad experience of our own hearts to tell us how easily this may be done, how easily the Giver is lost sight of in the gift, the Creator in the creature; what oblivion of Him is continually seeking to creep over us every one. Even those who desire to remember Him have continually to upbraid themselves that they forget Him too often, do not set Him at all so constantly before them as they ought. How, then, must it be with those who have no such desire? who, if they think upon God, are troubled, say to Him, when He meets them at unawares in their lives, as wicked Ahab said to the prophet Elijah, "Hast thou found me, O mine enemy?" and are then best pleased when they are able not to think of Him at all?

But these who forget Him, the true God, they must still have their god. No man can be without his god; if he have not the true God, to bless and sustain him, he will have some false god, to delude and to betray him. The Psalmist knew this, and therefore he joined so closely the forgetting the name of our God, and holding up our hands to some strange god. For every man has something in which he hopes, on which he leans, to which he retreats and retires, with which he fills up his thoughts in empty spaces of time; when he is alone, when he lies sleepless on his bed, when he is not pressed with other thoughts; to which he betakes himself in sorrow or trouble, as that from which he shall draw comfort and strength,—his fortress, his citadel, his defence; and has not this good right to be called his god? Man was made to lean on the Creator; but if not on Him, then he leans on the creature in one shape or another. The ivy cannot grow alone; it *must* twine round some support or other; if not the goodly oak, then the ragged thorn; round any dead stick whatever, rather than have no stay nor support at all. It is even so with the heart and affections of man; if they do not twine around God, they must twine around some meaner thing. Blessed is the man whose hope is in God; but whosoever is not hoping in

Him, is hoping in some idol ; is saying to money, or
to fame, or to pleasure, or to some other embodiment
of this present evil world, Thou art my confidence,
thou wilt make me happy ; or if not this, thou wilt
hinder me from being wholly unhappy.   A man's worship of these idols, one or more, may be very secret ;
he may withdraw it from the sight of others, down in
the deep of his heart ; he may withdraw it almost from
his own sight ; but it is there ; it is going on continually ; and there is One who sees and takes note of all.
And this brings me to the second branch of my subject, which is this :

God will search out these idols, these strange gods,
to which we lift up our hands, rendering to them the
service, the love, the fealty, the affection, which we
justly owe to Him, the God and Father of our Lord
Jesus Christ.   They are every one of them an image
of jealousy, provoking to jealousy ;* and He will not
fail to show them for what they are ; to show them in
their true nothingness, how unable to bless, how impotent to save ; He will make it plain that the man who
has trusted in them has trusted in a lie, in vain things
which cannot profit nor deliver ; in some wretched
Dagon, which, so soon as it is brought face to face
with the living God, presently lies along, a maimed
and mutilated stump, on the threshold of its own
temple.†

Brethren, is not this of which I speak, going forward
continually, God searching our idols out, dragging

---

* Ezek. viii. 3.   † 1 Sam. v. 3, 4.

them to the light, putting them, and us who trusted in them, to an open shame? We thought perhaps that our service of them was so hidden that none could know of it; we flattered ourselves that it would escape even his eyes; but it has not, and in due time He makes plain that it has not. Thus, one man is greedy of honor, of the world's reputation, to be highly spoken of and highly esteemed of men. If he could obtain this honor, he has cared little for the honor which proceedeth of God, has been well contented to go without this. Reputation has been his idol, his strange god, to which he has burnt his incense and lifted up his hands; but God has seen and searched it out; and this man, greedy of honor, living upon the world's praise, to whom this is the very breath of his nostrils, is brought by some fault or folly to discredit and dishonor, even before the world; his idol has been searched out, and perhaps before half his earthly course is done, lies in shattered fragments, never to be reunited again, at his feet.

Or a man's sin will assume sometimes another and a subtler form. It is not the honor of the world, but the honor of the church, which he desires, to be held in high reputation by good men, by the excellent of the earth. But even this may become a snare, it often has become a snare, when it has been forgotten that every man is but vanity, that God is the one fountain of honor, that He only weighed the spirits, that unless we have his "Well done," the "Well done" of all the saints that ever lived would profit us nothing. And how often God breaks this idol; and he who has duly sought this honor of men (for we may unduly seek the honor even of good men), he becomes, through some fault of his, or some misunderstanding of theirs, or both, an object of their dislike, their suspicion, and their scorn.

What need to speak of our other idols, which God in like manner searches out, and shows in their true vanity, and as having no help in them? One man trusts in his wealth: he says to his gold, Thou art my confidence; and this, in which he has trusted, makes itself wings and vanishes away; or else, in a bitterer mockery still, his wealth stays with him, but at the same time God mingles, from some other quarter, such a drop of bitterness in his cup, plants such a thorn in his pillow, makes for him a desolate and joyless home, takes away the desire of the eyes with a stroke, that he can have no pleasure in his worldly prosperity; and the world, as in cruel irony of its votary and servant, seeming to give him everything, yet in fact gives him nothing; for it has withholden the one thing which would alone have given worth to everything beside; and many a poorest hind that toils for his day's wages in the field has more joy in his life than he. What need of other examples of this? The ambitious man, who would fain live in the eyes of the world, is thrust back into some place of obscurity; and the proud man is overwhelmed with humiliations, is dragged as in the mire; and in these, and a thousand other ways, God searches out those secret idols of men, those strange gods, to which they have lifted up their hands, on which they have leant their spirits, when they should have lifted up their hands and leant their hearts only upon Him. He does it in anger, and He does it in love; in a loving anger, for the two may be most nearly united: in anger, that they should have forsaken Him, the fountain of living waters; in love, that He may draw them away from the broken cisterns which will hold no water, to drink of the waters of life, of those waters which should be in them a well of water springing up into everlasting life.

Oftentimes when the blow of this loving anger had lighted, when the man's idol has been overthrown, the world pities him as an innocent sufferer, or, at any rate, as one who has not provoked this chastisement by any special provocation upon his part. But he himself knows better. Reading his past life in the light of the present judgment, he is able to trace the secret idolatries which have been searched out at length, and which have brought this chastisement upon him. The arrow that pierced him, it was he himself that fledged it; and he sees it plainly; that his own sin has found him out, and that he is reaping in sorrow now, because he sowed in sin before. Others may miss, but he cannot miss, the mysterious links which bind his sorrow and his sin together.

But thirdly, why and how is God able so surely to do this, exactly to find out, as He so continually does, that wherein we have sinned the most, and to plague us in and through the same? not merely to burn our idols with fire and grind them to powder, but to strew this bitter powder on the very waters which we must drink?* The Psalmist tells us how: "For He know-

* Exod. xxxii. 20.

eth the very secrets of the heart ;—because there is no darkness nor shadow of death where the workers of iniquity can hide themselves ; because He is the same God who took Ezekiel of old, and showed him the secret idolatries of Jerusalem, and said to him, "Son of man, hast thou seen what the ancients of Israel do in the dark, every man in the chambers of his imagery? for they say, The Lord seeth us not; the Lord hath forsaken the earth," *—while yet the Lord, for all this, *did* see, and as He saw, avenged. And our chambers of imagery, He beholds them too ; and the darkness in which the worship of our idols may be conducted there, it is light, and no darkness, to Him. And those chambers of imagery, He will break them down ; unless we will be beforehand with Him, unless we will break them down ourselves, and throw down the idols, the images of jealousy which provoke Him to jealousy, with our own hands, before the day of his visitation has arrived.

For indeed, what are our lessons, or rather, what is our one great lesson from all which has been spoken ? It is this,—to beware of idols. With these weightiest words, as you may remember, with this affectionate exhortation, the beloved disciple concluded the apostolic admonitions of his first and longest epistle : "Little children, beware of idols." We may well beware of them ; for let us lay this to heart as certainly true, that the children of Israel, when they burned incense to Baal and to Ashtaroth and to all the host of heaven, were not laying up more certain plagues for them-

* Ezek. viii. 12

selves against the coming time, than we are for ourselves, when we lift up our hands to any strange god, and in heart (though it may not be outwardly in act) depart from the true and living God. The temptations to this are great, and are ever making themselves felt. The false gods of this world, they may be worshipped with an unrenewed and worldly heart. The worship of them falls in with all that is worldly and sensual within us, just as Moloch of old could be worshipped by the cruel, and Ashtaroth by the impure—their worship indeed *was* cruelty and impurity—while the God of Israel, He said to *his* worshippers, "Be ye holy;" He demanded of them then, as of us now, that they should lift up to Him holy hands, should worship Him in spirit and in truth. The temptation, therefore, is great, to worship some golden image which the prince of this world has reared, and to which he summons all to bow down; or if not that, yet some peculiar idol, which we have secretly enthroned in the profaned sanctuary of our heart; and who that knows his own heart will dare to say that it is easy to resist this temptation, in all the thousand subtle forms which it knows how to assume? Indeed, we could never do it, if we had not on our side One who has said, "If thou wilt hearken unto Me, there shall no strange god be in thee, neither shalt thou worship any other god;" who has promised us again, "The idols I will utterly abolish." Well for us if He do but abolish them; if we have had grace given us to separate ourselves from our strange gods, saying like Ephraim, "What have I to do any more with idols?" and to return, though it may be naked and wounded, to Him who stript and smote us, but stript that He might clothe, and smote that He might heal. Well for us, if the grace is given us so to use a time of visitation; but if, on the contrary, we stay upon our idols still, even after He has shown them to be nothing worth; if we cleave to them, make common cause with them, are angry with Him who robs us of them, crying like one of old, "Thou hast taken away my gods which I made, and what have I more?"*—if we continue thus mad upon them, what help is there then, but that in the end He should abolish us and our idols together; which just judgment of his, may we never by our sins provoke.

* Judg. xviii. 24.

SERMON XXIV.

THE GROANS OF CREATION.

For the earnest expectation of the creature waiteth for the manifestation of the sons of God. For the creature was made subject to vanity,
not willingly, but by reason of him who hath subjected the same in
hope, because the creature itself also shall be delivered from the
bondage of corruption into the glorious liberty of the children of
God. For we know that the whole creation groaneth, and travaileth in pain together until now. And not only they, but ourselves
also, which have the firstfruits of the Spirit, even we ourselves groan
within ourselves, waiting for the adoption, to wit, the redemption
of our body.—Rom. viii. 19–23.

IT is plain that the truths with which the great Apostle is here dealing are large and magnificent, reaching from one end of time to the other; that he is
embracing in the circle of his vision the wants and
woes, the hopes and expectations, not of the church of
God alone, but of the whole world, so far as it yearns
for, and thus shows itself capable of, redemption. At
the same time, it must be owned that the very grandeur
of his thoughts, the lofty and unusual courses in which
they are travelling, shed a certain obscurity over his
words; and thus, no doubt, many read them, or hear
them read, and attach little definite meaning to them.
We may very fitly, therefore, occupy ourselves with
them to-day, and inquire a little what their precise
scope and intention is.

All, I think, will acknowledge that the right understanding of the passage must mainly depend on our seizing the true meaning of the word "creature," which recurs in it four times; for though we have on one occasion varied the word, and used "creation" in our Version, there is no corresponding variation in the original. What, then, is this "creature," which was made subject to vanity, all parts of which groan and travail in pain together until now, which waits for the manifestation of the sons of God, which shall one day be delivered from the bondage of corruption, and become a sharer in their glorious liberty, or the liberty of their glory? I will not trouble you with the various explanations which have been offered; least of all, as all better interpreters are now pretty well agreed upon the matter. They find a key to the answer in the fact that the creature is in this very passage set over against the church of the redeemed; not only it, the creature, groans and travails, "but ourselves also, which have the firstfruits of the Spirit, even we ourselves groan within ourselves." The creature, then, is every thing capable of redemption, but which is not as yet redeemed; all which is outside of the church of Christ, and has more or less the consciousness, or the dim instinct at any rate, that it is outside, that it is submitted to a bondage of corruption, that it has been made subject to vanity, that it was meant for something better than its present condition is; and whose yearnings and cries and voices of misery, whose groanings and travailings, are indeed feelings after an unknown Christ, and after such a deliverance as He alone can bring in.

Now if the creature, in St. Paul's use of the word here, be thus inclusive, if it embrace all this, it is plain that the heathen world must be a part, and a large, indeed the largest, part of it. And may it not be said with highest truth of it, that it "groaneth and travaileth?" What voices of pain and distress reach us from the whole heathen world, from all the world, whether nominally Christian or not, as it is out of Christ, and ignorant of Him. What confessions of emptiness and vanity, of misery and despair. Some here present will have read, no doubt, collections of Greek and Latin epitaphs, as they have been gathered one by one from the tombs and monuments of those dead for whom the Son of God had *not*, as yet, brought life and immortality to light. It is when reading them, I think, that one best understands all the force of the Apostle's words, when he characterizes the heathen as "without hope in the world;" for with what a blank despair did *they* commit their beloved to the earth, following them to the brink of the dark grave, and there seeming to part with them for ever, and to exchange with them an everlasting farewell.

Think, too, of the institutions of heathen lands. In Christian lands the arrangements of society are sometimes unjust enough; but in heathen they often are nothing less than the permanent embodying of the tyranny of the strong, of the oppression of the weak; polygamy, for instance, is such; and slavery, again, is such. What cries of anguish have ascended, yea, are ascending now, into the ears of the Lord God of Sabaoth from the whole surface of a suffering earth; and these oftentimes the cries, not of some merely momentary anguish, of some mighty, but at the same time swiftly passing, calamity,—an earthquake, or a pestilence, or a war,—but of some woe, some cruel wrong, reaching from generation to generation, crushing out the life of the children as it did that of the fathers before them, and as it will do that of the children's children after them. Surely the world out of Christ groaneth and travaileth in pain. Take some single item in the catalogue of its woes ; take, for instance, the slave-hunts, which, as far back as our records reach, have spread through the whole of central Africa the sense of utter insecurity, terror and desolation and death. Try to realize any single fact of one of these expeditions, such an incident as no doubt somewhere in that vast continent occurred last night, and will this night occur again,—the peaceful unsuspecting village surrounded in the darkness, the blazing huts, those that defend themselves slain, the survivors borne chained away, one half of them gradually whitening the desert with their bones, the remainder separated from all they loved, and sold to a bitter bondage over the seas, from which only death should set free. Then multiply this fact ten thousand times, and that ten thousand times ten thousand again, and you may have some feeble image of the contributions to the world's woe which a single source will yield. Good right had the poet, looking back at all the matter for weeping which the world's history has afforded, to exclaim,

"Ocean of Time, thy waters of deep woe
Are brackish with the salt of human tears ;"

no wonder that the inspired Apostle should declare, "the whole creation groaneth and travaileth in pain together until now."

But it may be asked, if we apply, in part at least, this which St. Paul here affirms of the "creature" to the heathen world, where is the "earnest expectation" of the creature, whereof he also speaks. Does not the world, as it is out of God, and far from God, hug its chains, the chains of superstition and error with which it is bound, turn upon those who would fain loose or break these chains for it, reject, repel, stone them and drag them out of its cities? However heavy and crushing may be the weight of the world's woe, as it is alienated from God, can it be said that there is any cry after a redemption going up to God from it? any earnest expectation that a Deliverer and a deliverance may be in store for it?

In one sense, certainly, this cannot be affirmed. There is no cry which understands itself, which knows what it means; it is a blind longing at the best. And yet there is a sense, and a very sublime one, in which Christ is "the Desire of all nations;" and when you read of cruel rites and hideous sacrifices practised by heathen nations,—of priests of Baal cutting themselves with knives, Indian fakirs suspending themselves on hooks, worshippers of Molock passing their children through fire,—you have a right to say, what these men wanted to know was the cross of Christ. They felt, and felt rightly, that sin, to be forgiven, must be atoned; that there must be somewhere a sacrifice; only they have made a hideous mistake in regard of the quarter from whence the sacrifice should come. But for all this, there is a wonderful significance in these sacrifices of theirs, these offerings of their dearest and their best, of the fruit of their body for the sin of their soul. Unconscious what they did, they yet witnessed for the necessity of the cross of Calvary ; and each blind heathen now who devises sacrifices of expiation for his sin, tormenting himself or tormenting others, false and detestable as these sacrifices may be, he is yet groping in darkness after the cross of Christ, crying, though in most inarticulate voice, for that one sacrifice which can alone take away the sin of the world.

We may say the same in respect of the voices of anguish and despair which go up from the world as it is crushed under the weight of intolerable woe. The utterers of those voices may not understand them, nor what they mean ; but He knows, who dwelleth on high ; or rather He gives to them a far higher meaning than any which properly they possess. He translates them, and, translated and transfigured by Him, they become prayers, even prayers such as this : " O, that Thou wouldst rend the heavens, and come down ; that Thou wouldst cause thy kingdom to come, thy will be done upon this woeful earth below as it is in thy blessed heaven above." In such a sense as this the Apostle can speak of " the earnest expectation of the creature waiting for the manifestation of the sons of God " and of the Son of God ; even as we know that a day is coming when He shall appear, when He shall take away the covering that is on the face of all nations, the veil which is upon many hearts ; when, in the words, so significant, of the Psalmist, "All the ends of the world shall remember themselves, and be turned to the Lord;" they shall remember themselves, and remember Him; and all their long forgetfulness of Him, the true Lord of their spirits, shall be as a miserable guilty dream that has forever passed away.

Nor may we leave out of sight that there is sometimes a still distincter longing after a redemption, which makes itself felt and heard in a heathen land,—a "Come over and help us," which even men can understand. Who has read the recent travels of our great African discoverer, and will deny this? How weary, in parts at least, is Africa of itself! how weary of its cruel customs, of its bloody wars! What a pathetic cry was that with which one of its tribes, hunted and scattered and peeled, met him,—"We are weary; give us rest, give us sleep;" for under this image of sleep, of the calm unbroken sleep, these children of nature set forth to themselves the highest blessings they could conceive.

But to pass on: the creature in this passage, while it means first and chiefly the heathen, means also, as is generally agreed, something more than the heathen. It is a larger, more inclusive term. St. Paul ascribes here a groaning and travailing, not to *men* only, but to *things*. Nature too has been made subject to vanity, has had a yoke and bondage of corruption imposed upon it, yearns and longs to be delivered from this yoke, may be said to be itself looking forward to the day of the restitution of all things, when, at the great sabbath of the world which shall at length arrive, it shall put off the soiled and work-day garments which it has so long worn, and put on glorious apparel once more. And this is no fancy, that such a change, such a regeneration of nature, such a restoration of its original glories, shall one day be. The world in the midst of which we live, is not now what it was as it came from the hands of its Creator. Harsh discords and disharmonies have found their way into it; and make themselves everywhere to be heard. What means, for instance, the volcano, with its clouds of ashes and streams of liquid fire, carrying death and destruction to the peaceful towns and villages that reposed in fancied security at its base? What mean those fierce throes and shakings of the earth, which cause whole cities to topple down on their dwellers, and to crush them beneath their ruins? What the wild tornadoes, which strew the coasts with wrecks of ships and the corpses of men? What, again, the pestilential marsh, the very breath of which is fatal to all human life? Or turn your eyes to another province in the kingdom of nature,—to the world of animals. Do we not encounter the same discords, the same disharmonies there? Much, very much, to tell us that the state of Paradise has disappeared not for man only, but for the whole creation, whose destinies were made dependent upon his, which fell when he fell, and can only rise again when he rises. What intestine war is ever raging in this province of nature's kingdom; how many animals live only by the death of others. Behold through a magnifying glass a drop of water, and you will find in it a little world of terror and agony and suffering, the pursuer and the pursued, the tyrant and the victim ; there in little, as around us in large, the signs and tokens of something greatly amiss ; echoes in the natural world of the mischiefs which sin has wrought in the spiritual. For man, when he fell, did not fall alone ; God had set him as the lord and king of the earth, in whom all its glories should centre, in whom they all should be summed up. Only a little lower than the angels, and crowned with glory and honor, he was to have dominion over the works of God's hands ; all things were put under his feet. But when he rebelled against God, this lower nature rebelled against him. The confusion which sin had introduced into his relations to God, found its echo and counterpart in the confusions of nature's relations to him ; all became out of joint ; he dragged all after him in a common ruin. Glimpses, indeed, of the beauty of Paradise still survive ; fragments of that broken sceptre, which man once wielded over the inferior creation, still remain in his hands. But much, very much, has disappeared.

It has disappeared, but not forever. With Christ's first coming there went already signs and prophecies of a restored dominion of man over nature. Christ bids the angry winds and waves to be still, and they obey Him. St. Paul shakes off the venomous beast from his hand, and finds no harm. And the promise is, " Ye shall take up serpents ; and if ye drink any deadly thing, it shall not hurt you."* And yet all these are

* Mark xvi. 18.

rather prophetic pledges and intimations of what shall be, than a gift actually in hand. A day, however, is coming,—our Lord calls it the "regeneration,"* that is, the new birth of nature, even as there is already a new birth of man,—when the curse shall be lightened from the earth, as it has been already lightened from the spirit of man, and will, by and by, be lightened from his body; the day when He who is now making man new, shall make all things else new; when the wilderness shall blossom like the rose; when there shall be no more curse; when the wolf shall dwell with the lamb, when the leopard shall lie down with the kid; when they shall not hurt nor destroy in all God's holy mountain ;† and that holy mountain shall be as wide as the earth itself. This is "the glorious liberty of the children of God," into which the whole creation is yearning to enter; that is the bondage of corruption from which it is longing to be free.

Such was the aspect under which all things that he saw and heard around him presented themselves to the great Apostle's mind; on all sides a groaning and travailing world, full of labor and full of sorrow, because full of sin and full of guilt; and yet not laboring and sorrowing altogether in vain, seeing that all things were working together for a mighty issue and a crowning result; and these pangs of creation were, so to speak, the birth-pangs of that glorious time; these voices of the suffering creature were in his ear, though they knew it not themselves, cryings after a Redeemer,

* Matt. xix. 28.   † Isaiah xi. 6–9.

that He might come, and turn all the discords of the world into harmonies, stanch all the fountains of its woe, and make all its confusions and miseries to cease; and cryings too which should not always remain unheard.

My dear brethren, have *we* any sense of that whereof the Apostle had so strong a sense, the imperfection of the things which now are; any earnest longing for Him who can alone redress the wrongs of the present time; make the crooked straight, and the old new, and the weak strong, and the sick whole? For observe, this longing, this yearning, this groaning, this travailing, St. Paul does not ascribe it to the creature only, but goes on, "And not only they, but ourselves also, which have the firstfruits of the Spirit, groan within ourselves, waiting the adoption, to wit, the redemption of body." As there is imperfection and incompleteness everywhere else, so also there is even in redeemed man. In one sense he is complete: he is complete in Christ; made perfect as touching the conscience. But in another sense even he is incomplete; he is waiting the redemption of his body. That is underlying still the bondage of corruption, and as such it is exposed to a thousand hurts and harms; it pines with sickness, it is racked by disease, it wastes with age, it is torn by the shot, it is gashed with the sword; and, worse than all this, it is a body not merely of death, but of sin; the haunt of corruption, which is hard to subdue, and impossible, while we are here, altogether to expel. No wonder, then, that St. Paul should declare how that we too, even we, who have the firstfruits of the Spirit, who are ourselves "a kind of firstfruits of 'God's creatures,"* should oftentimes groan within ourselves, mingle notes of sadness with our anthems of praise, and be enabled to understand the world's woe by tasting some portion of it ourselves.

I cannot now make,—you must make for your own selves,—the application of what has been said. Only let me ask you one question: Can it be well with us, can all be right with us, if this language which the Apostle here speaks is to us altogether strange, altogether unintelligible; if we have no consciousness of a bondage of corruption, no groaning within ourselves that we may be delivered from this bondage, and as no yearning after a deliverance, so also no yearning after a Deliverer; in other words, no earnest need of our own heart and soul and spirit bringing us to Christ the Lord?

* Jam. i. 18.

SERMON XXV.

ST. PAUL THROUGH THE LAW DEAD TO THE LAW.

I through the law am dead to the law, that I might live unto God.
—GAL. ii. 19.

A THOUGHTFUL reader of Holy Scripture, above all of the Epistles of St. Paul, must have been sometimes surprised, perhaps a little puzzled, at the two very different manners in which the law is spoken of there, with, for the most part, so much good ascribed to it, and yet sometimes so much harm; it being generally pronounced such a blessed thing to be under the law, while yet, occasionally, such a blessed thing to be delivered from it. I need hardly remind you of the excellent things which are spoken of the law; it is " the law of the Lord," " an undefiled law," " giving light to the simple," " converting the soul," " holy and just and good."* The Apostle Paul it is who speaks these last words in its praise; and now listen to the same Apostle Paul, how he seems to speak against it; there is almost nothing too hard for him to say about it: " The law worketh wrath,"† " The strength of sin is the law ;"‡ he congratulates the Romans, and himself with them, on their deliverance from it, " We are delivered from

---

* Rom. vii. 12.   † Rom. iv. 15.   ‡ 1 Cor. xv. 56.

the law, that being dead wherein we were held."* He implies that obedience to God is thus, and only thus,—that is, through this deliverance,—made possible for any man : "Sin shall not have dominion over you ; for ye are not under the law, but under grace ;"† with much more to the same effect, which your own memories will easily suggest.

Shall I ask you, which of these statements is true ? You would answer at once, both are true ; both must be true ; and these seeming contradictions must be capable of reconciliation. It can only be while we dwell on the surface of things that there can even appear to be any opposition between one declaration of Scripture and another. This would be your answer, as it is mine. The actual reconciliation of what is spoken for, and what seems spoken against, the law, we shall arrive at best by attaining first a clear understanding in respect of what this law is, which St. Paul declares can never bring any man to perfection, can never produce in him any true holiness, any genuine and hearty conformity to the will of God, cannot overcome sin, but will strengthen it rather, and in the end can only hang over to the just and terrible judgments of God.

By this law, then, we are to understand not the Mosaic law alone, still less the ceremonial portion of it alone ; and those who snatch at this last interpretation, as though the Apostle did but charge that with impotency and inability to justify, do thereby declare that they have wholly failed to enter into the spirit of St.

---

* Rom. vii. 6.   † Ibid. vi. 14.

Paul's Epistles, and are missing, it is much to be feared, truths most vital for themselves. The law here, being primarily the Mosaic law, is not that alone, but every law which is nothing more than a law, every revelation and utterance of God as He commands and threatens; eminently, indeed, that "fiery law" which he spake once at Sinai; but with that, each other distinct utterance of his, as He speaks in and to the consciences of men, saying, If thou breakest these commandments, thou art under a curse, thou art worthy of death, and thou shalt die. Now St. Paul affirms that this commanding, threatening law can never of itself make a good man, can never make a holy man, can never make a man that shall love God with all his heart, that shall love his neighbor as himself. It might scare him, it might terrify him; it might drive his sin deeper down into the inmost recesses of his heart; it might bring him to such a sense of his own guilt and misery, that he should curse the hour of his birth, that hell should seem ever to yawn beneath him, and a threatening hand, ready to strike, seem ever suspended above him. It might bring him to see the holiness of God, but as the holiness of an enemy, of one whom he had made his enemy by his own unholiness, and one therefore whom he would fain flee from, if this might be, forever.

It might do all this; but more than this it could not do. For this law, I mean this law contemplated apart from other revelations of God, has in itself no secrets of peace, no secrets of power. It has no seats of peace; nothing by which it enables the sinner to make good the past; to feel that his conscience is cleansed from dead works; to look up to God as his Father, forgiving, pardoning, blotting out all this past, setting his heart at liberty, and so enabling him to run in the way of God's commandments. As little has the law any secrets of power. It gives no strength; it does not address the man through his affections or his will; it draws him with no cords of love. It is a bare menacing letter, saying to him, Do this, or, not doing it, thou shalt die; demanding much, but at the same time imparting no strength to enable him to fulfil the demands which it makes.

And even this is not all. To call the law impotent would oftentimes express only a part of the mischief whereof it was the occasion. The commandment coming, would not seldom of itself stir up the opposition which was slumbering before, awake up for the first time a rebellious principle in the heart of man, so that the very forbidding him to do the thing should arouse in him the desire to do it. This, the *irritating* power of the law, provoking by a spirit of contradiction the very evil which itself forbade,—just as a rock flung into the bed of some headlong stream, would not arrest the stream, but only cause it, which ran swiftly yet silently before, now furiously to foam and fret round the obstacle which it found in its path,—this irritating power of the law, itself a most fearful testimony of the depth of man's fall, St. Paul often dwells on, above all in the seventh chapter of the Romans: "I was alive," he says there, " without the law once," counted myself alive, was not conscious of the deep antagonism between my will and the will of God; "but when the commandment came, sin revived," started up from its seeming trance into fierce activity, into an open rebellion, "and I died."* So too in another place, "The motions of sins, *which were by the law*, did work in our members to bring forth fruit unto death."† But even where it was not thus, the law imparted no strength to a man enabling him to meet its claims, but left him exactly where he was before; or, indeed, not so, but invested with a new responsibility; for "where there is no law, sin is not imputed," and where there is law, it is imputed; henceforward, therefore, not a sinner only, but a transgressor.

This is the law which St. Paul is so zealous against, about which he says so many hard things; and yet not zealous against it in itself, not speaking hard things of it, so long as it keeps in its own sphere, moves within its own bounds; so far from this, that, writing to Timothy, he says, "The law is good, if a man use it lawfully."‡ And how "lawfully"? If he lays it on his flesh, and represses by it, not the inner evil lustings of his heart, for that he will never do, but the grosser outbreaks of his corrupt nature; if he learns by it what the whole compass of his duty is, and how greatly he has come short of it; if he regards it as the awful utterance of God's perfect holiness, the pattern shown in the Mount of what man ought to be, and of what he has not been; if it serves as a schoolmaster to bring him to Christ; if it drives him to the mercy-seat, to lay hold there on the horns

* Rom. vii. 9.   † Ibid. vii. 5.   ‡ 1 Tim. i. 8.

of the altar, to shelter himself under the shadow of the Cross from the wrath of God which is revealed from heaven against all unrighteousness of men. Such is the proper sphere of the law; and St. Paul is only zealous against it when it forsakes this, the region which God has assigned it in the economy of our salvation, and is allowed to intrude into another; when the man begins to regard it as the power in which he is to accomplish his obedience, and to do the works of God; as that which, being fulfilled, should prove the meritorious cause of his salvation. Then indeed St. Paul was zealous against the law, exactly because he was zealous *for* the law, because he desired to see the righteousness of the law fulfilled in us, and because he knew that no man ever did in the power of the law accomplish obedience and bring forth fruit to God; because he knew that for this a higher principle of life is needed, and one which no law could ever impart, for it is the gift of the Spirit of God.

This was the central conviction of the Apostle's life; therefore was he so deeply indignant with the false teachers among the Galatians, who had brought his converts under the bondage of the law again; who had transplanted them, his young and tender plants, from the rich and fertile soil of the grace of God, where they would have sprung up freely, and brought forth fruit abundantly, into the cold and barren and hungry soil of the law; where, if they did not perish outright, they would yet pine and wither, grow dwarfed and stunted, and bring no fruit to perfection. And hoping to extricate from their bondage these misled

Galatians,—"bewitched" he does not scruple to call them who could make so miserable an exchange,—he sketches for them the spiritual story of his own past life, summing up the entire result in the two verses, of which my text forms the first : " I through the law am dead unto the law ; " or better, " died to the law, that I might live unto God."

Let us take the first clause, that which contains the chief difficulty, first ; reading his words here by the help, and in the light of, other words of his own elsewhere. There was a time, he would say then, when I made the same experiment which you, who have gone back from Christ, and would fain be justified by the law, have been persuaded to make ; when, at my first awakening to an earnest, serious view of my relation to God, and of the obedience which He might justly demand of me, I sought in the law, and in my keeping of it, righteousness and peace, favor and acceptance with Him. But the experiment was a failure. The law could show me the good afar off, but it could not enable me to attain to the good it showed ; while yet it judged, threatened, and condemned for not attaining. Revealing to me the holiness that was in God, and the unholiness which was in me, it brought me for a while to the very verge of uttermost despair. But this attempt of mine, a failure in one way, was not a failure in another. " I, through the law, died to the law." I gave up, after a time, as a hopeless matter, the being justified by it. I found and perceived that it could condemn, but never absolve me ; could kill, but never make alive. I bade farewell to it : I extricated myself from it, and from the condemnation and curse which it pronounced upon me; even as I was able to do this, for I now knew of One who had come into my place, even Jesus Christ the righteous, who had kept the law which I had not kept, who had borne my curse, had been crucified for me, had condemned my sin in his own flesh, had at once condemned and forgiven it;—for was there not the most awful condemnation of it in all that He bore, a manifestation of the righteousness of God? and yet while He condemned, at the same time He also forgave it; for if He became a curse, it was for my sake; that, becoming such, He might bear, and bearing bear away, all the curse which I must else have borne. And now henceforth I look to his cross, and I see my sin crucified with Him, nailed to the same cross to which He was nailed. It is my sin no longer, for He made it his sin; and the debt which I could not pay, He took on Himself, and He paid it there. I am thus free from the law, or dead to the law, henceforth.

He was indeed dead to the law in two ways. First, he no longer sought in it the motive power which should enable him to bring forth fruit to God. It had itself cured him of this delusion. Henceforth he knew a more effectual motive, the love of Christ, that should constrain him to obedience, being in itself precept and power in one. And secondly, he was loosed from the law, dead to it, in that he no longer sought to be accepted with God through, and on the ground of, his observance of it. For he had found by a mournful experience that it wrought not acceptance, but rejection;

a terror of God, and not a confidence toward God; that by the works of the law should no flesh be justified. While yet this dying to the law, as he goes on in the second clause of my text to say, was not a dying to all law. The law of the spirit of life took the place of the law of a dead, yet threatening, letter. He put one yoke off him, but in the act of this he put another on him. In fact, he only could get rid of one by assuming the other, even the yoke of Him, whose yoke is easy and whose burden light. He died to the law; but he died to it that he might live unto God.

With such an experience of his own as this, it is nothing wonderful if St. Paul could ill endure that his beloved Galatians, they too already receivers of a new life, quickened long ago by a new power, delivered from the law that they might keep the law, justified freely by God's grace, that out of love to their Justifier, their crucified Lord and God, they might do those things which they never would or could have done out of fear of their lawgiver and condemner,—if, I say, he could ill endure that they should leave the riches of this grace, and submit themselves to the penury of that law; should forsake the strong, and attach themselves to the weak; should quit the blessed shelter of the mountain of the beatitudes for the rugged steeps of Sinai, its thunders, its lightnings, and its doom.

And you, too, my brethren, you see your calling. For you also it stands true, that you are not under the law, but under grace; and you also should be able to say with Paul, "I through the law am dead to the law." The words contain an answer to two errors, both very

current in our day; errors seeming opposite to one
another, and yet growing out of the same root; so that
the answer to one is the answer to the other. The first
is theirs who count that the end for which the Son of
God came into the world was, that God might accept
from us henceforth a poorer obedience than that which
He demanded before, and be satisfied with less; that
Christ came to make the narrow way not so narrow,
the strait gate not so strait. Is it not even so? Are
we not oftentimes tempted to think thus of Christ, as
the mere bringer-in of an easier law, as having come
to let men off from the stricter obedience which God
had hitherto required, the Only-begotten of the Father
having, in fact, for this taken flesh, and lived and died,
that men might lead poorer, meaner, earthlier lives
than before? This is one error. The other, opposite,
yet akin to it, that the chief end for which Christ came
was to give a stricter law than Moses had given, to
draw the reigns more tightly, to impose a severer rule
and discipline than that which men, through the hardness of their hearts, had been hitherto able to bear.

These are errors both; for indeed Christ's gospel is
neither one of these nor the other; neither a laxer law,
as those would affirm, nor a stricter, as these; being,
in truth, not a law at all, but rather a new power com-
municated to humanity; a new hiding of the heavenly
leaven in the lump of our nature; the casting of fire
upon earth, the new fire of a heavenly love, and of the
Holy Ghost, who is love; which should enkindle the
cold hearts of men, and burn up in them the dross,
which the law indeed could make them aware of, but

which it never could burn out from them. It was the
coming in of new spiritual forces into the world. It
demanded more from man, but it also gave more; it,
in fact, demanded nothing which it had not first given.
You see, then, your calling, that unto which you are
summoned, even the obedience of faith : you see why
peace is preached to you for the past, even because
holiness is demanded from you for the future. You
see what the law can do for you, and what it cannot ;
and where the gospel must come in. Use them both,
but at the same time have a good care that you use
them both aright ; and that you do not confound, but
keep them apart ; not applying the one where you
ought to apply the other ; for on this results most disastrous might follow.

Use the law, its terrors, its threatenings, as a bridle
on the flesh, on its lower appetites and desires. Use
the law to convince and to condemn you ; to beat you
out of your refuges of lies, and all your vain confidence
in yourselves ; to show you your sin. Listen to it in
the length and breadth of its commandments, every one
of which, spiritually apprehended, you have broken, in
the terrible sanctions with which the Lord has fenced
it, and sworn that He will avenge its breach ; listen,
till you hear the thunders of Sinai rolling ever nearer
and nearer, seeming at length to pause right above
your head, and only to wait for a word ere they break
in ruin there. But when thou wantest to find the secret of peace,—yea, when thou wantest to find the
secret of strength, be thou as Paul, "through the law
dead to the law." Refuse to know it, to acknowledge

its jurisdiction, for it will surely deliver thee to thy enemies. Say like Paul, "I appeal unto Cæsar." In it there is no peace, in it there is no strength. It can tell thee of no pardon; it can lend thee no strength for the fulfilment of one even of its own lightest requirements. All this is to be found in another, in Christ Jesus, and in the faithful looking unto Him. The law, when regarded apart from Him, is like that fabled Medusa's head, which froze them that looked at it to stone. But Christ thaws those frozen hearts again, causes the pulses to play, and the genial life-blood to flow in them once more. See, then, that thou do not confound these two,—the law, the utterance of God's holiness, the rule of man's life, the sinner's condemnation,—and the gospel, the power in which this obedience is to be accomplished, the dispensation of the Spirit, the message of pardon and peace; showing all mercy to the sinner, while at the same time it demands of him that he shall show no mercy to the sin.

SERMON XXVI.

THE DUTY OF ABHORRING EVIL.

Abhor that which is evil.—Rom. xii, 9.

HOW many, my brethren, shun evil as inconvenient, who do not abhor it as hateful; while yet the abhorrence of evil here demanded of us implies a great deal more than that shunning, which satisfies, as we often think, every claim which can be made upon us. To abhor evil is to have it in a moral detestation; to shrink back from it with a shuddering horror, as one would shrink back from a hissing, stinging serpent which of a sudden lifted itself up in his path; for it is this shuddering horror that our word implies; which, strong as it is, is certainly not a whit stronger than the word of the original. It is this duty which I desire to urge on you this day; the duty incumbent on the Christian man of entering into God's mind concerning evil, of seeing it in the light in which He sees it, of having the whole moral and spiritual nature engaged in active and lively repugnance to it, so that he shall never, looking abroad upon the evil which is in the world, looking within himself upon the evil which is in his own heart, regard this evil around him or within him with a careless, indifferent eye, shall never think of sin lightly, or speak of it jestingly,—it is only fools

who make a mock at sin,—but ever more regard it as
the abominable thing which God hates, and which therefore his children, who have his mind, and are ranged
on his side in the great conflict between light and darkness, are pledged and bound to make no terms with, but
evermore to hate, detest, and defy.

And, indeed, this vigorous abhorrence of evil has
been the mark and note of God's saints and servants
in all times, and from the very beginning. Let me
rapidly gather a few notable proofs. More than forty
years had elapsed since that cruel and treacherous murder of the Shechemites by Simeon and Levi; but with
what a fresh indignation, with what a still lively abhorrence, as though it had been the crime of yesterday,
does the aged Israel on his deathbed disclaim any part
or share in that bloody act, and detest and denounce
it: "O my soul, come not thou into their secret;
unto their assembly, mine honor, be not thou united."*
Then, too, in a life which had many flaws, I mean in
that of Lot, the most honorable testimony which is
anywhere borne to him is this, that he was "vexed
with the filthy conversation of the wicked;" that he,
"dwelling among them, in seeing and hearing, vexed
his righteous soul from day to day with their unlawful
deeds."† And St. Peter nearly connects his deliverance from the doom which overtook the guilty cities
with this his righteous abhorrence of the evil things
which were wrought in them.

Still more plainly and signally does this appear in

* Gen. xlix. 6.　　　　　† 2 Pet. ii. 8.

him, whom among all the saints of the Old Testament we know the best, I mean, of course, David. Hear him, as he is speaking before a heart-searching God : " I hate the works of them that turn aside ;"* " Do I not hate them, O Lord, that hate Thee ?"† with many more utterances to the same effect. The same voice finds its utterance in other Psalms, which, though they be not David's, yet breathe and share the spirit of David. How often, for example, and how strongly, in the 119th Psalm : " I hate vain thoughts ;‡ not merely, I avoid them, and would willingly be rid of them, but my whole moral nature rises up in active hostility against them ;" or, again, " I beheld the transgressors, and was grieved ;"§ it was not, that is, a thing indifferent to him, but pain and grief that men were breaking God's law, transgressing his commandments.

And as with these, so no less with the righteous kings of Judah in later times, the Asas, the Hezekiahs, the Josiahs. What the others gave utterance to in word, these, as occasion offered, uttered and expressed in deed. When, after some great falling away of the people to idolatry, they restored the true worship of Jehovah, they were not satisfied with merely abandoning the groves, and forsaking the temples of the false gods, and ceasing to burn incense to them therein ; but we read of their cutting down the groves, breaking in pieces the images, stamping and burning them in the fire,¶ turning to basest uses the idol temples,‖ defiling

---

* Psalm ci. 3.

‡ Ver. 113.

¶ 2 Chron. xv. 16.

† Ibid. cxxxix. 21.

§ Ibid. cxix. 158.

‖ 2 Kings x. 27.

with dead men's bones the altars on which incense had been burned to them ;* for so did they embody in righteous acts, visible to all men, their fulfilment of the precept of the Apostle, " Abhor that which is evil."

But most signally of all this abhorrence of evil comes out in Him of whom it is written, " Thou lovest righteousness, and hatest wickedness ; therefore God, thy God, hath anointed Thee with the oil of gladness above thy fellows."† It is this, you will observe, which is avouched of Him, namely, that he *hated* wickedness ; it was not merely that He kept Himself aloof from it, passed it by, had nothing to do with it ; but that He *hated* it. His whole moral nature was in active and continual warfare with it. That " Get thee behind Me, Satan," uttered once to the adversary in the wilderness, was the voice of his heart at every instant, was the key-note to which his whole life was set. The zeal of his Father's house consumed him, so that, though once only, or at most twice, He may have driven out the profane intruders from the Temple of his Father, yet the spirit which dictated these outbreaks of holy zeal was the spirit in which his whole life was lived, his whole ministry was accomplished. Ever near to his heart was the holy indignation which He felt at the dishonor done to his Father's name ; the holy hatred which he felt, not of the world, for that was the object of his tenderest pity, but of the pollutions of the world, in the midst of which He was moving ; and in his entire exemption from which pollu-

---

* 2 Kings, xxiii. 20.　　　† Psalm xlv. 7 ; Heb. i. 9.

tions He was "separate from sinners," though united to them in every thing besides.

If, brethren, it is indeed thus, if all holy men have felt this abhorrence of evil, and the holiest have felt it the most strongly, and Christ, the Holy One of God, more than all the rest, it may be well worth our while to inquire whether we have any of this righteous passion in our hearts ; for surely as He was, so ought we to be in the world.   The inquiry is by no means superfluous. This is an age of feeble, languid Christianity, as I fear we must all confess.   Those who are slightly touched by the power of the truth, on whose lives it exercises a certain beneficial influence, are many, perhaps more than in any other period of the church.   But it is much to be feared that what we have gained in breadth we have lost in depth.   Those whom the truth mightily takes hold of, who are content to be fools for Christ, who would be content to be martyrs for Christ, who love the good with a passionate love, who hate the evil with a passionate hatred, are few ; while yet it should be thus with all.   Let me suggest to you two or three tests by which we may try and form a judgment of ourselves, whether we can in any measure be said to abhor that which is evil.

And first, how fares it with us in regard of our temptations ?   Do we parley and dally with them, willing to entertain them up to a certain point, and to have thus, as by a certain foretaste, some shadow of the pleasure of the sin without the guilt of it ? do we plot and plan how near to the edge of the precipice we may go without falling over ?   Or do we rise up against ·

temptations so soon as once they present themselves to us, knowing them afar off, keeping them at arm's length, indignant with ourselves that they should so much as once have suggested themselves to our minds, and resolved of God's grace that there is nothing more that they shall do ; that at any rate the temptation shall not lay its cockatrice's egg in our hearts, to be hatched one day into the fiery flying serpent of accomplished sin? This is a sign of abhorring evil, when it is thus repelled at its first advances ; when the remote approaches to sin are counted, if not actually as guilty as sin itself, yet to be shunned and watched against with an equal care.

But, again ; the light in which a man regards the old sins into which he may have been betrayed is instructive, as furnishing an answer to this question, Does he really abhor what is evil? When a man looks back on sins which he has committed in times past, and though he would not indeed now *do* the same, yet feels a certain complacency in the circumstances and details of them,—in his old debauch, in the excesses of his youth ; when his forsaken sins thus fill him with any other feeling but that of shame and self-loathing, as exprest in those words of St. Peter, " The time past of our life may suffice as to have wrought the will of the Gentiles ;" this is too certain a proof that he has not truly learned to abhor what is evil ; that, however he may have left off certain sinful acts which he once committed, the pure hatred of evil, such as the Apostle requires of us, is not in him.

But another important element in this self-examination whether we be abhorrers of evil or no, is this : In what language are we accustomed to talk of sin, and of the violations of God's law? Have we fallen into the world's way, taken up the world's language in speaking about all this? Is the man sunk in impurest lusts of the flesh, the seducer of innocence, the violator of the holiest sanctuary of family life, called a man of pleasure? Do we speak good of the covetous, whom God abhorreth? Do we in these, and many like ways, put, as the world does, sweet for bitter and bitter for sweet? If we do, this is only too sure a sign that we do not abhor evil, else we should not call it by the name of good ; if light was indeed light to us, and darkness darkness, we could not so confound these, and call them by one another's names.

But, once more ; is the sin which is in the world around us a burden to our souls and spirits? I am not speaking of our own sin, for that must be a burden, if we have anything of Christ and of his spirit in us, but the sin which is around us. Could we with any truth take up that language of the Psalmist, " I beheld the transgressors, and was grieved " ? or, again, " Mine eyes run over with tears, because men keep not Thy law " ? or that which found its yet higher fulfilment in the Saviour Himself, " The reproaches of them that reproached Thee are fallen upon me " ? * When we look abroad on the world, and see the works done against the words of God's lips, does this fill us with any heaviness, with any indignation ? is it any part of the

---

* Ps. lxix. 9 : cf. Rom. xv. 3.

burden of our hearts, the sorrow of our lives? Is there any feeling in us, that when Christ is wounded we are wounded; any of the spirit in us which was in Paul and Barnabas, when they rent their clothes because of the dishonor they saw about to be done to God, in giving his glory to another?* Could any testimony be borne to us like that which, amid many grievous shortcomings, was borne to the angel of Ephesus, "But this thou hast, that thou hatest the deeds of the Nicolaitanes, which I also hate"?† Or do we rather feel, that if we can get pretty comfortably through life, and if other men's sins do not vex, cross, inconvenience, or damage us, they are no great concern of ours, nothing which it is any business of ours to fight against? I say, if it be thus with us, we have not yet learned the meaning of the words, "Abhor that which is evil."

One or two practical observations in conclusion. Seeing, then, that we ought to have this lively hatred of evil, that, tried by the tests which have been suggested, there are probably few, if any, among us who have it to the extent we ought, how, we may very fitly inquire, shall we obtain it? St. Paul tells us how, when in the same breath he bids us to "abhor that which is evil," and to "cleave to that which is good." Do not miss, I beseech you, the energy of that word "cleave." This, too, expresses, but it does not do more than express, the energy of the word in the original. Cling, the Apostle would say, to the good as

<hr>

* Acts xiv. 14.   † Rev. ii. 6.

something from which you will not be divided, from which nothing shall divorce you. We all know how the ivy clings to the wall or to the tree, casts out innumerable little arms and tentacles by which it attaches and fastens itself to it, seeking to become one with it, to grow to it, so that only by main force the two can be torn asunder. It is something of this kind which is meant here. In such fashion cleave to that which is good;—and if " to *that* which is good," then, as the sole condition of this, to *Him* that is good, who is *the* Good, *the* Holy, *the* Just One.

It is only in nearer fellowship with Him, and by the inspiration of his Spirit, that we can learn our lesson of hating the evil. It is in his light only that we can see light, or that we can see darkness. It is only light which reveals darkness; it is only holiness that condemns unholiness; it is only love which rebukes hate. Here, therefore, is the secret of abhorring the evil, namely, in the dwelling with and near the good, and Him who is the Good. From Him we shall obtain weights and measures of the sanctuary whereby to measure in just balances the false and the true; from Him the straight rule or canon which shall tell us what is crooked in our own lives, what is crooked in the lives around us. While our conversation is only or chiefly with men, we can have no high standard of what is pure, or lovely, or true. It is conversation with God, conversation with Christ, which alone supplies that standard. How must Moses have felt, when, having been forty days with God in the Mount, he came down from thence, and, as he drew near the

camp, heard the shouts of riot and revelry, these impure accompaniments of idolatrous worship, rising up
from the plain below!*   At any moment they would
have shocked him; but how must they have shocked
him now, fresh from his long communion with his God,
from the silence of the holy mount, from the awful
vision of Him, whose throne is on the sapphire pave-
ment of heaven, who charges his angels with folly,
which had been vouchsafed him there.

Be with God in the mountain of contemplation and
prayer, and it will fare with you as it fared with
Moses.   Fellowship with God in Christ, an often
pressing into his presence, and seeing of his face, a
cleaving to Him whom the young ruler might not call
'good," because he did not recognize Him as God,†
but who brought, as *we* know, goodness down from
heaven and planted it on earth; who has made it
something which is very near to every one of us; who
is Himself the Holy and the True;—this, with the il-
lumination of that Holy Spirit whose special office
it is to reprove all works of darkness,‡ will teach us
the right abhorrence of evil; so that no familiarity
with it shall make us patient toward it, or reconcile us
to it, but that it shall still be to us what it is to the
holy angels, what it is to the holy God, the abominable
thing which our soul hates.   "O ye that love the Lord,
see that ye *hate* the thing which is evil."

* Exod. xxxii. 17, 18.   † Matt. xix. 17.
‡ Eph. v. 11–13.

SERMON XXVII.

CHRIST WEEPING OVER JERUSALEM.

And when He was come near, He beheld the city, and wept over it,
saying, If thou hadst known, even thou, at least in this thy day, the
things which belong unto thy peace! but now they are hid from
thine eyes.—Luke xix. 41, 42.

THREE times, and three only, during the days of his
flesh, it is recorded of the Son of God that He
shed human tears: once at the grave of Lazarus his
friend, where, touched and moved by the sorrow of so
many round Him, Himself too a mourner among
mourners, "Jesus wept;" once in the garden of Gethsemane, where, as the writer to the Hebrews tells us,
He, our great High Priest, "offered up prayers and
supplications, with strong crying and tears, unto Him
that was able to save Him from death;" and once,
which is the occasion that will occupy us to-day, as He
descended the Mount of Olives, and saw stretched beneath his feet the city, so near its destruction, and yet
so unconscious of its doom. Then, too, "when He was
come near, He beheld the city, and wept over it."
And, Man of sorrows as He was, these three times, so
far as we know, were all; so that his tears lay not, as
do the tears of so many, near to the surface, ready to
start forth on every slight and trivial occasion, but
were drawn from deep fountains; and when he wept,

we may confidently ask, Was there not a cause? when He shed tears, we may be quite sure that there was matter before Him worthy of tears ; for nothing but an infinite sorrow, a matter of unutterable sadness, would have drawn those precious drops from his eyes.

Let us, then, my brethren, seek to give some account to ourselves of what the motives were of that passionate grief which at this moment more than at others the Lord felt and uttered, and where the stress of his sorrow lay. Let us inquire what lessons of comfort, what lessons of awful warning, these tears of his are charged with for us. For Jesus the Lord is our teacher, not merely by all that He said, but by all that He did. There is not a gesture, an emotion, a look of his, a look of love, or a look of anger, or a look of compassion, recorded in Scripture, which is not recorded there for our learning, which has not its own instruction for us, if only we would patiently consider these lesser traits as well as the broader features of his divine life and ministry.

And first, where was the stress of his sorrow, the pang that wrung Him, and wrung Him so nearly, at that peculiar moment? Assuredly it lay not in the outer circumstances of that immediate time. Beautiful for situation, the joy of the whole earth, the holy city lay beneath Him, as he stood upon the crest of Mount Olivet. And as his eye could scarcely have beheld a fairer sight, so too his ears were filled with the loud hosannas of the multitudes, who, with branches of palm-trees in their hands, and strewing their garments in the way, greeted and welcomed Him as the King of

Israel, the Messiah waited for so long. It was indeed one of the few festal moments in the earthly life of the Lord. A gleam of glory lit up for a moment that earthly life before the thick darkness of Gethsemane and Calvary had closed around it. It was the triumphal entry of a king into the metropolis of his kingdom ; and the proud unbelieving city, which had so long despised and rejected, seemed now ready to welcome with open arms Him who should turn iniquity from Jacob.

And yet, in the midst of all this joy and exultation, and for Him who was the object and the centre of it all, there was sorrow in his heart ; nor only that burden of habitual grief, that burden of a world's sin, which lay evermore on Him, and made Him the Man or sorrows that He was, but the anguish of a sharper and a nearer grief. And what was that ? His own words will best declare : "If thou hadst known, even thou, at least in this thy day, the things which belong unto thy peace! but now they are hid from thine eyes." He measured the worth, or rather He estimated the worthlessness, of those greetings which greeted Him now. He knew that all this joy, this jubilant burst, as it seemed, of a people's gladness, was but as fire among straw, which blazes up for an instant, and then as quickly expires, leaving nothing but a handful of black ashes behind it. He knew that of this giddy thoughtless multitude, many who now cried, " Hosanna, blessed is He that cometh in the name of the Lord," would, ere a little week was ended, join their voices with the voices of them who exclaimed, " Crucify Him, crucify Him : we have no king but Cæsar ;" and He wept, not for Himself, but for them, for the doom which they were preparing for their city, for their children, for themselves.

He knew, and this was a sadder thought still, that there was no part of this dreadful doom but might have been averted. There were things which belonged to Jerusalem's peace, and which would have secured it, if only she would have known them. They were things which He had brought with Him. The guilty city, the murderess of the prophets, she that had been a provocation almost from her first day until now, might have washed her and made her clean from all that blood and from all that filthiness ; she might have become, not in name only but in deed, "the city of peace," if only she would have consented first to be " the city of righteousness," to receive aright Him who had come, " meek and having salvation," and bringing near to her the things of her everlasting peace. There was no dignity, there was no glory, that might not have been hers. She might have been a name and a praise in all the earth. From that mountain of the Lord's house the streams of healing, the waters of the river of life, might have gone forth for the healing of all the bitter waters of the world. But no ; she chose rather to be herself the bitterest fountain of all. As she had refused in the times past to hear God's servants, so now she refused to hear his Son, stopped her ears like the deaf adder, made her heart hard as adamant, that she might not hear Him.

And now, which was the saddest thought of all, the
13*

days of gracious visitation, during which He was walking up and down in her streets, during which she might, if she would, have seen his glory, full of grace and truth,—these days were ending, or had indeed already ended, for many; the things which belonged to the peace of her children, they would not know them; and those things were being forever hid from their eyes. He who knew what was in man, knew that for the great mass of that people it would be so. He who sees all, saw in his mind's eye those forty years of impenitence and pride, of hatred toward Him, the ascended Lord, with all the messages of defiance sent after Him, —"We will not have this man to reign over us,"— those forty years of the cruel persecution of his servants, during which that people should fill up the measure of their iniquity; and then He beheld that day when the great King should send his armies, for they were *his* armies, the rod of his wrath, however they might be also the armies of Rome, and destroy the city of those murderers.   Already He beheld Jerusalem compassed with foes; He saw with prophetic eye the Roman engines shaking the walls; He heard with prophetic ear the tramp of the Roman legions as they advanced to the assault. He saw all; the sword devouring without, and the sword devouring within; the famine consuming what the sword had spared; the tender and delicate woman fulfilling the hideous prophecy of Moses, and eating her own offspring for the want and straitness of all things in the siege ;* "the

* Deut. xxviii. 56, 67.

abomination of desolation" (whatever that might be) " standing in the holy place ;" and all which is involved in the fierce madness and wild despair of a people, which, having been the people of God, had rejected Him, and had been in return rejected by Him. He saw all, and comparing this, the portion which Jerusalem was making for herself, with the portion which He would have made for her, " when He beheld the city, He wept over it."

And these tears of the Son of Man, with the words which accompanied and interpreted these tears, have they no lesson, no instruction for us? They have many lessons, much instruction. Bear with me, while I endeavor to bring some portion of this home to your hearts.

And first, there are things which belong unto our peace; things which it most deeply concerns us to know ; things which it were matter of weeping even for the Son of God, were He now upon earth, if we refused to know them. And what things are these but the same which Jerusalem in that her day might have known, and would not,—the things of Christ? Happy the world may count him, happy he may count himself, but I say that miserable is every man, who has nothing between himself and judgment except that little inch of time which he is still permitted to call his own ; miserable indeed, who does not know these things of his peace, being the things of Christ, the worth of his all-atoning sacrifice, the power of his blood to cleanse the conscience, of his Spirit to sanctify our spirits ; who does not know the reconciliation with the Father which is the fruit of these. Such are the things of our peace. Whatever else the world can give us, it cannot give us these; and yet not to have these, is to be, however we may disguise the fact from ourselves for a while, most miserable of all; to be preparing wrath and doom, tribulation and uttermost anguish for ourselves.

But then, secondly, we learn that there are times of gracious visitation, when these things are brought nearer to us than at other times, when above all it behoves us that we embrace and make them ours. Nations and individuals have alike these their times of gracious visitation, which it vitally concerns them that they do not miss, that they do not allow to slip by them unimproved. It was, as we have seen, such a time of visitation for Israel when her King walked up and down in the midst of her, speaking such words as none other had ever spoken, doing such works as none other had ever done. Then was the " one year more," during which the heavenly Husbandman was digging about the roots of the fig-tree, barren too long; and then, if it had borne fruit, well; but because it did not, He therefore cut it down.

But while we wonder at their blindness and their guilt, who would not know this time and improve it, let *us* beware lest *we* come under the same condemnation. There are moments and crises of our lives, which are *our* times of visitation, upon which vast issues, oftentimes the whole issue for eternity, depend. Times of a great joy, or of a great sorrow, when the Lord of our life gives us some crowning blessing, the keystone of the arch of our happiness, or when He takes this keystone away, and that arch, which seemed a moment since so strong, falls in ruins at our feet ; times of some signal outward deliverances, when the sickness of a great fear, the bitterness as of death for some whom we loved, passes from us ; times when God shakes the rod over us, but, it may be, withdraws it again, or times when He suffers it to alight ; seasons of trying pain, of weary sickness, of unlooked-for recovery ; when He makes us rich, or when He makes us poor ; times of spiritual trouble, when the spectres of our old sins rise again from their graves to trouble and to haunt us, or when those old sins evidently find us out, bring us to an open shame even before men ; all these, and many more, are times of visitation, which it infinitely concerns us to know. God is then speaking to us more than at other times ; alluring us into the wilderness, that He may talk with us there. He is singling us out from the crowd. As the prophet had a word for Jehu, and singled him out from his fellows,—" I have an errand to thee, O captain,"*—so God has a special word for us at such times as these. And what is that word? Give Me thy heart. If thou hast served Me in times past, yet serve Me better now ; with a purer service, with a more devoted aim, with a singler eye, with more frequent and more fervent prayer, with a freer dedication of thy means, thy time, thy affections to Me. Or if in time past thou hast been serving vanity, serving the world, serving sin, yet count that time to be enough, and more than

* 2 Kings ix. 5.

enough; look back at it and its doings with a holy indignation, and now serve Me, who hold thy soul in life, and have sought by these gracious leadings to lead thee to the knowledge of Myself, whom to know is life everlasting.

Whoso is wise will consider these things, will not allow these times to escape him unobserved, unimproved. They are angels of God, whom he will detain and welcome; angels, sometimes, it may be, with dark and threatening countenances, "very terrible,"* but always with hands full of gifts and full of blessings. For these critical seasons may not return; there is certainly one of them which will be the last; and even if they do return, the same inconsideration, the same lack of watchfulness in respect of God's dealings with us, which lost us the first, would probably in like manner lose for us the second and the third. And when at last this long course of God's dealings with us, and messages to us, is exhausted; when the things of our peace, because we refused to know them, have been forever withdrawn from our eyes, what will remain for us then? We know what remained for Jerusalem, what doom was reserved for her and her children. Jesus wept over the guilty city, but He did not the less destroy it. There was no weakness in those tears. It was because He meant against the guilty city all with which He threatened it, that therefore He wept over it. There would not else have been any cause or argument for tears.

* Judg. xiii. 6.

And He means all which He threatens now. We are sometimes tempted with a temptation like this: God, who is a God of love, who is a God of infinite compassion, will never execute those terrible sentences which He has pronounced against impenitent sinners. He means but to scare them, if thus it may be done, from their sins; and if He fails in so doing, He will in one way or other find out for them a way of escape. It is a subtle temptation, lurking in the background of many minds, which yet hardly acknowledge it to themselves: one by which multitudes contrive to persuade themselves that they have no such need of earnestly mortifying sin, of seeking Christ while He may be found, of pressing upon others the knowledge of his one saving name. But against all these perverse disputings of men we would set the one awful fact, that He who shed over Jerusalem those tears of love, who uttered those words of an infinite pity, it was even He, the same, who, when the city continued impenitent and unbelieving, without faith and without repentance, sent his armies and destroyed it.

THRONGING CHRIST, AND TOUCHING CHRIST.

And Jesus, immediately knowing in Himself that virtue had gone out of Him, turned Him about in the press, and said, Who touched my clothes?   And his disciples said unto Him, Thou seest the multitude thronging Thee, and sayest Thou, Who touched Me?

—MARK v. 30, 31.

FEW things strike us more in the record of our Lord's miracles of healing, than the infinite variety of the circumstances by which they were attended. They have each its several and distinct physiognomy; so that there are hardly any two which in their minor details repeat one another. Features, indeed, of resemblance they all have.   They are all outcomings of the grace and power and infinite pity of the Son of God, who in our flesh walked up and down among the suffering children of men.   But, with all this, how different they are; nor is this hard to account for.   The richness, the opulence of the Lord's spiritual life, the deep sympathy which He had for all forms of suffering and sorrow, brought Him in contact with the suffering and the sorrowing on a thousand new and unexpected sides; while the wisdom which caused Him to vary his gracious dealings according to the varying needs and necessities of those who applied to Him for help, ever seeking, as He did, to make the healing of the body minister to the healing of the soul, this manifold wisdom must explain why one was healed in this way, and one in that ; why one obtained a blessing at once, and another only after much asking ; one by a word spoken from a distance, and one by the actual touch of those sacred hands ; one through the intercession of friends, and another in reply to his own prayer.

Thus how totally unlike every other miracle of healing is that wrought upon the poor woman whom my text has no doubt summoned up before your mind's eye. Grievously afflicted, she had sought, but had sought in vain, during twelve long years, for help and healing. What a picture in a few strokes our Evangelist draws ; and, indeed, there is no such painter as he : "She had suffered," he tells us, "many things of many physicians, and had spent all that she had, and was nothing bettered, but rather grew worse." Many painful remedies she had tried; but they were ineffectual as they were painful. Many physicians had undertaken her cure, but presently brought to the end of their art, were obliged to confess that this cure exceeded their power. Bandied about from one to another, elated sometimes by a little hope, which was presently to be dashed by a great disappointment, her means of living quite wasted and gone, spent in a vain pursuit of health which seemed now more remote than ever, her case appeared as sad and despairing a one as could well be conceived.

I know of only one sadder ; which yet *is* sadder, because sicknesses of the spirit are worse than sicknesses of the body ; I mean the case of some poor struggling sinner, who, conscious of sin, of a mighty power of evil overmastering him and bringing him into bondage, has, after some vain attempts to be his own healer, his own deliverer, gone here and there to the makers of human systems, has been promised by one after another of these help and healing, deliverance from evil, strength to resist it, power to overcome it, but has found, alas, after brief dreams of liberty, that he is a captive still; a miserable man, doing the evil which he hates, and hating the evil which he does; ever sinking deeper and deeper into bondage, the cords of sin being ever drawn more tightly round him, and he ever more hopeless of extrication from them; those helpers whose help he once sought, and who promised him so much. the wise men and philosophers and moralists of this world, having nothing bettered, but rather left him worse than they found him, miserable comforters that they were, and physicians of no value. That were a sadder case still; and yet it is a case so little uncommon, that I can well believe one and another here present to-day will acknowledge it to be their own. To them I shall presently return; but now to proceed with the history which we have begun.

In this her extremity, in this her blank destitution of all hope, the woman heard of Jesus, of his grace and power; and how these two, his ability to help and his willingness to help, went hand in hand; and what she heard, she believed. The star of hope, which seemed to have set forever, rose once more in her heart; she said within herself, "If I may touch but his clothes, I shall be whole." Was not that faith indeed?

To believe of the Lord Jesus, that if only she put herself in relation with Him, strength and health would stream forth from Him to her ; to believe that there dwelt in Him such fulness of all grace, as that virtue and healing grace would freely flow upon her, or upon any, who brought themselves, however remotely,—touching, it might be, but the hem of his garment,—into this faithful contact with Him ; was not that one of the noble audacities of faith ? And what she purposed to do, she did. " She came in the press behind, and touched his garment, and straightway the fountain of her blood was dried up, and she felt in her body that she was healed of that plague." She could not mistake the fact. It witnessed to itself. The pulses of a healthful life were beating in her veins once more. She was, and she knew it at once, healed of that plague. Truly hope maketh not ashamed.

And you, I would beseech you also to try, as many as have not tried already, whether this, which was true for her in the lower sphere and region of things natural, is not still more gloriously true in the higher sphere of things spiritual. What is your plague, the plague of your own heart, for which as yet you have found no healing anywhere, after all your toils and tears, but only disappointment, defeat, and now well-nigh despair that it will ever be healed at all ? I cannot tell what it is, but you can ; you know it only too well. You know the secrets, the mournful secrets, I am bold in most cases to call them, of your own spiritual life ; the strength of corruption, the tyranny of sin, the way in which old sores, which seemed healed for a while, have broken out afresh, and with a worse malignity than ever. You have cried, perhaps, with Paul, " O wretched man that I am, who shall deliver me from the body of this death ?" but you have stopped there ; you have never been able to take upon your lips the triumphal rejoinder which at once he puts in, " I thank God through Jesus Christ our Lord," for the freedom which I have obtained through Him. Well, you have tried many things ; but have you tried the one thing which Paul tried, which this woman teaches you to try ? many ways of spiritual health, but have you made trial of this ? Have you ever come to Christ, as she came, and made proof whether He would not heal you, He would not deliver you ? Perhaps you will say, Yes ; I have not turned my back on any of the ordinances of the church ; I have said my prayers, have joined in public worship, and, as it may be you will add, I have drawn nigh to the holy table itself ; but there has been no strength, no virtue, in these ordinances for me. They have left me as they found me ; my conscience still uncleansed from its guilty stains, my corruptions still unsubdued, the plague of my heart still the same ; and now I am persuaded that what I am, I must continue to be ; that for me, if there is any progress, it can only be from bad to worse ; and I must carry this conscience not cleansed, this spirit not healed, with me to the grave, and to those dark judgment-seats which lie beyond the grave.

Ah, brethren, let none say this. You complain that the very ordinances of Christ's church have proven barren to you, as unfruitful to you of good as everything else, dry channels by which no streams of blessing were conveyed to your souls. See whether there be not in what follows of this very history an explanation of that barrenness and unprofitableness whereof you complain, and whether this history does not also suggest a way in which these may be removed. I beseech you, then, to go along with me in the further consideration of this most instructive narrative. We heard how the poor woman felt in herself that she was healed of her plague. The Evangelist proceeds : "And Jesus, immediately knowing in Himself that virtue had gone out of Him, turned Him about in the press, and said, Who touched my clothes? And his disciples said unto Him, Thou seest the multitude thronging Thee, and sayest Thou, Who touched Me? And Jesus said, Somebody hath touched me ; for I perceive that virtue is gone out of me." What I wish to urge on you, and O, that I could urge it as it deserves to be urged, is the mighty difference, it may be a difference for us as of life or death, between " touching" Jesus and " thronging" Him ; the multitude " thronged" Him ; only this faithful woman " touched" Him. There was nothing to the outward eye which should distinguish between her action and theirs. Jesus was moving now, as he so often did, in the midst of an eager, busy, and rudely curious multitude ; He had just been summoned to the house of the ruler Jairus, that He might heal his dying daughter, or, as it proved, raise his dead. As the Lord set forth upon that errand of mercy and power, " much people followed Him and thronged Him." Peter and the other disciples could see nothing to distinguish this woman from any other member of that eager, inquisitive, unceremonious multitude which crowded round Him, as was their wont; so that, as you have just heard, Peter, who was always ready, and sometimes too ready, with his word, is half inclined to take his Lord up and rebuke Him for asking this question, " Who touched me ?" a question which had so little reason in it, seeing that the whole multitude were thronging and pressing upon Him at every moment and on every side.

But Christ reaffirms and repeats his assertion, " Somebody *hath* touched Me." He knew the difference ; He distinguished at once, as by a divine instinct, that believing *one* from the unbelieving many. There was that in her which put her in connection with the grace, the strength, the healing power which were in Him. Do you ask me what this was ? It was faith. It was her faith. She came expecting a blessing, believing a blessing, and so finding the blessing which she expected and believed ; she came saying, as we just now heard, " If I may touch but his clothes, I shall be whole." But that careless multitude who thronged the Lord, only eager to gratify their curiosity, and to see what new wonder He would next do, as they desired nothing, expected nothing, from Him, so they obtained nothing. Empty they came, and empty they went away. It may very well have happened that among that crowd there were more than one sick and suffering, holden with some painful infirmity or inveterate disease ; but there went forth no virtue from the Lord to them. And why not ? because they thronged Him, and did not touch Him ; because faith, which is as the electric wire along which the spark of divine healing should have run, was wanting on their parts, and because, therefore, their contact with the Lord was merely external and accidental, and had in it no real significance whatever.

O my brethren, is there not here the explanation of much, of only too much, in the spiritual lives of men,—the explanation of barren sacraments, of fruitless prayers, of church-going, of sermon-hearing, which, after twenty or thirty years, leave us where they found us, not a whit holier, not a whit more conquerors of our sins or masters of our corruptions, not a step nearer to God and heaven, than we were at the beginning? We are of the many that throng Jesus, not of the faithful few who touch Him. We bear a Christian name, we go through a certain round of Christian duties ; we are thus brought outwardly in contact with the Lord ; but we come waiting for no blessing, and so obtaining no blessing. We enter his house, and we never say, " How dreadful is this place! This is none other but the house of God, and the gate of heaven." We walk with Him by the way, but we never so commune with Him that our hearts burn within us. We approach his table, but not saying to ourselves, The Lord has appointed to meet me here, that He may dwell with me and I in Him ; and I will be satisfied with no blessing short of this. In everything there is coldness, formality, routine. Faith is wanting, faith, the divine hunger of the soul, the emptiness of the soul longing to be filled, and believing that it will be filled, out of God's fulness ; and because this is so, therefore there goes out no virtue from Him to us ; it is never given to us so to touch Him as that immediately we know in ourselves that we are whole of our plague.

You who complain, you who, it may be, murmur, that the ordinances of God's church are so little fraught with grace and strength for your souls, is it not at least possible that the explanation of all this barrenness and unprofitableness may be here, in the fact that you have been thronging Christ, and not touching Him? Only come to Him now, saying, If I may but touch Him, I shall be whole ; only come, looking for good, and you will find good ; expecting mercy, and you will obtain mercy ; bringing your heart to be healed, and it shall be healed. When you read, when you meditate, when you hear, when you pray, when you partake of the holy Communion, so do it that Christ shall be compelled to say, and believe me He will rejoice in the compulsion, " Somebody hath touched Me." He will not now need to turn round and to inquire who hath done this thing. He will have seen thee afar off, thy first timid approaches to Him, thy nearer and bolder advances, the faith which brought thee at length into immediate contact with Him. He was only waiting for this, that so virtue might go forth from Him to thee ; and thou, who camest fearing and trembling, who camest, it may be, behind Him, as hardly daring to own either to thyself or others what thou wert looking for from Him, shalt go away strengthened, reassured, healed, an open confessor of the faith; boldly declaring in the face of all what God hath done for thy soul, as this woman declared what He had done for her body; thou too whole of thy plague, thine iniquity pardoned, and the ever-flowing fountain of thy sin and thy corruption stayed.

14

SERMON XXIX.

And He withdrew Himself into the wilderness, and prayed.—LUKE v. 16.

WHEN we read in this, and in so many other passages, that our blessed Lord in the days of his flesh offered prayers unto God, it greatly concerns us that we do not accept an explanation, only too commonly suggested, of these his prayers. It is sometimes said that Christ our Lord prayed by way of example, that so He might teach us the duty of prayer; and that his prayers had no other purpose and meaning but this. Doubtless He *was* our example in this, as in every other point. But his prayers were no such hollow unreal things as we must needs confess them to have been, if such was the *only* intention which they had. An explanation such as this would go far to introduce a fatal hollowness and insincerity into all our manner of regarding Him and his gracious work for us; as though that work had been the scenic representation of a life, and not the life itself; done for the effect which it would produce upon others, instead of being in every part the true outgrowth and genuine utterance of those conditions of humanity under which He had been willing to come. Our Lord, the head of

"

the race of men, but still man as truly as He was God, prayed, as any one of his servants might pray ; because in prayer is strength, in prayer is victory over temptation, in prayer, and in the grace of God obtained through prayer, is deliverance from all evil. He prayed, because He came in his human nature to live upon his Father's fulness, and not upon his own ; to draw life from Him, and not to find it in Himself ; to teach us that this was the true glory of the creature, not to set up for itself, not to attempt to live an independent life of its own, but evermore to live *in* God and *from* God.

Very instructive too is the manner in which this notice of his having withdrawn Himself into the wilderness and prayed, is, in the chapter from which my text is taken, interposed between, and in the midst of, his active ministries and labors of love. It follows close upon the record of some of these labors, others again of these follow close upon it ; that time of his brief withdrawal from toil being, so to speak, a breathing-time, a time of refreshing, in which He revived and renewed his strength, and, this done, returned to that toil again.

And such times were needed in that life which He lived upon earth ; for that life was not a flying from the world, lest *it* should stain and defile *Him*, but a mingling *with* the world, that He might cleanse and purify *it*. The career of a John Baptist, a preacher in the wilderness, whom men might seek and find, but who did not himself seek them ; this might be, and was, good ; but yet, at the same time, there was a more excellent way even than this, the way which Christ chose. No preacher in the wilderness He; but in crowded streets, at marriage-festivals, in the concourse of cities, amid all the busiest haunts of men, wherever there was a want to relieve, or a woe to assauge, or a sin to rebuke, He was there, shedding round Him the healing influences of his presence and his power. And yet such a life as this, lived *for* men and *among* men, noble and blessed as it was, needed that it should have its breaks, that the burden of it should not be continuous. Even He whose spiritual strength is so immeasurably greater than ours, whose whole life was in some sort one long connected prayer, even He needed, from time to time, to be more especially alone with God, to draw new strength and joy from a more fixed contemplation of his heavenly Father's face.

And if this was needful for Him, how much more for all others; for as He was in the world, so are we; the only difference being, that we lie open to the injurious influences which it exerts, as He neither did nor could; that the evil in the world finds an echo and an answer in our hearts, which it found not at all in his. In a world where there is so much to dissipate and distract the spirit, how needful for us is that communion with God, in which alone the spirit collects itself at its true centre, which is God, again; in a world where there is so much to ruffle the spirit's plumes, how needful that entering into the secret of his pavilion, which will alone bring it back to composure and peace; in a world where there is so much to sadden and depress, how blessed that communion with Him, in whom is the one source and fountain of all true gladness and abiding joy; in a world where so much is ever seeking to un-hallow our spirits, to render them common and profane, how high the privilege of consecrating them anew in prayer to holiness and to God.

Is it not even so? Would you measure in some sort the gains of this communion with God to which we are admitted and invited, consider only what we may gain by communion with good and holy men, and then conclude from this less to that greater. Consider, I say, the elevating, ennobling influences which it exercises on the character to live in habitual intercourse with the excellent of the earth, with those whose conversation is in heaven, the tone of whose minds is high and lofty and pure. Almost without being aware of it, we derive some of their spirit into ourselves; it is like an atmosphere of health which we unconsciously inhale. But how much more must this be the case, how far mightier the reactive influence for good, when we continually set before us, when we live in fellowship with Him, who is the highest, the purest, and the best; in whom all perfections meet, from whom all true nobleness proceeds; when thus, I say, our fellowship is not with men, who have caught a few glimpses of the glory of God, but with God Himself, from whom all greatness and glory proceed.

And yet, necessary and blessed as this fellowship and communion are, by the confession of all who have any experience in the divine life, we must needs acknowledge sadly that here is a privilege to which men require to be invited and exhorted again and again;

that, transcendent dignity and honor as this is, namely, to be allowed to speak with the great King, it is not always so felt by all. Nay, who is there that does not know, by mournful experience, the tempta tions, even if he has grace given him in the main to overcome them, which beset him here? the excuses which suggest themselves for praying seldom, for praying briefly; other matters ever seeking to encroach upon this prime matter; the time allotted to it, too brief perhaps at the first, being ever in danger of still further curtailment; pleasure at one time, and business at another, and indolence at all times, weariness at night and sloth in the morning, the company of friends, the attraction of books,—these, with a thousand other real or fancied demands on our time, seeming all in one vast conspiracy to thrust our prayers into by-corners of the day, if not to thrust them out of the day altogether; until at length prayer, if it survives at all, survives as a slight and barren form, from which all strength and vigor have departed; a mere peppercorn rent of our time paid to Him who has given us all our time; a mockery rather than a reverent service of the living God.

But how serious, how disastrous, the consequences which must then ensue. For prayer, it is as the ladder which Jacob saw, with angels ascending and angels descending upon it. But if there be no ascending angels, there will presently be none descending; if there be no prayers nor supplications going up to heaven, there will in a little while be no grace or blessing coming down from heaven. In vain will heaven and earth have been linked together as by a golden chain, let down from the throne of God, binding to that throne this earth of ours, if, after all, we count ourselves and this world which we inhabit but as blind atoms floating blindly and at random through an infinite space.

Ah, brethren, how many departures from God, ending in a total shipwreck of faith, have begun in the secret chamber. In some sense, they have all begun there. If only we could look into the inner records of some young man's life, who, trained in a Christian household, and himself seeming to have well begun, has yet after a while forfeited the promise of his youth, gone forth and forgotten the sanctities of home, and the faith pledged not to God alone, but to father and mother and sister;—still loved, and to be for ever loved, but with a tearful aching love, how unlike the proud love which regarded him once;—could we look, I say, into that story, here, I am sure, would be most often found the secret of all. He counted that he could do without that which the Saviour Himself would not do without—that he could live on his own resources, that he could lean upon his own strength. The hidden life of the soul, that life which is hidden with Christ in God, was neglected; and thus whatever in him of good was once lost, was lost for ever, the first impulses to a holy life, to an earnest resisting of sin, being spent and exhausted, no other came in their room; little blemishes in the character, which might once have been easily removed, grew into huge faults; small sparks of temptation, which might have been trodden out at the first, into fierce flames, setting on fire the whole course of nature. And all this will have come to pass through neglect of secret communion with God, through suffering the life of prayer first to languish, and then to die out in the soul.

But they, on the other hand, who wait upon the Lord renew their strength. They find in this waiting upon Him that which answers every need and satisfies every yearning of their souls; and this whether as respects others or themselves.

And first, in respect of others. I cannot dwell here on intercessory prayer as it deserves to be dwelt on; and yet, in this hour of England's trouble, of an anxiety so deep for many among us,* I would fain not leave some words unsaid, which may be words in season for some. How often it must happen that we can reach them whom we love, to do them good, in no other way except in this way of prayer. Our beloved have passed forth from under our eye, from the protecting shadow of our roof. They go in and out before us no more, as they did of old. We think of them as they move under other skies, amid strange faces, exposed to novel temptations, among dangers which we can only dimly guess of, and which no forethought of ours could avert. We think of them, it may be, in stormy seas, beneath fiery suns, amid treacherous foes, upon distant and doubtful battle-fields. How good is it then that, when powerless in all else, we can still pursue them with blessing, and bear them in prayer

---

* This Sermon was preached in June, 1857, a few days after the first tidings of the Indian mutiny.

before *his* throne, who can shield and shelter in every danger and temptation, so that none of these shall by any means hurt them.

And in respect of ourselves, we have here that which will answer all our needs at every turn and crisis of our lives.

Thus has God in his good providence made a hedge around us, has He kept all evil from our dwellings; have others been smitten, but not we; has He given us benefits and blessings, which we are only in danger of not feeling for the same reason that we do not feel the pressure of the atmosphere upon us, namely, that this pressure is so equable upon every side as not to be perceived; here is that in which our thankfulness may embody itself the best, if only we remember that with the duty (too often forgotten) of giving thanks there must go hand-in-hand that other duty (still more often neglected) of living these thanks as well.

Or, has He made a breach upon us; has the cup of pain, which comes to all, come also to us and to our lips; have we too discovered, that with the heritage of Adam's sin we have the heritage of Adam's sorrow, however for a moment it might have seemed as though we were to be exempt; where but in Him who smites, where but in the Smiter shall we find the Healer; where but in his hand who has made the wound, the balm and the medicine that can make us bear its present smart, and expect its future cure?

Or, are there times when all things here seem hollow and unreal, with vanity and emptiness written upon them; times when there seems to us, as there seemed once to the royal preacher at Jerusalem, no profit to a man of any labor wrought under the sun, but vanity of vanities, and all vanity ; what help is there against this, the worst sickness of the soul, save in laying hold of Him who is not hollow, not unreal, not a shadow nor a dream, who abides for ever, and who causes his servants to inherit substance ; what help but in laying hold of Him, as He can be only laid hold of in prayer ?

Or, again, are there other times when the world threatens to become too much to us, the near hillocks of time to hide from us the more distant mountains of eternity, earth's tinsel to outshine heaven's gold ; it is in God, in the light of his presence, as we press into that presence, that all things assume their due proportions, are seen in their true significance, the tinsel for tinsel, the gold for gold, that the hillocks subside, and the mountain-tops reappear, that the shadows flee away, and the eternal substances remain.

Or, is there some unwelcome task to be done to which duty plainly points, but which we would fain avoid, some cross which our God would have us to take up, but from which we shrink with a shuddering fear ; it is only in Him from whom all strength proceeds, who bore his own cross so meekly up the hill of scorn, that we shall find a strength which is equal to this need.

Or, do we need (and who is there that does not need ?) that peace which is above all peace, that purged conscience which only the precious blood of the Lamb slain before the foundation of the world can impart, it is in prayer to the Father of mercies, as He may be approached through his dear Son, that this boon and blessing, the best even in the rich treasury of heaven, this conscience purged from sin, from its guilt, its stain, and its power, can be obtained.

To sum up all which has been said :—consider the great High Priest of our profession, who Himself showed the way of obedience to his own precept, " that men ought always to pray, and not to faint :" consider too for ourselves the blessedness of being allowed to bathe our spirit's wings as in living streams, of running and not being weary ; of being able to bring everything that is distorted within us, that it may be made straight ; everything that is weak, that it may be strengthened ; all that is dark, that it may be illumined ; all that is rebellious, that it may be subdued ;—consider this, and Who it is that invites, beckons, entreats, commands us to this ; and then consider how great at once our guilt and our folly must be, if, with such a throne of grace provided for us, we only approach it languidly and rarely ; if, with such powers of the world to come brought within our reach, we do not earnestly lay hold of them ; how just our doom will be, if, when God was ready to give, we did not care to ask ; if, when He was waiting to be found, we were not willing to seek ; if, when heaven's door would have opened to our knocking, we counted ourselves so far unworthy of eternal life, or rather counted eternal life so little to us, that we did not care so much as earnestly to knock at that door.

SERMON XXX.

THE LONG-SUFFERING OF CHRIST.

Thy gentleness hath made me great.—PSALM xviii. 35.

LONG-SUFFERING, or slowness to anger, is the
glory of man, as it is the glory of God. It is the
glory of man, as is well declared in those words of the
wise king of Israel, " The discretion of a man deferreth
his anger, and it is his glory to pass over a transgression ;" words which, like all the words of this book
of Proverbs, the more we meditate upon them, the
more their wonderful depth and wisdom will appear.
Weak and violent men,—and commonly those who
are one are also the other, weakness and violence
going hand in hand, and completing one another,—
are swift to wrath, unable to defer it, unable, where
this behoves, to lay it wholly aside, and to pass over
a transgression. But the wise, and those for whom
any glory may justly be claimed, are very far from
this impotence of mind. Not that they cannot on
just occasion, in the cause, for instance, of God and
of his outraged truth, be angry. But they will be
slow to anger ; not roused to it without a cause, or
on every slight and trivial provocation ; and still
slower to execute the suggestions of anger, as knowing how easily these may be precipitate, or excessive ;

(324)

and even where they are not violations of strict justice, still violations of that charity which " suffereth long and is kind."

But it is of this long-suffering, not as it is the glory of man, but the glory of God, that I desire this day to speak. It is indeed a constant attribute of Him; one which He evermore in Scripture claims for Himself, which those who speak good things of Him evermore claim for Him. When the Lord, on a very solemn occasion, namely, the second giving of the law, passed before Moses, and proclaimed to him his Name, what was the Name which He proclaimed? It was this, " The Lord, the Lord God, merciful and gracious, long-suffering, and abundant in goodness and truth ; keeping mercy for thousands, forgiving iniquity and transgression and sin."* This is the chief passage ; but there are also many more to the same effect, which will easily suggest themselves to your remembrance.

But this slowness to anger, this long-suffering or forbearance on God's part toward those who provoke Him every day, and in the face of all their provocations, what, it may be asked, does it particularly declare concerning Him, that He should thus claim it as a part of his excellent greatness?

It declares, in the first place, his *power*. He has no need to hasten his work, lest if He do not execute a sentence at once, He may not be able to execute it at all, the offender in some way or other eluding his grasp, and escaping beyond his reach. There can be

* Exod. xxxiv. 6.

no fugitives from his justice who fills heaven and earth, to whom all the ages and all the worlds belong. What he does not punish now, He can punish by and by; what he does not punish here, He can punish there; what not in this world, in the next. He is, in the words of the Psalmist, "strong and patient;" patient, because He is strong, because all power belongeth unto Him. What need for him to be in a hurry? He may well defer his anger who has all time and all eternity in which to work out the counsels of his will, whom none can escape, being as He is Lord and absolute disposer of men alike on this side of the grave and on the other.

But the long-suffering of God declares better things than these, tells of attributes in Him more glorious even than his power. It is a declaration of his *love*, not willing that any should perish, but that all should come to repentance. Here is the true secret of Christ's forbearance with sinners. He knows what powers of the world to come are at work in his church for their conversion, and, being converted, for their perfect restoration to spiritual health and strength; the efficacy of that blood which He once, and once for all, shed upon his cross, the prevailing might of that intercession which He is evermore carrying forward in heaven. He knows the effectual operation of the Holy Spirit in quickening those that were even dead in their trespasses and sins. He knows how the man who is standing out the most obstinately against Him now, who is most fiercely in arms against his own blessedness, may to-morrow throw down his arms, yield himself vanquished, and suffer himself to be led, like Paul, a trophy and captive of the divine power and love through the world.

And as the eye of the cunning lapidary detects in the rugged pebble, just digged from the mine, the polished diamond that shall sparkle on the diadem of a king ; or as the sculptor in the rough block of marble, newly hewn from the quarry, beholds the statue of perfect grace and beauty which is latent there, and waiting but the touch of his hand,—so He who sees all, and the end from the beginning, sees oftentimes greater wonders than these. He sees the saint in the sinner, the saint that shall be in the sinner that is ; the wheat in the tare ; the shepherd feeding the sheep in the wolf tearing the sheep ; Paul the preacher of the faith in Saul the persecutor of the faith ; Israel a prince with God in Jacob the trickster and the supplanter ; Matthew the apostle in Levi the publican ; a woman that should love much in the woman that was sinning much ; and in some vine of the earth bringing forth wild grapes and grapes of gall, a tree which shall yet bring forth good fruit, and wine to make glad the heart ; so that when some, like those over-zealous servants in the parable, would have Him to pluck it up, and to cast it without more ado into the wine-press of the wrath of Almighty God, He exclaims rather, " Destroy it not, for a blessing is in it ;" and is well content to await the end.

And even where this proves not so, where the riches of that grace and long-suffering appear to have been spent in vain, wasted upon obdurate sinners, who despise these to the last, still the manifestations of that grace and long-suffering shall not therefore have been for naught. They shall have served their purpose, and if not that purpose which He most desired, which was nearest his heart, namely, that of bringing men to repentance and to life,—if not that, yet another ; I mean that of clearing the righteousness of God. For God in his infinite condescension is not content with merely *being* just and righteous in all his ways ; He desires to approve Himself such, and that his justice and righteousness and goodness should so plainly appear to all the world, so lifted above all cavil, that none should be able, with the less apparent grounds of reason, to call it in question. And thus, in regard of the final condemnation of wicked men, and that severe and terrible doom which He shall one day execute upon them, He will be clear when He is judged ; every mouth shall be stopped. No one shall be able to say that the long-suffering of God had not waited for him ; or that, however guilty, he had, like the wretched Haman, been hastened and huddled to his doom.*

So far from this, nothing is more remarkable than the slow advent of the divine judgments. The king's wrath may be as messengers of death, but because it is so, therefore it is long before the King of kings suffers his whole displeasure to arise. Note, I beseech you, the way in which He warns before He threatens, threatens before He strikes, strikes lightly before He strikes heavily, strikes heavily before He causes that blow

---

* Esther vii. 8–10.

which shall leave no room for another to descend. Note how this is so everywhere, in Scripture, in the lives of others, and in your own. Note it in Scripture. If God brings in a flood on the world of the ungodly, it is only after his long-suffering has waited for them while the Ark was a-preparing ; * and though his Spirit, as on that occasion He declared, should not always strive with man, "yet his days," that is, his days of grace, "shall be an hundred and twenty years." Again, " the iniquity of the Amorites is not yet full ;"† therefore they are allowed still to abide in the land, and their excision root and branch is for centuries deferred ; they must fill up the measure of their sins before their judgment can arrive. The guilty cities, Sodom and Gomorrah, cannot perish before God has gone down and seen whether they have done altogether according to the cry of it ; ‡ words spoken after the manner of men, yet with a blessed truth behind them, that, namely, of the extreme deliberation with which the divine judgments proceed. And this patience, this long-suffering, this deliberation, they are, as I have said, if possible, for the salvation of man ; and if not for this, if he is resolute to perish, if he has made a covenant with death and hell which he will not break, then for the vindication of God, that He may be justified in his doings, and clear when He is judged.

My dear brethren, spared to see another Lent, that season when it so well becomes us to consider the relation between our sins and God's judgments on the one

* 1 Pet. iii. 20.   † Gen. xv. 16.   ‡ Gen. xviii. 21.

hand, our sins and his mercies on the other; if such as I have described it is the meaning of God's forbearance with us sinners, it concerns us very nearly that we inquire what interpretation we have put, or are putting, upon it. Plainly there are two ways in which it may be accepted by us. There is a blessed use, and also a most wicked abuse, which we may make of it. Surely he makes a wicked abuse, who, through a seeming impunity, is emboldened in sinning; begins to argue that the eyes of the Lord are *not* in every place, beholding the evil and the good; that He does *not* set a difference between him that serveth Him and him that serveth Him not; that all things come alike to all; the man who says to himself, I have done evil, and no harm has happened to me, and in this thought strengthens himself to do it again. It is only too frequent an abuse of God's long-suffering. " Because sentence against an evil work is not executed speedily, therefore the heart of the sons of men is fully set in them to do evil."*

But this tardiness of vengeance, this lame foot with which it seems to lag and halt after successful wickedness, this fact that sentence against an evil work is not executed immediately, means something very different from that which it is thus taken to mean. It is no pledge of safety to the sinner. It argues no listlessness, no moral indifference to the eternal distinctions between good and evil on the part of Him who is the Judge of the whole earth, and by whom actions are weighed.

* Eccles. viii. 11.

Neither is it that He is talking, or pursuing, or on a journey, or sleeping, and therefore could not avenge, if He chose, with the quick recoil and prompt backstroke of justice, his own violated law.

But what does it mean? It means, first, that Christ has died, died for sinners; and thus the decree, "In the day that thou sinnest thou shalt surely die," has been suspended for *all* sinners, and may yet be reversed, if thou wilt repent and believe, for thee. It means, that there is yet room for thee to say, What have I done? to take words, and turn to thy God, and thus to have all thy sins blotted out, done away, cast into the deep of the sea, not mentioned against thee any more. But shouldst thou, alas, put these benefits away, this long-suffering of God means also, that He who fills heaven and earth, who is from everlasting to everlasting, can afford to wait. Why should He not? Where wilt thou go where his hand cannot reach thee, where his justice cannot overtake thee? Wilt thou take the wings of the morning, and dwell in the uttermost parts of the sea, He is there. Wilt thou climb up to heaven, or dig down to hell, He is there also. Flee *from* Him thou canst not. To flee *to* Him is thy only way of deliverance.

Oh, then, if one is here present to-day who is at this moment despising the riches of the goodness and forbearance and long-suffering of God, arguing from past impunity to future, blessing himself in his heart, and saying, "I shall have peace, though I walk in the imagination of mine heart, to add drunkenness to thirst,"*

* Deut. xxix. 19.

believe nothing of the kind. The judgments of God which thou art defying may be slow in arriving, but they arrive at last, and oftentimes only the more terrible for their delay. The old heathen, whom we often think of as so dark, were yet not so dark but that they understood this; for they had a proverb, "The mill of God grinds late, but grinds to powder;" and we have our own to match it, "Vengeance has leaden feet, but iron hands;" leaden feet to mark how slow its approaches often are, iron hands to signify the crushing weight with which it comes down at the last. Take, then, oh, take this forbearance of God to thee as He intended, as He still intends it. He by it leadeth thee to repentance. He does not drive, He does not drag, He does not compel; thou mayest, alas, resist if thou wilt; but He leadeth thee to repentance, draws thee, if only thou wilt follow. Kiss the Son, lest He be angry indeed; consent to be blessed by Him, to be pardoned, to be healed; consent to be one of those who shall say to Him through the ages of a blissful eternity, "Thy gentleness hath made me great."

But whether thou wilt or no, a few words I must say, ere we close, to *you*, brethren beloved in the Lord, who *have* understood what the meaning of this long-suffering of Christ to you might be, who have had grace given you to profit by it, to you whom his gentleness has made great. See, I would say, that you greatly praise Him for this. If you do not praise Him, no other will. The sinner, so long as he is in his sin, understands nothing of this forbearance of Christ; though he is himself then the most signal and immediate object of it. He must have come out of his sin before he perceives anything of this. Then, indeed, he will never cease to admire the long-suffering which has spared him and saved him; as the man who has come out of his drunkenness stands in wonder and awe at the perilous places, the abrupt edges of precipices, on which he walked just now, and knew not that God kept him back when there was but a single step between him and death. Exactly so, men must have come out of their sin before they can praise God, who spared them in their sin.

Meanwhile you must praise Him on their behalf and on your own. And, ah, when you praise Him on your own, when you praise the long-suffering which waited for your repentance, do not limit the times of his forbearance to those times of your former ignorance, as though you had not experienced and had not needed that same forbearance since. Thou hast needed, and wilt need it to the very end. True, thou dost not any longer drink up iniquity like water, nor do evil with both hands earnestly, nor sin presumptuously and with a high hand against God. But yet measure back in memory the way which thou hast trodden since thou hast known Him, his grace, his loving-kindness, since He met thee with the kiss of peace, and put on thee the new robe, and called thee by a new name; and then ask thyself where thou wouldst now be, if that hour of reconciliation had been the final limit of his forbearance; if thou hadst not had ever since to do with a Saviour of infinite forbearance; if He, an Advocate with the Father, who first made for thee a way to the throne of grace, had not kept that way continually open, which thou by thy later sins wouldst else long ago have effectually blocked up and obstructed again.   For number up, if thou canst, the provocations with which thou hast provoked Him since the day that thou knewest Him— thy heartless prayers, thy wandering devotions, thy careless communions; all thine excess in things permitted; all thy allowance of things doubtful; all thy dalliance with temptations; thy vain thoughts, and covetous desires, and proud imaginations; thy murmurings, thy disputings, thy discontents; all thy rash, foolish, uncharitable words; all thy harsh judgments and speeches about others; all in which thou hast sought ease for thyself and shunned labor, evaded the Cross of Christ and the reproach of Christ,—the thousand forms of thy sin;—number up all these, each of them, it may be, severally small, yet not small as committed against so great love, and, alas, making up by their multitude what they may have wanted in their weight; and then ask thyself what would be thy place now in the church of the redeemed, what would be thy place hereafter in the church of the glorified— would it be a place at all—except for a forbearance higher than heaven?—and see that thou bless and praise God, not merely that thou hadst once, and in times past, to do with a Lord of infinite long-suffering, but that thou hast to do with such an One now, and wilt *have* such, as thou wilt *need* such, even to the end.

SERMON XXXI.

DAVID'S SIN, REPENTANCE, PARDON, AND PUNISHMENT.

And David said unto Nathan, I have sinned against the Lord. And Nathan said unto David, The Lord also hath put away thy sin; thou shalt not die. Howbeit, because by this deed thou hast given great occasion to the enemies of the Lord to blaspheme, the child also that is born unto thee shall surely die.—2 SAMUEL, xii. 13, 14.

THE story of David's great sin, of the great forgiveness which blotted out that sin, of the great punishment in this present time which, notwithstanding, followed that sin, all this is familiar to us ; yet not so familiar but that we may find in it lessons which, if old, are also new, which may again and again be profitably prest home upon our hearts. Some of these I shall endeavor to draw out from this Scripture, and, as I would fain trust, for your profit and for mine.

When we read, then, the history of David's fall, what surprises and somewhat perplexes us, at the first, is, the apparent suddenness of it. There seems no preparation, no warning. It is as though the sun, with no announcement beforehand, should suffer a total eclipse at noonday. It will generally happen that these falls, sudden and inexplicable as to a remote or careless observer they may appear, are yet explicable enough. Some careless walking, some worldly habits,

some self-indulgent ways, these sufficiently account for
a catastrophe which, with all its seeming suddenness,
had yet, in fact, been long in preparing. Neglected
duties, slurred over or omitted prayers, unmortified
corruptions, pride, self-confidence, worldliness, these
had eaten into and eaten out the heart of the man's
religion ; and thus, when the blast of a sudden temptation struck him, he fell ; as a tree decayed at the
core might fall in an instant, although to a careless
beholder it had showed, only an instant before, as
green and strong as any tree in the forest.

But, indeed, if we look closely at David's history,
and with the anxious scrutiny which such a case deserves, we shall perceive that it furnishes no exception.
If only we look back to the first verse of the chapter
preceding, we shall find the explanation there ; not
obtruded, not thrust upon us, for that is not the way
of Scripture ; but yet an intimation sufficiently given
of this, namely, *how* it came to pass that the man of
God, the man after God's own heart, should have ever
given room for words like these to be written about
him : "But the thing that David had done displeased
the Lord."*   We find it written there, " At the time
when kings go forth to battle, David sent Joab, and
his servants with him, and all Israel, and they besieged Rabbah, but David tarried still at Jerusalem."†
Had he gone himself, "at the time when kings go forth
to battle," instead of sending Joab, how different
would have been the issue of all. Had he been endur-

<hr>

* 2 Sam. xii. 27.   † 2 Sam. xi. 1.

ing hardness with the armies of Israel, these temptations to luxury and uncleanness would probably never have come near him; certainly he would not have succumbed beneath them. But he whom adversity could not break, who had kept himself true to God when he was chased like a partridge on the hills, was giving way under the flatteries of prosperity, the seductions of ease.

What teaching, my brethren, is here. Surely if the Scripture has said, "In the day of adversity consider,"* it might have said, indeed it has said in a thousand ways, In the day of prosperity beware. When all things are going well with thee; when thou hast no trouble anywhere, no thorn in the flesh, no least cloud in the firmament above thee; when it seems as though God had made an hedge about thee, and about thine house, and about all that thou hast, on every side; when the world speaks thee fair, and thy very enemies are at peace with thee,—then be thou ware. This time, which thou countest perhaps a time of no trial at all, may be indeed the time for thee of thy chiefest trial of all; whether thou wilt be still quick and earnest in prayer, when that prayer is not wrung out from thee by some pressing and urgent need; whether thou wilt be still watchful over thyself, when there is so much to persuade to unwatchfulness; whether thou wilt still gird up the loins of thy mind, when there is so much that would lead thee to ungird them. If thou sittest still when thou oughtest to be going forth to the battle of

* Eccl. vii. 14.

15

the Lord, if thou puttest others to labors from which thou shrinkest thyself; who can say how near the day of thy fall may be? Suddenly, in an instant, some great sin, matter of grief for the church and of mockery for the world, shall overtake thee. Or, if not this, yet worse than this; all thy good resolutions, thy holy practices, shall thaw and melt away under this sun of worldly prosperity; and though thou fall not, as David fell, into one notorious transgression, yet, for thee more perilous still, the world may, little by little, draw thee back altogther into its own bosom, assimilate thee wholly to itself. Take, then, this for a first lesson, that prosperous times are perilous times. "In all times of our wealth, good Lord, deliver us."

But here is another teaching; the way, namely, in which sins are linked to one another, in which, as by a terrible necessity, one leads on to a second, and the second to a third, and so on. David, giving way to his lust, meant to be an adulterer; but he did not mean to incur the woe pronounced against him "that giveth his neighbor drink, that puttest thy bottle to him, that makest him drunken also;'* still less did he intend to be a murderer. "Is thy servant a dog, that he should do this great thing?"† would assuredly have been his indignant reply, if any had shown him this in the prospect, this as the goal towards which he was bound. It is still the same. The tempter shows but a single step. It is only this one thing, and then thou mayest stop; only thus far, and then thou mayest

---

* Hab. ii. 15; cf. 2 Samuel xii. 13.   † 2 Kings viii. 13.

pause, or go back, if thou wilt. But it never proves so. The great enemy of souls is in nothing more skilful than in breaking down the bridges of retreat behind the sinner. Wrong may become worse wrong, but it never becomes right. " Let them fall from one wickedness to another ;"—one has said, and has well said, that this curse is the most fearful one pronounced anywhere in the scripture ; sin punished with worse sin ; the sinner handed over from crime to crime ; thinking to do a little evil, and finding himself inexorably bound in to much. Oh, how often has this repeated itself in the history of men.. They have launched themselves a little, it was to be only a very little, from the safe shore of God's commandments ; and currents and tides and eddies, of which they knew nothing and dreamt nothing, have presently caught them, and borne them quite out of sight of land, to be swallowed up in quicksands or dashed on rocks ; in one way or another to make miserable shipwreck of all. Close walking with God is the only safe walking.

Then do not miss this lesson,—the ignoble servitude to men in which the sinner is very often through his sin entangled. Mark, for it is very instructive, how David becomes in fact the servant of Joab, from the moment that he has made Joab the partaker of his evil counsels, the accomplice of his crime. And Joab feels this, and will make David feel it too. What covert irony and scorn is couched in the message in which the ungodly captain announces to the king* that

* 2 Sam. xi. 20.

his will has been accomplished, and Uriah is no more. Then note the insolent and taunting speeches which Joab in aftertimes addressed to David, but which the king did not venture to resent;* the acts of violence, directly contrary to the king's will and honor, as, for instance, the murder of Abner,† in which he allowed himself, but which David as little ventured to punish. We can only account for all this on one supposition. There was a guilty secret between the two; Joab had but to speak the word, and David would stand a con- victed murderer before all his people. Joab was, therefore, David's master. Let no man in this sense be thy master. Let no man know that of thee, which if he chose to reveal, would cast thee down from the fair esteem and reputation which thou enjoyest before men. That man in his worldly position may be as the dirt beneath thy feet, but he is indeed thy master; se- cretly thou tremblest before him; and he knows this, and will make thee feel that he knows it. So live, so walk, a child of light and of the day, that thou need- est fear nothing, though every man should proclaim in market-places and on house-tops the very worst about thee that he knows.

And yet once more; note the darkness of heart which sin brings over its servants. David is not en- tangled merely in the sin of a moment, borne away by the passion of an instant, then to look back with hor- ror and dismay at what in his brief madness he has done. For well-nigh a whole year he has lain in his

---

* 2 Sam. xix. 5–7.   † Ibid. xviii. 5, 14; xx. 10.

sin, for a large part of this time in his double sin, each of them a damning one ; and yet all the while his conscience is in a death-like sleep, so that it needs a thunder voice as from heaven, the rebuke of a prophet, to rouse him from this lethargy. And who was it that thus slept this sleep of death ? Was it a common man, one who had never known what it was to walk near to God and in the light of his countenance ; one who had never had any clear insight into the length and breadth and spirituality of God's law ; one who had never been jealous with a godly jealousy over himself and all his ways ? It was none of these. Rather, it was one who had testified in so many ways his insight into the length and breadth of the law of the Lord, his sense of God's favor and the light of his countenance as better than the life itself. Wonder of wonders, it is he who thus lies so long, dead in his trespass and his guilt. So strange is the deceitfulness of sin ; to be compared to nothing more fitly than to that vampire-bat which we read of in the West Indies, that sucks the blood of the sleeper, and ever the meanwhile fans him with its mighty wings, that he may not waken, but still sink and sink into deeper slumber, though his very life-blood is being drained away. Was there any likelihood that David would have *ever* wakened, if God had not sent him that message ; shown him, who could see so clearly the mote in another's eye,* the beam in his own ; if the words of the prophet, "Thou art the man," had never rung in his ears ?

<hr>

* 2 Samuel xii. 5.

19*

"Thou art the man." Arrows shot at a venture have sometimes found their way through the joints of a sinner's armor ; but here was an arrow, shot with so true an aim that it could not miss its mark, or fail to come home. Promptly on that word follows another word, even the unreserved confession of the royal culprit, so striking in its simplicity, " I have sinned against the Lord ;" and then on that the free forgiveness of a gracious God, " The Lord also hath put away thy sin ; thou shalt not die." Many things are here to observe ; and first, the blessing that goes along with a full, free, unreserved confession of sin, being, as this is, the sure token of a true repentance. So long as a man puts himself on the defensive with God, seeks excuses for himself, would justify himself in whole or in part, so long there is no real, certainly no thorough, work of grace in his heart. The Spirit has not convinced him of sin ; he has not yet seen the glory, the all-sufficiency, of Christ, else he would not seek help in the fewness of his sins, but in the multitude of God's mercies in Christ Jesus ; he would not say, as he is now saying, Heal my sin, *for it is small ;* but, as the Psalmist said, " Heal my sin, *for it is great.*" Go through all Scripture and you will everywhere find, that where repentance is sincere, there confession is ample. The man gives all glory to God, and takes all shame to himself. This is, in one sense, all that a man can do after he has offended. He cannot do away the least tittle of his offences ; he cannot pay off a single penny of the ten thousand talents in which he is indebted ; but he can put his mouth in the dust, and say, " Righteousness belongeth unto Thee, but unto us confusion of face;" but he can say, "I have sinned against the Lord;" and until he says this from his heart, his sin remaineth. He hides it, and therefore God will lay it bare; he makes little of it, and therefore God will make much; he does not judge it, and therefore God will.

What a motive here for coming to Him with true hearts; concealing nothing, extenuating nothing, justifying nothing; keeping back from Him not one of the hurts and sores of our souls; though we could not endure to show them to the dearest and most trusted friend that we have, lest he should loathe and abhor us, that we should yet show them unto Him. He will not loathe and abhor; He is the same gracious God upon the throne of heaven, who on earth touched the leper, and suffered Himself to be touched by the woman that was a sinner. He will touch the leprous spot in our souls, and even there, at his cleansing touch, the flesh will come again as the flesh of a little child; and that sin which, unconfessed, and therefore unforgiven, should have appeared to our endless confusion on that day, shall now be put quite away, sought for and not found; for He shall have cast it behind his back, into the depths of the sea, into any place where it shall not appear any more for ever. So blessed are the fruits of free, unreserved, hearty confession of sin.

And yet, my Christian brethren, while it was thus in regard of the eternal penalty of David's sins, while he who has fully confessed is fully forgiven, there is still, as concerns this present life, a sad "howbeit" behind : "Howbeit, because by this deed thou hast given great occasion to the enemies of the Lord to blaspheme, the child that is born to thee shall surely die ;" and with this the prophecy of a woe reaching much further, of sorrows searching far more deeply, than this of a new-born infant's death : "Now, therefore, the sword shall never depart from thine house. . . . Behold, I will raise up evil against thee out of thine house," with more to the same effect. You see how it fared with him. God restored his favor to him ; David walked again in the light of God's countenance ; he was most truly his child ; forgiven, cleansed, received back. It was not that God forgave him only partially, and so punished him still. There is no such thing as a partial forgiveness ; it is yes or no ; God forgives all or none ; a man is in his sin, or he is not in his sin. David was not in his sin ; God's word by the prophet had absolved him from that ; and yet this stroke came upon him at once, and in a little while those others which were behind it ; for this was only the beginning of sorrows, and far sadder and more searching were behind. The sword never did depart from his house ; evil did rise up against him from the bosom of his own family. It is hardly too much to say, that his after story, to the end of his life, is a scroll written within and without with lamentations, and mourning, and woe.

Do you ask how this could be, how this was reconcilable with the free and full forgiveness which he had just received? In this way. God had taken from him the eternal penalty of his sin ; He had said,

" Thou shalt not die ;" but He had never said, Thy
sin shall not be bitter to thee. Nay rather, it should
be bitter. He should see the stamp and visible im-
press of his own sin in all the thousand shapes of suffering and anguish which should visit him henceforth.
He had violated the awful sanctities of the family
life ; had defiled the wife, and slain the husband with
the sword ; all was measured back into his bosom ;
quarrels, incests, rebellions, murders, stroke upon stroke,
breach upon breach, blood touching blood, fearful
crimes more fearfully avenged,—these, as they fill up
the pages of the after history of David, declare to us
that the word of the prophet was not spoken in vain,
that it did not fall to the ground ; that the thing
which David had done had displeased, and greatly
displeased, the Lord.

Would God we might all lay to heart as they deserve the most serious and most solemn lessons which
are here ! God may forgive his children their sin ;
yea, if they claim forgiveness aright, in the one prevailing name, He will forgive them, He must forgive
them ; his faithfulness and his justice are pledged to
it ; and yet, for all this, He may make their sin most
bitter to them here ; teaching them in this way its
evil, which they might else have been in danger of forgetting, the aggravation which there is in the sins of a
child, in sins against light, against knowledge, against
love. Ah, brethren, how easily may we be laying up
sorrow for ourselves against a day that is coming,
weaving dark and sombre threads into the innermost
tissue of our lives, stripping bare those lives of some

richest blessing in the future, which now in very faithfulness our God must withhold from us. Oh, then, if we would lead happy Christian lives; if we would not thus sow to ourselves large harvests of a future sorrow; if we would not hush the voices of joy in our homes; if we would spare ourselves many a stroke, many a wound, which will else come upon us, let us seek to lead holy lives, fleeing from sin as from the face of a serpent. The sins of God's saints and servants, let them not embolden us to sin; for we see how they were plagued for their offences. Rather let those sins of theirs be motives to us for watchfulness, motives for fear, motives for a close and careful walking with God. If David, after all his acquaintance with the things of God, was betrayed by a corrupt and treacherous heart, what may not I fear from the corruption and treachery of mine? If he, a standard-bearer, fell, how shall I, the least and weakest in the host of the Lord, hope to stand, unless I lean on some higher and better strength than my own? This mournful story of David's sin will not have been written in vain for us, if it thus sends us in more humble, earnest, frequent prayer to God; if we take the precept of the Apostle, "Be not high-minded, but fear," as for us the moral of all.

SERMON XXXII.

WHAT WE CAN, AND WHAT WE CANNOT, CARRY AWAY WHEN WE DIE.

He shall carry nothing away with him when he dieth; neither shall his pomp follow him.—PSALM xlix. 17 (Prayer-Book version).

I REMEMBER an eastern legend, which I have always thought furnished a remarkable, though unconscious, commentary on these words of the Psalmist. Alexander the Great, we are there told, being upon his deathbed, commanded that, when he was carried forth to the grave, his hands should not be wrapped, as was usual, in the sereloths, but should be left outside the bier, so that all men might see them, and might see that they were *empty;* that there was nothing in them; that he, born to one empire, and the conqueror of another, the possessor, while he lived, of two worlds, of the East and of the West and of the treasures of both, yet now when he was dead could retain no smallest portion of those treasures; that in this matter the poorest beggar and he were at length upon equal terms. This was his comment, or the comment of those who may have devised this legend, on the text of the Psalmist, "He shall carry nothing away with him, when he dieth; neither shall his pomp follow him." This was his anticipation of the declaration of the Apostle, "We brought nothing into this world, and it is certain we can carry nothing out."

And we may here fitly ask with Solomon, " What can the man do that cometh after the king?". If it was thus with that mightiest king, shall it not, by much stronger reason, be thus with meaner men? They too must leave what they have gotten to others ; for they cannot carry it away with them, one jot or tittle of it, to that other world for which they are bound. And that word *leave*, which I have just employed, how striking is the use we make of it in our common conversation, when we are speaking of the disposition of his property which some one who is lately dead has made. We say, perhaps, he has *left* a good deal, *left* a good estate to this son, a large portion to that daughter. We do but use the word as a synonym for *bequeathed*. But what unconscious irony there is in the phrase ; what a profound lesson, as there is in so many of our common phrases, if we would but give heed to it. Yes, indeed, he *has* left it ; as others, many of them far mightier than he, have left whatever they called here for a little while their own ; as Dives has *left* his purple and fine linen, and that other rich man his " much goods laid up for many years,"* and Ahab his ivory palaces, and Pharaoh his " treasures of Egypt," and Alexander the wealth of two worlds,—he has *left* it, and not for a little season, but for ever. Surely such phrases as these, *leaving* a fortune, *leaving* a good estate, which

* Luke xii. 19.

are so common in men's mouths, have a deeper significance than we are' wont to give them ; witness for
most solemn truths, if we would but listen to, and lay
to heart the witness which they bear. We do, indeed,
in this common language of ours, unconsciously set
our seal to the words of the Psalmist, " He shall carry
nothing away with him, when he dieth ; neither shall
his pomp follow him."

Nor may we suppose, when we hear such words as
these, that they are merely warnings to *rich* men, to
those who have much to leave. They are warnings to
all men. A man may cleave to a few things as closely
as to many, to a hut as passionately as to a palace ;
may forget or abuse his stewardship in the dispensation of one talent as effectually as in the dispensation
of ten. When Christ said, " Take heed and beware
of covetousness," He was not speaking to a select few
among the rich and great of the earth, but to a mixed
multitude, and one gathered mainly from the humbler
classes of society. It is "*the love* of money" which is
" the root of all evil ;" and all may be guilty of this
inordinate love ; alike those who have it, and those
who desire to have it ; those who exult in treasures
which they have, and those who pine for treasures
which they have not. It would be a very serious
mistake, if warnings like the present were assumed by
those who heard them to be addressed to one class
alone. They are addressed to all. The inordinate
desire of the things of this world ; the temptation to
trust in them rather than in the living God ; to forget
that in anything which we have here we are not pos-

sessors in fee, but tenants-at-will, liable, therefore, to be turned out at any moment ; this temptation is common to us all, being as it is the birth of that natural corruption, of that mind averted *from* God and *to* the earth, which is not one man's more than another's, which is every man's. And when the hour has come, it is as true of the beggar as of the king, that " he shall carry nothing away with him, when he dieth." If the one must leave his sceptre and his crown, the other must leave his staff and his wallet,—each must leave his all ; and who will dare to say that the beggar has not sometimes quitted his rags more reluctantly than the monarch his robes ; those who might seem to have almost nothing to leave in this life sometimes cleaving to it with a passion as intense, or, it may be, far intenser, than those who might seem to have almost everything to leave ? The lessons, therefore, of my text. and the considerations which it suggests, are for all,—high and low, rich and poor, great and small, one with another.

Let me set before you what appear to me one or two of the most important of these considerations. They shall be thoughts of comfort and encouragement ; for sadly as this announcement may present itself to us at the first, writing vanity on so many of the toils and hopes and accumulations of men, yet, looked at a little closer, it is not so sad as it appears.

For, in the first place, that a man shall carry away nothing with him when he dieth, is true only of his earthly goods ; which are, therefore, not *goods* in the highest and truest sense of the word. The tinsel, the

trappings, of men's outward existence, " the glories of
their birth and state," these, indeed, must all be stripped
off ; these must be laid aside in the vestuary of the
grave. But these are not all. There are other garments besides these : the garments of the soul, the
robe of humility, the marriage vestment of faith and
love, the raiment that has been made white in the
blood of the Lamb ; and as many as have put on these,
woven in the looms of heaven and with threads of
light, shall never be found naked and unclothed. In
like manner those that have listened to the loving
counsel of Christ, and bought of Him gold tried in
the fire that they may be rich, the precious treasure of
the knowledge of Him, these never shall be poor,—
no, not when they leave all things here. There is
something which they *can* carry away with them, when
they die ; not their worldly wealth, if they had such ;
in regard of that, the notable words of the Italian
proverb, " Our last garment," meaning our winding-
sheet, " is made without pockets," are as true for them
as for others. Of the largest worldly treasure they
shall carry away with them not so much as the single
penny which the blind heathen placed in the mouth of
their dead, that with it they might pay their passage
over the dark river that, in the dream of their imagination, encircled the shadowy kingdom of the grave.

But all of Christ and of Christ's which they have
made their own, all of his image, of his lineaments and
likeness, which has been stamped upon their souls, all
the graces which they have won, which have been in-
wrought in them, which have become part and parcel

of themselves, and of their new nature over which the grave has no power,—all these shall be a possession for ever. Instead of having to quit these at the summons of death, they shall then possess them by a much firmer, stronger hold than at any time they possessed them before. All is made sure for eternity. Here, then, is a thought of encouragement, of strong consolalation, that it is only the meaner things of earth which lie under the bondage of corruption, on which the sentence of vanity is written, which refuse to accompany their owners on that long last journey which, one day or other, every man must make. Whatever was of true value and dignity; whatever was really worth the winning; whatever was akin to the divine and immortal in man; whatever came to him from God through Christ,—and this includes every good and perfect gift,—of that nothing can rob him. He *shall* carry it away with him when he dieth, to be his riches, his treasure in the life eternal, as it was his riches and his treasure here. Surely our lesson from all this is contained in the words of the Saviour, " Labor not for the meat which perisheth ; " not, that is, first and chiefly for this, " but for that meat which endureth unto everlasting life." Seek to make that your own which has the stamp of God, and therefore the stamp of eternity, upon it.

But a second consideration, and a most practical one, which suggests itself, is this, that, even in regard of these earthly things, while it is quite true that a man can *carry* nothing of them away with him *when* he dies, he may *send* much of them before him while he lives. The Apostle Paul declares no less, when urging those who are rich that they be glad to distribute, he proposes this as a motive, that they will be thus "laying up in store for themselves a good foundation against the time to come."[*] Observe, I beseech you, the boldness of St. Paul in the language which he here uses. He is not afraid of being called a legalist, a preacher of good works, instead of a preacher of faith. He knew that he was not so; that he had said, in another place, "Other foundation can no man lay than that is laid, which is Jesus Christ;" a foundation which *we* do not lay, but which is laid for us. But having said this, having declared it, indeed, in a thousand forms, he did not shrink from employing the language which I have just quoted, namely, that men, by large and liberal giving, should be "laying up in store for themselves a good foundation against the time to come;" a foundation, indeed, which is only a good one when it rests on that other, that deeper foundation, which no man lays for himself, but which is laid for us of God, namely, the finished work and the perfect righteousness of Christ. We can carry nothing away with us, if we put off all to the last; but we can send as much as we will before us, if only we set about it in time, and have the heart and courage to trust God in the matter.

Supposing you were bound to some distant land, that it was no matter of choice, but of necessity, that you should travel thither, never to return again, and that, however well furnished here, there seemed no

* 1 Tim. vi. 19.

means of transmitting funds for your support when you arrived there, bills of exchange, letters of credit, and the like, not reaching so far ;—supposing it was impossible, from one cause or another, to carry these funds with you ; would you not, under these conditions, rejoice if one whom you could perfectly rely on offered and engaged that whatever you committed to him you should find there ; if he announced to you that he had channels of communication, though you had not ; that by help of these secret channels, whatever you placed in his hands should thus reappear for your behoof when you needed it the most? I ask, would you not welcome such tidings with a lively joy? Well, then, this is exactly what God says. This world is the land which we must leave; where we are only pilgrims and strangers for a time. At our death we set forth on the journey which we must all take ; that mysterious world beyond the grave is the land to which we are inevitably bound. We can carry nothing with us there ; we can send many things before us there ; that is, if we have courage, courage to believe God, to trust in his promises, in his faithfulness, in his truth ; to be sure that nothing is lost which is committed to Him ; no prayer, no alms-deed, no act of self-denial, no tear of penitence. He has bottles for these tears, books of remembrance for those deeds of love ; He is not unrighteous, to forget the least of these things that is wrought for his name's sake.

Be rich then, my Christian brethren, *toward* God ; be rich *with* God. These are the only durable riches, the only riches which a man can keep for ever ; all other either leave him, or he leaves them. I know that exhortations of this kind, especially exhortations to a large and liberal return to God of those things which He has so freely given to us, are in general appended to sermons dedicated to some charitable object. It seems to me very desirable that they should be sometimes not associated with these. Without having any hard thoughts of the preacher, it is easy on such occasions to persuade ourselves that he is making much of the duty for the special purpose before him, and that he would not press it so earnestly at another time; or else to satisfy ourselves with a slight and momentary response to his appeals, and then to relapse into our ordinary habits of selfish expenditure, of laying up treasures for ourselves, and not for God.

Believe me, such casual, desultory giving, giving merely when we are asked, and because we are asked, under the stress of a momentary excitement; instead of deliberately laying out our income and our expenditure beforehand on a scheme which would enable us to give liberally and give constantly, is for the most part of very little worth indeed. Sum up the whole amount of it at the end of the year,—I trust you do keep an account of your charities, that you may know how small they are,—and what a paltry and miserable sum-total it will prove. On some single pleasure, on some single amusement, on some single superfluity, on some single "need-not," as our ancestors strikingly called it, you will very probably have spent more, perhaps many times more, than on God's church and on God's poor.

If you desire, my Christian brethren, at all to fulfil God's will in regard of the earthly mammon whereof you are the dispensers here; if you would not be fools for eternity, however wise and prudent you may be accounted in time, beggars in that coming world, however rich and prosperous in this present; make this a fixed resolution, and keep it, that some well-defined portion of your income shall be devoted to God. I presume not to say how much. That is a matter for the conscience of every man. It belongs to the freedom of the gospel that each man must here be a law unto himself; only beware lest this freedom become a snare. But having determined this proportion, do not go back from it. Diminish not the firstfruits of your hand. Increase them if you will and if you can, but do not diminish. I would by no means conceal, that such a rule as this, honestly laid down, and honestly carried out, as in the sight of God who is not mocked, will cost you something; that it may oblige you to make a less figure in the world than otherwise you would have done, to abridge yourself of some pleasures, to exercise some habits of self-denial. But what is it we want? Is it that our offerings shall be such as shall cost us nothing, as shall not interfere in the least with the pride of our life, as shall leave us every one of our indulgences untouched? I fear it is often so. But it is not this which God's Word demands, which Christ, who gave *Himself* for us, requires, even as He has a right to require, at our hands; it is not by aid of such that we shall ever lay up in store a good foundation against the time to come.

SERMON XXXIII.

WALKING WITH CHRIST IN WHITE.

They shall walk with Me in white; for they are worthy. He that overcometh, the same shall be clothed in white raiment.—REV. iii. 4, 5.

HOLY SCRIPTURE is full of promises. Eternal life is set out to us there in a thousand alluring forms, under a thousand attractive images, such as appeal to our affections, our imaginations, our hopes. We are not barely and coldly told that it is an infinite good, and then left to realize as we best can, by aid of our own fancies, that good to ourselves; but the goodness, the glory, the beauty, the blessedness of it, are brought home to us by a thousand gracious assistances which God's Word itself supplies. Eternal life, it is to eat of the hidden manna, yea, of the tree of life in the midst of the Paradise of God; it is to be a pillar in the temple of God that shall go out no more; it is to be a citizen of the New Jerusalem, the city which comes down out of heaven from God; it is to receive at Christ's hands a crown of life; it is to sit with Christ upon his throne; or, as here in my text, it is to walk with Christ in white, even in the pure and shining garments of immortality.

And it was most graciously ordered of God, who

has given these Scriptures to his church, that they should be thus full of these glorious promises ; that life eternal should be thus set forth to us in all these alluring, winning, enticing forms, which kindle our affections, which captivate our imaginations, which draw our hearts. There are promises in abundance on the other side. The devil is a great promiser ; the world is a great promiser ; the flesh is a great promiser ;—lying promisers all, liars from the beginning, who keep none of the promises which they make to the children of men ; but evermore deceive, delude, and betray them ; but still their mouths are full of promises. Satan says, Eat of the tree of knowledge of good and evil, and ye shall be as gods. The world, pointing to some of its painted toys, its gilded vanities, says, All these will I give thee, if thou wilt fall down and worship me. The flesh says, To-morrow shall be as to-day, and much more abundantly ; you shall never tire of my joys ; you shall never draw dry the fountains of my delight.

And who that knows anything of the deceitfulness of his own heart but will confess the power and potency which these promises exert. We may have proved them false and deceivable a thousand times, and yet they are still able to attract and to allure, too often to deceive and to betray. What need, then, that mightier promises should be set over against these, more potent lures, magnets of heaven over against these magnets of hell. What need that against the false splendors of the world should be set the true glories of heaven, so that those other might have no glory by reason of the glory which excelleth. Therefore is it that there are in Scripture such exceeding great and precious promises,—God setting against the shows of earth the substances of heaven ; the gold of heaven against the tinsel of earth ; pleasures which never fade against pleasures that are but for a season ; crowns of life against crowns that wither in a day. He multiplies these, that by them we " might be partakers of the divine nature, having escaped the corruption that is in the world through lust ;* that we, laying hold of the promises of Him that cannot lie, may not be drawn aside by the promises of him who is a liar from the beginning, and never more a liar than when he promises any good to his victims and his slaves.

We have here to do with one of these promises of Him, all whose words are true : " He that overcometh, the same shall be clothed in white raiment." But we must not so dwell upon the promise as to overlook the conditions of the promise. It is made to him " that overcometh." Overcometh what? This is not hard to answer. Overcometh what Christ overcame, the world ;† overcometh what Christ did not need to overcome, himself,—the pride, the malignity, the selfishness, the sensuality, the thousand forms of sin which are lodged in his own bosom. He who in the strength of God, and through the grace of his Spirit, is a conqueror of all these, the same, that one and not any other, " shall be clothed in white raiment," shall walk with Christ in white.

<hr>

* 2 Peter i. 4.   † John xvi. 33.

But this walking with Christ in white, this being clothed in white raiment, what is the exact import of this wonderful promise? It is worth our while to study it; for it is the character of God's promises, the closer they are looked at, the more they are accurately examined, by so much the more rich and the more glorious do they appear. White, I would first call you to observe, is everywhere the color, so to speak, the livery of heaven; and more noticeable in this Book than in any other; for we read here of the "white stone," the "white horses," the "white robes," the "white cloud," the "white linen," the "white throne."* But not in this Book alone. It is the same, though not to the same extent, everywhere else. Do angels appear to men, and are we told any thing of their outward appearance, they are clothed in white: so the angel at the sepulchre, he is clothed, according to St. Mark, "in a long white garment;"† and in St. Matthew, his raiment is "white as snow."‡ And these last words lead me to observe, that the white of heaven is not that dull dead hue, rather the absence of color than anything else, which, on this poor earth of ours, sometimes goes by this name; but the heavenly white is a shining white. The angel whom St. Matthew and St. Mark describe as clothed *in white*, is said in St. Luke to have been "in *shining* garments,"§ as that angel who appeared to Cornelius was clothed, "in *bright* clothing."¶ Compare with these notices the

* Rev. ii. 17, vi. 2, xix. 14, vi. 11, xiv. 14, xix. 14, xx. 21.
† xvi. 5. ‡ xxviii. 3.
§ xxiv. 4. ¶ Acts x. 30.

several records of our Lord's transfiguration. Take, for instance, St. Mark's: " His raiment became shining, exceeding white as snow, so as no fuller on earth can white them."*

What shall we understand by these shining garments of Christ and of the angels, and the promise of the same to the perfected saints in glory? The language recurs too often to allow us to explain it away, or resolve it into a mere figure; while yet we cannot ascribe a literal fulfilment to such words; for, as we all must feel sure, there can be properly no garments in heaven. These pertain only to the necessities, the humiliation, the pride, of our present existence. The Scriptures which speak of the white raiment of the saints or of the angels may best be understood by such an utterance as that of the Psalmist, where of God he says, " Thou deckest Thyself with light, as it were with a garment."† Light, then, is itself a garment; and the spiritual, or glorified body—that, no doubt, and nothing else—shall be the garment of light, the white raiment of the saints, to which such frequent allusion is made. Nothing outside of them, nothing now to be taken up and now laid down, but the very bodies which they wear,—bodies in which mortality shall have been for ever swallowed up in life,—shall contain in themselves the fulfilment of this promise of the Lord. They too, like Him, shall then be light, and in them, as in Him, there shall be then no darkness at all; and, in sign and token of this,—of sin overcome,

---

* Mark ix. 3.
† Ps. civ. 2, Pr. B.

16

of the very dregs of sin for ever cast out,—they, as He, shall clothe themselves, or rather shall have been clothed by Him, with light as with a garment.

Friends and brethren, do these promises move us? have they any attraction for us? would we fain have these bodies of weakness and dishonor, of sin and death, which we bear about with us now, these bodies of our humiliation, transformed and transfigured into the likeness of Christ's body of glory? And if we would, how may this be, and how shall this be attained? I will endeavor to give a reply.

And, first, while those garments of light, that vesture of life, is only put on in the day of the Lord Jesus, it is not for all this something wholly disconnected from that body, that investiture of the soul, which now we wear; and we must above all things beware of regarding it so. This body rather is the germ and seed of that; and, as the butterfly from the worm, that must unfold itself from this. But these present garments of our souls, what spots, what stains, what defilements, are upon them! How little is there in them which gives pledge of such an issue; how much that seems to give pledge of a very different issue from this. One thing, then, is sure—only those garments which have been *made* white in the blood of the Lamb will *show* white upon that day. If, then, we would walk with Christ in white then and for evermore, the first condition for this is, that we come with a heartfelt " Woe is me!" with the confession, " Unclean, unclean!" to that Rock which was cleft for us; to that sacred Side which was pierced for us; and in the water and the blood which flowed out from thence, in the one fountain open for uncleanness, wash away all our guilty stains. And this not once, but continually; drawing near again and again, that we may be partakers of that precious blood of sprinkling; again and again crying, as those who need an ever-repeated cleansing, "Purge me with hyssop,"—the hyssop, that is, which has been dipped in the blood,*—"and I shall be clean; wash me and I shall be whiter than snow." Know you anything, O my friends, of such a coming as this to Christ; of such a washing of your garments now in the blood of the immaculate Lamb? Unless you do, be sure of this, you will never know what it is to have those glorious garments of which Christ speaks in my text given you, and to walk with Him in his heavenly kingdom. They who have not purified themselves on the *third* day, on the *seventh* they shall not be clean; that third day being this time that now is, the seventh the eternal Sabbath that shall be.†

But this is not all. This is the first condition, but it is by no means the only one. The garments which have been made white in the blood of the Lamb, we must subsequently keep them, to the best of our ability, from all after spots and stains; for Christ is not a minister of unrighteousness, but a minister of righteousness and of holiness; He came to bless us in turning us away from our iniquities, to save us *from* our sins, and not to save us *in* our sins, which surpasses even his power. When I say, "to the best of our

* Lev. xiv. 6, 7. † Numbers xix. 12.

ability," you must not misunderstand me. I do not mean to the best of our natural ability ; for in spiritual things, in the things of God, natural ability is no ability at all. I refer to the ability which comes directly from Him, which is his immediate gift and grace ; and I say that to the best of this our ability, that is, by stirring up his gift which is in us, we must endeavor to keep our garments—in other words, to keep ourselves—unspotted from the world. See what is said in the verse immediately preceding my text : " Thou hast a few names even in Sardis which have not defiled their garments ;" and then follow the words, " and they shall walk with Me in white : for they are worthy." Note who they are that shall walk with Him in white. Such as " have not defiled their garments," such as have hated the garments spotted by the flesh. And why these ? " For they are worthy." Scripture does not shrink from this language, " they are worthy," and therefore neither should we. There is a worthiness in God's saints, a meetness or fitness for the inheritance of the saints in light :—though that worthiness is itself of God's free giving, would never have been at all unless He had implanted it ; and not merely of his giving, but also of his most gracious allowing, in that for Christ's sake, and having respect to his perfect obedience, God allows that which of itself would not for an instant have endured his searching gaze. I am afraid we sometimes shrink from this language, from dwelling on words like these, " they shall walk with Me in white, *for they are worthy*," not, as perhaps we fancy, out of any jealousy for God's honor, not out of any fear lest the entire freeness of the salvation which is by Christ Jesus should be called into question, and some other merits mingled with His; but because declarations like these imply that there must be an earnest watching against sin on our part, a striving to cleanse ourselves from all impurities of flesh and spirit, that without holiness no man shall see God. But so it is. There are some that will walk with Christ in white, and it is those who are worthy. Are you candidates for these garments of light? You hear, not from my lips, but from the lips of the Lord, the sole conditions on which they may be yours.

And this holiness,—seek it, I would beseech you, not at its outward circumference, but in its central point, in Christ; let Him dwell in your hearts; let Christ be in you, the hope of Glory. What a phrase of inexhaustible wonder is that of the Apostle, " Christ in you, *the hope of glory ;"** and how directly does it bear on this very matter which has occupied us to-day. If these white garments indicate the future glorification of the bodies of God's saints, how can those bodies pass through this transcendent change, how can they be transmuted and glorified, except through the mighty power of Christ, of Christ dwelling in them, subduing all things to Himself, and Himself effecting this marvellous transformation? Not else assuredly. Thus Christ *in us* is our "hope of glory." He is the pledge of a glory that shall be; a glory that is hidden now, but shall be manifest hereafter; according to that

---

* Col. 1. 27.

other word of St. Paul in the same Epistle, ' When Christ, who is our life, shall appear, then shall ye also appear with Him in glory.'* The faith, the love, the truth, the purity, which were in God's saints, which Christ by his Spirit had wrought in them, but which were all more or less concealed from the eyes of others, yea, and from their own, by the covering of the flesh, the earthen vessel in which this treasure was contained, shall then burst through the covering which concealed them ; shall then flash forth, as Gideon's lamps flashed forth when the pitchers which had hid them hitherto were broken.† That which was before inward shall in that day of manifestation become also outward, visible, seen of all men. "Then shall the righteous *shine forth ;*"—observe that "shine forth," for it is exactly that which I would press upon you ;— they, many of them God's hidden ones till that day, shall " then shine forth as the sun in the kingdom of their Father," living epistles of Christ, shut once, but opened now, and to be read of all men. Christ in you, Christ in you *now*, He is the one hope, the one pledge, of such a glory to be revealed in you hereafter ; so, and so only, will you ever walk with Him in white.

And if not in white, how else ? and if not with Him, with whom ? Ah, brethren, there is a sadder, a sterner side of this truth of my text, and I must not, I dare not, wholly overlook or omit it. Those who have *not* overcome the world, those who *have* defiled

<hr>

* Col. iii. 4.   † Judges vii. 19.

their garments, and never sought to cleanse them again, in what shall they be clothed?

They also shall be clothed with their bodies, for there is a resurrection of condemnation no less than a resurrection of life; but those bodies, dark and not luminous, ugly and not beautiful, shameful and not glorious, food for the undying worm, and fuel for the unquenchable fire; for they are bodies which shall have stamped and written upon them, to be read of men, to be read of angels, the hideous records of all the evil which was done *in* them, which was done *by* them. Would you willingly be clothed with such bodies as these? Would you rise, as the prophet Daniel declares to us some will rise, to shame and everlasting contempt; not one evil thing which you have ever thought, or spoken, or done, but, having left its mark, its stamp, its scar, its cicatrice behind, then visible to every eye? I know you would not. Would you be content to have the polluted garment of sinful flesh cleaving to you for evermore, making you one pollution? I know you would not. And yet I say to you, (would that one might leave it unsaid, would that it were not to say!) that if you, if any of you here, is a lover of pleasures rather than a lover of God, choosing friendship with the world and enmity with God, walking after the flesh and not after the Spirit; much more, if you are allowing yourself in any open, in any secret sin, which plainly separates you from Christ and the benefits of his salvation,—you are in fact choosing all this, choosing this shame, this dishonor, this contempt, this scorn, this tribulation, this anguish;

when you might have chosen glory, honor, immortality, to stand before the throne, to see his face who sits upon it, to have his name written in your forehead, to walk with Christ in those white and shining garments which saints and angels wear.

THE END.